HARRY STONE

THAT
MONSTROUS
REGIMENT

The birth of women's political emancipation

HARRY STONE

THAT MONSTROUS REGIMENT

The birth of women's political emancipation

MEREO
Cirencester

Mereo Books

1A The Wool Market Dyer Street Cirencester Gloucestershire GL7 2PR
An imprint of Memoirs Publishing www.mereobooks.com

THAT MONSTROUS REGIMENT: 978-1-86151-313-7

First published in Great Britain in 2015
by Mereo Books, an imprint of Memoirs Publishing

The address for Memoirs Publishing Group Limited can be found at
www.memoirspublishing.com

The Memoirs Publishing Group Ltd Reg. No. 7834348

The Memoirs Publishing Group supports both The Forest Stewardship Council® (FSC®) and
the PEFC® leading international forest-certification organisations. Our books carrying both the
FSC label and the PEFC® and are printed on FSC®-certified paper. FSC® is the only
forest-certification scheme supported by the leading environmental organisations including
Greenpeace. Our paper procurement policy can be found at
www.memoirspublishing.com/environment

Typeset in 10/15pt Bembo
by Wiltshire Associates Publisher Services Ltd. Printed and bound in Great Britain by
Printondemand-Worldwide, Peterborough PE2 6XD

Contents

✻

Part I 1542-1558: The First Ladies

Part II 1559-1568: The Ladies Muster

Part III: The Cockpit of Europe, 1569-1575

to French princes - Treaty of Blois - Elizabeth allows volunteer support for the Netherlands - Catherine's children shake off her influence - Charles sympathises with the Huguenots - Catherine's adoption of murder and the St. Bartholomew massacre - Siege of Rochelle – Elizabeth favours Spain - Popish plots against Elizabeth and English Parliamentary precautions - Anjou is imprisoned and his first escape - Anjou surrounds Paris - Treaty of Beaulieu - Philip refuses Anjou's marriage to his daughter - Anjou's second imprisonment - Elizabeth proposes engagement renewal - Catherine loses power to Henri's favourites - Anjou to London - Elizabeth's Spanish shipping raids renewed - Drake knighted - the Pope calls for Elizabeth's assassination.

Part IV: 1576–1587, Spanish Silver

Philip increases his silver income and takes Portugal - Drake raids Lisbon - Margaret reinstated in the Netherlands - Anjou has Henri's tacit support in the Netherlands and liberates Cambrai - Elizabeth rebuffs Anjou's new advances, his treacherous behaviour - Guises sign the treasonable Joinville treaty with Philip - Elizabeth takes positive action in the Netherlands - the Babington Plot and Mary's execution - Henri loses his struggle with Guise - The night of the barricades – Henri flees Paris - murder of Guise - death of Catherine and Henri.

Part V: Elizabeth Defiant, 1588-1603

Philip and Elizabeth prepare for the Armada - the English and Spanish navies - the Armada battle - Elizabeth resumes raids on Spanish ports - spread of world trade - Philip invades France and Elizabeth sends troops to Brittany - Navarre converts to Catholicism and takes Paris - Elizabeth a sole survivor - Essex and ghosts from the past - death of Elizabeth.

OTHER BOOKS BY HARRY STONE

※

Adult Bedwetters and Their Problems - a cause of homelessness

Better Charity Management

The Casebook of Sherlock Doyle - true mysteries investigated by Conan Doyle

The Century of Musical Comedy and Revue

Ski Joy - a social history of winter sports

Slippery Slopes, - a cartoon guide to happier skiing

Stage Effect Sensations

Writing in the Shadow - resistance publications in occupied Europe

PERIODS OF AUTHORITY

	NETHERLANDS	SCOTLAND	ENGLAND	FRANCE
1507-1530	Margaret of Austria			
1531				
1532	Mary of Hungary			
1533				
1534				
1535				
1536				
1537				
1538				
1539				
1540				
1541				
1542				
1543		Marie of Guise		
1544				
1545				
1546				
1547				
1548				
1549				
1550				
1551				
1552				
1553				
1554			Mary Tudor	
1555				
1556				
1557				
1558				
1559			Elizabeth I	
1560	Margaret of Parma			Catherine de Medici
1561				
1562		Mary of Scots		
1563				
1564				
1565				
1566				
1567				
1568				
1569		Mary Imprisoned		
1570				
1571				
1572				
1573				
1574				
1575				
1576				
1577				
1578				
1579	Margaret of Parma			
1580				
1581				
1582				
1583				
1584				
1585				
1586				
1587				
1588				
1589 - 1603				

PART I

1542-1548
THE FIRST LADIES

John Knox should really have known better when writing about his "Monstrous Regiment of Women". "How abominable before GOD", he thundered, "is the Empire or Rule of Wicked Woman, yea, of a traitress and bastard." His tirade, which appeared in his pamphlet "First blast on the Trumpet", was politically incorrect even in 1558. He was in exile in Geneva at the time, so he must have been well aware that in the Netherlands two Governesses, Margaret of Austria and Mary of Hungary, had already become acknowledged throughout Europe as highly-skilled practitioners in international diplomacy. Indeed, they were the first women to reach such status in the modern world. No - instead he chose to pour out his wrath upon Scotland's Regent Marie of Guise and Mary Tudor. Yet both were almost completely under the thumb of their men.

Moreover his choice was ill timed, because both ladies were quite evidently nearing the end of their lives.

Knox was also showing duplicity over what should have been his Christian belief. All down history Kings happily engineered war on the assumption that they would win and so could claim their victory as proof their rule was favoured by God. The ladies, in contrast, preferred to settle their international problems through marriage or, more precisely, through engagement. So, in all logic, he should have blessed them as peacemakers.

Margaret of Austria was the first woman in this gender revolution. She had the advantage of having been born into the Habsburg family. While most empires have been created through waging war, the Habsburgs accumulated their estates through marriage. Consequently the family were able to dispense with the normal way of securing an empire. Instead of executing the leaders they had conquered, they made them their relations. So they were quite used to having women as major players in their empire. It was a policy they were to pursue most successfully for a further three centuries, until eventually their Austrian Hungarian Empire was blown to pieces by the First World War.

Even so it was a significant decision when, in 1531, the Emperor Maximilian appointed his daughter Margaret as Governess of the Netherlands. It was no mean appointment. At that time the Netherlands was one of the richest countries in Europe and included Antwerp, the most important port in the world. Its spectacular ascendency in overseas trade had turned it into a European centre for financiers and bankers.

On being appointed Governess, Margaret quickly confirmed her ability by out-manoeuvring those heavyweight bullies Henry VIII and Cardinal Wolsey. She inveigled them into signing an agreement over the wool trade which was blatantly to the advantage of the Flemish weavers. She did, however, hold very strong prejudices as regards nationality. She had great love for England. Indeed she had been in the running for marriage to Arthur, heir to Henry VII. She had also greatly come to like Thomas Boleyn while he had been Ambassador to her court at Malines. He, in turn, had been filled with admiration at the sophistication and culture of her household. This was why he sent his daughter Anne for her 'finishing' in etiquette and parlez vous. And that, of course, had proved highly successful - even though the end had been so tragic.

In contrast, she hated the French. Again this was entirely personal, for she had been brought up to believe Francis I would be her husband. Then, while she was still in her teens, he jilted her, and even more demeaning, he went on to marry her stepmother.

Margaret charmed everyone with her beauty and her open, radiant face. Once, when she was visiting a Spanish provincial town, the crowd waiting to welcome her was so dense it was feared she would be crushed, so she had to stay outside until after nightfall, when it was hoped there would be fewer people. She brought this charm to the negotiating table and with it an effective calm to the squabbling factions in the Netherlands. By the time she retired, after more than twenty years, she was held in the highest esteem, not only in the Netherlands but throughout Europe.

No doubt emboldened by this success, when in 1533 Charles V, now head of the Habsburgs, had to appoint her successor, he chose his sister, Mary of Hungary. A small, slight woman, her bulging eyes, heavy eyelids and full lips made her look disdainful. Unfortunately her appearance was an accurate reflection of her character. In contrast to Margaret's charm, humour and open frankness, Mary was implacable, and seemed to take pleasure in humiliating those around her.

She had been born actually in the Netherlands and had remained there until she was eight. But on returning at the age of 25, any hope that she might be sympathetic to the people she was to rule proved to be very wide of the mark. Her loyalty was totally and exclusively devoted to Charles. Originally she had, like the other women, been completely ambivalent over the different faiths. As a result a large proportion of her household had come to include Calvinists. However, when Charles made it a condition that she should purge her household of heretics, she showed not the least compunction in sacking the lot.

She started off at a disadvantage for, although she had been brought up by Margaret, she still had little or no practical knowledge for the job. Her inexperience was immediately apparent, for even in her inaugural speech she muttered, as though embarrassed to raise her voice. Even those close by could not hear her. Charles fully realised the situation and, after having supervised her arrival, he remained by her side, guiding her for almost a year. And when he did leave, he left her surrounded by a multitude of advisers so as to give her little latitude.

Besides a state council, she had a privy council and a finance council and to prevent her from doing anything rash, he had given the state council power to overrule any of her decisions. Her task was made the more difficult since nearly all these appointees were new; most of those who had been advising Margaret had retired at about the same time as she had.

Mary had not been Governor long before she too was confronted with marriage problems. Three years earlier, Charles had suggested to James V of Scotland that he might like to marry Dorothea, daughter of the exiled King of Denmark, who was now under Habsburg care. James had refused, saying the age difference was too great. Now it looked as though he was going to marry a French woman. This would be an alliance with the enemy. So Margaret told him this was not at all a good idea and that he should think again about marrying Dorothea. Instead James took offence and sent the acid response that while he agreed the princess was now older, so was he. His objection therefore remained. Then, as feared, he went on and married the French woman.

The second marital problem arose in 1538 and concerned Henry VIII. Having ruthlessly disposed of his third wife, Henry was proposing that Christina, another Danish princess, should become his fourth. Christina was the Governess's niece and ward. So it was up to her to keep the delicate balance between not offending the powerful Henry yet protecting her niece from his advances. She wrote laconically to her brother Charles: "It is to be hoped, if one can hope anything from such a man, that if this one bores him, he will find a better way of getting rid of her. I believe that most women would not appreciate it very much if this kind of habit became general, and with reason. And although I have no inclination to expose myself dangers of this kind, I do after all belong to the female sex, so I shall also pray God that he may protect us from such perils".

So Mary dragged her feet over all the necessary preliminaries to such an extent that at last the English ambassador asked her direct if her intentions were genuine. With extreme diplomacy she simply lowered her eyes and blushed, which he correctly interpreted as a sign that she was not.

Soon Henry's rapaciousness was again testing her negotiating skills. In 1532 the Ottoman Empire was threatening Europe, and the brunt of defence fell upon Charles with his Mediterranean coastline. At the same time, Henry VIII was threatening war. It was up to Mary to persuade Henry to forget all the resentment he might still be harbouring over the way she had stalled over his wish to marry Christina. She had to persuade him it was his duty as a Christian, regardless of denomination, to rally round and help fight the Ottoman heathens. She was certainly successful, for the English Ambassador wrote in his report, "if His Majesty had heard the Queen of Hungary's words and seen the engaging expression on her face he would undoubtedly be inclined the more generously to do whatever he thought best". It brought brilliant results, for within ten days Henry had signed a treaty of reciprocal support.

But Mary's troubles were far from over. Henri of France could never let things be. He was bent on settling old scores with Charles. Mary foresaw that this would lead to another outbreak of war and it would almost certainly mean the invasion of her region of the Habsburg realm. But when she asked for help, typically Charles did not reply. So, with her usual energy, she made a tour, inspecting all the defences of Artois, Namur and Luxembourg. She ordered all

Frenchmen to leave the country and instructed the innkeepers to keep records of their guests so that she could check against possible spies. Above all, she raised funds from the ever-reluctant Dutch. She made it clear that it was their area that was threatened. As a result they proved to be comparatively forthcoming.

It was just as well. France did indeed invade. Now everything seemed against Mary. A short while before, she had hoped to improve relations by asking Charles to replace the Spanish generals with native Dutchmen. For once, he had obliged. And now that the crucial time had come, they were fighting more among themselves than against the enemy. She herself had to impose a scorched earth policy, devastating large tracts of the country.

Still the French advanced, and she was just about ready to give up. She wrote to Charles begging him, not for the first time, to relieve her of her post. Her plea is interesting for the light it throws on the problems confronting even a skilful woman in office during the 16th century. Of course her letter contained an element of despair, for she was by this time over 50 years old and had spent more than 20 years struggling with all the problems of authority. In her own words:

"I am of the opinion that whoever acts as a regent for a ruler must have more understanding of affairs than the person who governs on his own account [by which she meant an anointed sovereign] and is therefore only responsible to God. If he does whatever lies within his power, he has done his duty. But a regent has to account not only to God but also to his sovereign and his sovereign's subjects... experience has taught me that a woman is not suited to the purpose, neither in peacetime nor in time of war. Your majesty is himself in a position to judge that I have often done more than was fitting for my position and vocation as a woman.

"Your Majesty also knows what insurmountable difficulties we would have met with if you had not been in the country yourself during the last war. Difficulties which I could not have removed because as a woman I was compelled to leave the conduct of the war to others.

"Your Majesty will nevertheless be able to understand that it is difficult for someone like me, who has served you till the end, to have to think in my old age of learning my ABC all over again. It is suitable that a woman of fifty who has served you for at least twenty-four years, should content herself for the rest of her life with one God and one master. Moreover, I see in the Netherlands a young generation to whose ways I cannot and would not wish to accommodate myself. Loyalty and respect towards God and the Sovereign have deteriorated in such a way and the number of devoted servants is so small (a phenomenon to be observed not only in this country but almost everywhere) that not only would I not wish to rule over such people, even if I were a man and sufficiently capable, but I take so much offence at them that I do not wish to live even as a private person surrounded by people amongst whom I cannot do my duty either towards God or towards my Sovereign. I can assure your Majesty, and God is my witness, that I loathe governing so much that I would rather work for my living than occupy myself with it".

And again Charles refused.

But then came news that the French were retreating. She forgot all her worries and dashed around urging her recalcitrant generals to sort themselves out and make a proper effort: "Take the offensive, don't exhaust yourself bothering with sieges". A few days later she said, "If France will wait for just another fortnight, I'll show them for what purpose God gave a woman strength".

She was as good as her word. She girded herself in full war panoply, complete with black leather jerkin over her tabard. She set out for the front with a body of horse "to give the French a present". The English ambassador, who was in her suite, was much impressed.

He wrote back saying the French were indeed about to have a rude awakening. At the last moment her Council stepped in and forbade her to go into the firing line, but her leadership bore fruit and soon after her forces captured St. Pol.

Unfortunately, on her retirement, all the progress both she and Margaret had made towards the emancipation of women rulers fell into abeyance.

That aforementioned French woman, whom James V had married despite Mary's discouragement, was Marie of Guise. So it is little wonder that there was no love lost between them. The distaste was evidently mutual, for when Marie later asked for some favour from Charles V, it was Mary who replied with frigid formality that the request was invalid, since it had not been made "through the official channels".

Now in August 1542, Marie was pregnant. But all did not presage well. James lost the battle of Solway Moss against the marauding bully Henry VIII. Furthermore, he lost hope, for it left him isolated, with most of his leading nobles taken prisoner.

Probably suffering a mental breakdown, James took to his bed. There they brought him news that Marie had successfully given birth, but it was not the prince he had been hoping for; it was a girl. He simply turned his face to the wall, and within five days he was dead.

So here was Marie, a defenceless widow with a new-born babe in a foreign land. The relationship between Scotland and England had for long been fraught, for England realised it was only too easy for the Scots to be wooed into an alliance with either Spain or France. This would make their country an ideal springboard for invading England.

Henry had tried to counter this, and formed an alliance with the Scots by marrying his sister Margaret to James IV. But he was not best pleased when his brother-in-law refused to go along with him in throwing out the Catholics and embracing Protestantism. In due course Henry found his nephew, James V, no less obdurate. He refused to join him in plundering the Church lands. Then, when Henry summoned him to a meeting at York, James did not turn up, and the powerful English monarch suffered the humiliation of being kept waiting.

In fact James had been warned, and with good cause, that if he went he would probably not be allowed to return home. But in winning the battle of Solway Moss, Henry was following a strange policy. He must have known then that Marie was eight months pregnant and the birth would leave him with an ideal opportunity. If the child was a girl, she could marry his son Edward, and if it was a boy, there was his daughter Elizabeth. Despite this, Henry chose to use this latest victory as an opportunity to impress upon the Scots that any thoughts of alliance with another European country would bring down on them terrible retribution. He followed through his victory by burning and pillaging without mercy and far beyond the acceptable ravages of war. It was so incongruous to Henry's ambitions that the skirmish became known as the Rough Wooing.

Hardly had Marie begun suckling the child than the crude, unprincipled Scottish chieftains were making advances from every side. In the sixteenth century a baby princess was extremely vulnerable. Under the conventions of the time, her betrothal made her little more than a diplomatic bargaining pawn. But when the Princess was also heir to a throne, she became a magnificent prize. As had happened with the Habsburgs, the husband would take over the throne and the country would be added to his realm. Consequently princesses who were future queens were betrothed while still a baby and usually married just before puberty.

So Marie had hardly given birth before she and her daughter were being circled by fathers prowling as surrogate suitors. At the front of the queue was Henry VIII, anxious to book the young princess for his son Edward. And now he apparently considered all his recent outrages of no particular concern. Brushing them aside, he demanded the princess for his son. Indeed he seemed to think he already owned the girl. He demanded that she should be sent to London so that he could oversee her education.

Marie was perfectly capable of handling Henry. Indeed, he had proposed to her before she had married James. The fact that she had turned him down in preference for a minor royal in a benighted little country must have hurt his pride. Also, her witty aside must in due course have reached his ears. When wooing her, he had complimented her on her figure. Once out of hearing, she had remarked "Yes, but I have a slender neck".

Nor was she anybody's fool. She was, after all, the daughter of the mighty Duke Claude de Guise, whose family considered themselves to be second only to the King of France.

She was a remarkable character in her own right. She was tall and had "presence". She had courage too, for there were occasions when she appeared actually on the battlefield urging on her troops, yet she had the softness to remain feminine. She had charm, and this helped make her a successful conciliator and enhanced her ability at persuasion. From her family she had learnt prudence, tolerance and she was naturally intelligent.

When she had first arrived in Scotland, she had been horrified at the primitive state of the country, the houses and the people. But, careful not to deride her new country, she had gone to great lengths to praise wherever she could. She found Fife particularly charming and she was enchanted by the children.

And behind this lay a quick and shrewd mind. Almost at once she realised that if a woman in Scotland wanted something, she must ask for the opposite. It was a tactic that was to serve her well. Now she realised that to get anywhere, she must seem to pacify Henry. When he sent his ambassador Sir Ralph Sadler to inspect the babe, for there had been rumours she was a weakly child, Marie not only showed her to him but insisted on unwrapping the little girl until she was stark naked to prove she was healthy all over.

Marie also realised that Henry would demand something more practical. So in July 1543, the Treaty of Greenwich between Scotland and England was duly signed. It was in effect the peace terms following Solway Moss, but was never actually ratified by Parliament. Certainly the Scots won generous terms in response to agreeing to baby Mary's betrothal to Edward, with the marriage scheduled to take place when she reached eleven. If Edward died, leaving Mary a childless widow, she would return to Scotland, and England would recognise Scottish independence. Henry even agreed, though with considerable reluctance, not to insist on Mary going to England for her education until she was at least ten years old.

However, for any agreement with Henry ten years was a long time, and this too proved optimistic – indeed ten hours was barely sufficient. The very day after the signing, Henry received word from his ambassador that French ships had been seen anchored just off the Scottish coast. Henry immediately jumped to the conclusion that he had been duped and the French had come to carry off Mary. He demanded that she be brought to England. The Scots declined, saying the baby was suffering from "the breeding of the teeth".

Still apparently under the illusion that he had control of the child, Henry ordered his ambassador to separate the mother from her baby and said he should act as mentor. The response from the Scots was – nothing. So Henry had to content himself by arresting some merchant ships sailing to France and purloining their freight.

But Henry did not know the full situation. He did not know he had a rival much closer to home. The Earl of Arran also had a young son whom he considered admirably suited for Mary's hand. In pursuing his suit, he was quick to emphasise that as a girl child she could easily be pushed aside. But were she betrothed to his son, she would have a strong ally right there in Scotland, and it would prevent the crown being shared with a foreign King.

He also insisted he was next in line to the throne. In this, however, there was the problem of a blot on his escutcheon. There was considerable doubt as to whether the old Earl really was his father. If this was the case, then he would lose all reasonable expectations. So Arran felt that the engagement would be the perfect way of ensuring his son would gain the throne.

But whatever precautions Marie might take to protect her daughter, she could not exert complete control. As Queen of Scotland and a minor, Mary was the charge of the nation and a Regent. The Regent had to ensure her best interests, including decisions over her betrothal. Marie's problem was that the Regent could not be a woman. Of course Marie had considerable influence, but the royal family was inherently weak. The Stewarts lacked several of the regal assets then considered advisable. Their forbears were not lost in the mists of antiquity. The court contained several nobles who, although they had been created comparatively recently, still had almost as strong a claim to the throne. This made it necessary to be constantly watching for rebellion. When the Tudors had been in a similar situation they had murdered all likely rivals.

Besides being a woman, Marie had the severe disadvantage of being a foreigner.

Initially it looked as though the problem could be satisfactorily decided. Cardinal Beaton was a leading politician as well as a churchman and he was a family friend. He had presided over her marriage in Paris. He was also ardently pro-French, which meant he was anti English. He had the advantage of being one of the few people who were impervious to Henry's bribes.

It was at this crucial moment that Beaton chose to produce a paper which had undoubtedly been signed by James and which purported to make Marie and himself joint Regents for the little girl. This was immediately challenged by Arran, who declared that Beaton had browbeaten the dying man into placing his signature on a blank sheet of paper.

Then Henry pounced. After the battle of Solway Moss he had not followed the usual procedure of holding the greater nobles for ransom. Instead he had taken them back to London and held them as his "guests". There he had indoctrinated them to appreciate all the advantages that lay in having a firm Anglo-Scottish alliance. Now he felt was the opportune moment to free them so that their influence could shape the situation. To make sure they continued upholding his ideals, he kept them on a "pension".

Marie's fears proved to be only too real. These ex-hostages, together with Arran, who was also on Henry's payroll, discovered Beaton had been getting money from France to help finance himself as Regent, so they kidnapped him during a meeting of the privy council and had him imprisoned, and Arran had himself made Regent.

Now Marie found herself completely isolated in her need to protect her daughter. She strongly suspected the bribery and realised that she and her daughter were in a very delicate, if not dangerous, position. There was every likelihood Mary would be kidnapped or even murdered. Marie took all precautions and even arranged for the baby to sleep at the foot of her bed.

However, she could claim a degree of authority as the mother of the Queen. In recognition of this she was in 1544 elected Honorary Lady President of the council. This allowed her to oversee the welfare of her daughter. She was also in a position to blackmail Arran. If she divulged to Henry that Arran also wanted his son to be Mary's wife, Henry would cut off his "pension" and bring down upon him the full force of his fury. But Marie realised she needed to use every advantage if she was to control the situation.

For some while she flirted with Arran, that is until he discovered she was two-timing him with his nearest rival in line for the throne, the Earl of Lennox. Arran had no compunction in seeking revenge by trying to sell state secrets to the English. It also suited her to flirt with Patrick, Earl of Bothwell, who was so besotted he spent most of his fortune wooing her. She tried to flirt with the English ambassador, but he was too fly and realised what she was up to. She even confided in him that, having been married to a King, she could not now look lower for a husband. In other words she was open to advances from Henry again. But by this time Henry was too busy with Catherine Parr. So she tried to disarm him with her humility.

"It becomes me not" she said, referring to his interest in her daughter, "to play the dissembler with so noble a prince as His Majesty of England". Of course, that was exactly what she was doing. It was not long before she began undermining Arran's position. She made sure Henry got to hear of his rivalry for her daughter. She also made quite sure he heard it in Arran's exact words: that by the time Mary was of marriageable age, Henry might well be dead. She knew full well that Henry hated anyone mentioning the possibility of his death. Then in January 1544, all these elaborate subterfuges were disrupted by a completely new and unexpected development.

Catherine de Medici was pregnant. She had been married to the King of France for ten years without issue. It had been assumed she was barren and there had even been talk of "returning" her to her family in Florence. For Henry its significance was obvious. If the child was a boy, he would be a direct rival against Edward for Mary's hand. More than this, with Marie's strong French connection, she would almost certainly give the Dauphin preference among suitors.

It presented a fraught situation. Catherine had been born in 1519 into the mighty Florentine banking family. Her mother died twelve days later and her father six days after that. She was brought up first by her grandmother and when she died by her aunt, who also died while she was still a child. Her education was completed in a convent. Her fortune was so prodigious that even at the age of six she was, like Mary Queen of Scots, the object of interest to many great people anxious to have her affianced to their offspring. They had even included James V of Scotland and the future Duke of Milan.

In the end it was Henri, Duke of Orleans, second son of the King of France, who was chosen. The marriage took place when she was 14. It was truly spectacular. She was escorted to the coast of France by the Duke of Albany with 27 ships and a 300-oar galleon When she reached Nice, her procession was joined by the Pope and 13 cardinals

She had been married only four years when the Dauphin died and Henri became heir to the throne. But the French aristocrats made little effort to hide their contempt for "the merchant's daughter", particularly since her uncle, the Pope, had not kept his side of the bargain. Once he had her married off, he refused to pay the promised dowry.

Nor was her appearance in her favour. She was tall and stout with a red face, and her hair looked as though it was a wig. She had pale eyes which seemed to bulge and a big mouth. To add to these blemishes, her French accent was like that of a peasant. Surprisingly, she worked the most beautiful delicate embroidery and was a graceful dancer. Her character was in complete contrast. Death had robbed her, one after another, of the people she could look to for security and affection. It could have left her insecure, introverted and incapable of affection. But she emerged a remarkable woman. While still in her early teens, she completely won over her reticent, crabby old father-in-law, Francis I. He considered all women to be shallow and a waste of time. But the child Catherine was different. He enjoyed going for long studious walks with her. To please him, Catherine learnt Latin and Greek and unlike most ladies of the time, begged to be allowed to join his hunting parties. She introduced the idea of riding side-saddle and, to preserve her modesty when mounting a horse, she introduced women's knickers. She loved to shoot and play tennis with the ablest. She was described as the true daughter of Florence:"gay and brilliant; always ready to laugh, and her nimble repartee meant her rooms were always full of friends."

Despite such gifts, she suffered sorely on two counts. For seven years she was desperate to produce the required heir to the throne. Various potions she tried included drinking mule's urine and putting cow dung mixed with ground antlers of stags "upon her source of life". When there was talk that if she did not produce an heir soon she would have to be divorced and sent back to Florence she in desperation petitioned her father-in-law. For a woman of her age she wrote a letter of astonishing insight and grace. She quite understood that he thought it advisable not to wait any longer hoping for an heir to such a great kingdom. Her gratitude at having been accepted, even as a daughter-in-law, was so great that she would never resist the will of His Majesty but rather bear the great grief if she had to leave. Then either she would enter a convent or, if it was pleasing to His Majesty, remain in the train of the fortunate woman who was to take her place as the wife of her husband.

Francis was so moved by her plea that he told her to have no fear and said that since God had willed her to be wife of the Dauphin, he did not wish to make any change and that perhaps "it will please Almighty God in this matter to grant to you and to me the gift we so much long for".

Whether God was pleased or whether it was the pills of myrrh, prescribed by Jean Fernel, but in 1544 Catherine gave birth to a boy. The crisis was over and, as though to make up for lost time, a whole string of children followed.

Her second difficulty was not so easily overcome. The man she had married already had a mistress. It was a strange set up. Diane de Poitiers was 20 years older than the Dauphin. There must have been a degree of mother complex in this, and indeed Diane would sometimes admonish him and instruct him to leave her to stay the night with his wife and carry out his conjugal duties. She has been described as having masculine intelligence, which Henri, like his father, found infinitely preferable to the trivial chatter of the women at court. Even in an age when it was considered perfectly normal for a king to have a mistress, his excessive attention to Diane was an affront to Catherine. At court dinners, he would sometimes sit on Diane's lap and play on his guitar or with her breasts. But Catherine remained completely calm and retained her dignity. All the time she remained studiously courteous to Diane. She never took advantage of her official position, nor tried to influence the King politically. While she may not have loved her husband, she was very fond of him. Despite the loose morals of the court, there was never any suggestion of impropriety on her part.

The King had shown sufficient confidence to have entrusted her with the regency twice before, though it had been little more than nominal. But in 1553 the war in Italy demanded he should be absent for an indefinite time. He left her to carry out several delicate negotiations. By far the most important was to persuade Parliament to allocate more money. Beyond the natural resistance to such a request, Parliament was being awkward, demanding a full account of the considerable sum they had voted the last time. The delegates were expecting a strident and demanding diatribe.

For the occasion, Catherine dressed sombrely in black. Instead of regally commanding them to help, she took a humble approach, flattering them and asking them to aid their king. She emphasised the peril they were all in. Catherine's presentation was so clever, authoritative and persuasive that the hard-headed delegates were profoundly moved. They asked her to withdraw while they discussed the situation. Hardly had she done so than they were calling her back. Not only would they gladly grant her all the money she asked for but they would increase it.

"The queen thanked them in so sweet a form of speech that she made well-nigh the whole parliament shed tears from emotion. She told them that, remembering this their demonstration towards her, she would always consider them her clients and she promised to appoint her son, the Dauphin, to be their advocate and intercessor with the Most Christian King. Thereupon the Parliament adjourned greatly applauding Her Majesty and with it such marks of extreme satisfaction as to defy exaggeration and all over Paris nothing is talked of but the prudent and gracious manner adopted by Her Majesty in this business."

It was indeed just a foretaste of what this formidable and intriguing woman could do.

All this time, Marie had been busy strengthening her position in Scotland by manipulating the Earl of Arran. She had suggested that since Beaton was a Scot but had no son, he might well be persuaded to back Arran's claim for Mary's hand in preference to Henry. So Arran ignored Henry's machinations to have Beaton brought to London where he could deal with him direct. Instead, in July 1543 Beaton was mysteriously released from prison. Both were fearful that the child Queen might be spirited away to France, spoiling the plans Arran had for his son. Beaton also feared for the child's safety, since she was still within the reach of Henry. So they rallied 7,000 Catholics and marched to Linlithgow to collect the baby Mary and carry her off to the far safer castle at Stirling.

Henry's reaction was rather unexpected. He did not invade; he did not even try to bribe Arran with money. Instead he suggested that young Arran should be betrothed to his second daughter Elizabeth. Presumably Arran still held hopes for his Scottish cause, for, while expressing his appreciation of the high honour, he refused. Even stranger, Arran refused Henry's improved offer of gold and troops to help him take the throne by force. He explained that under such circumstances, the Scots would surely refuse to recognise him.

Not that such a reason would normally have bothered him. Arran's real reason for escaping Henry's control became clear that autumn. He realised Marie and her Catholic supporters were gaining popularity in Scotland. The fact that his professed Protestantism was linking him with the ogre Henry meant his influence could be lost. Should he instead claim reconversion to Catholicism, he would find favour not only with the populace but more particularly with Marie. He was even prepared to work with Beaton if it would further his cause.

Marie was perfectly agreeable to such an arrangement, for Beaton was by far the cleverer man and could manipulate Arran without him even realising it. Arran was further encouraged when the King of France, nudged no doubt by the Duke of Guise, said that if he returned to Catholicism and rejected any claim to the throne, they would create him 1st Duke of Chatelherault. Arran duly returned to the faith in September, 1543, conveniently in time to claim his part in the baby's coronation ceremony. He carried the crown, no less.

For Henry, this was the last straw. He took to arms again and in 1544 invaded Scotland, where his forces had little difficulty in reaching and sacking Edinburgh. Little Mary was hastily moved still further north to Dunkfield. But this time Marie had been able to negotiate sufficient funds from France to outbid Henry's bribes. For once she was able to induce sufficient "loyalty" among the Scottish nobles for them to work as a team.

The result was dramatic. In February 1545, the Scots actually defeated the English at Ancrum Moor. Even so, things were not good. Beaton's success in defying Henry was short lived. So was he. Building works at his castle at St. Andrews, were supposed to be under the tightest security. None the less, one day the workmen turned out not to be workmen at all but some lairds bent on revenge for the Protestant Bishop Wishart, whom Cardinal Beaton had caused to be burnt at the stake. They gave him only sufficient time to repent his sins before dispatching him.

One of the assassins was John Knox who was just beginning to make a name for himself with his outspoken and fiery sermons. He was caught and sentenced to be a slave in the French galleys.

In his absence, the popularity of Catholicism continued to grow apace. At the same time, the King of France was showing himself to be violently anti-English. So the English long-term fear that the French might at any moment arrive in Scotland to launch that much-anticipated attack from across the border was becoming ever greater.

Under Edward VI, the English bribes were now exceeding Marie's and they began notching up further successful excursions into Scottish territory. In 1547 they inflicted another defeat at Pinkie Cleugh.

The suggestion that the Scots had shown cowardice and had quickly given up is wide of the facts and largely invented to denigrate the Earl of Arran. Contrary to the popular report that he had "taken hastily to his horse" the first day of battle was inconclusive, even though the English were more numerous and better equipped and had the advantage of the long bow.

Added to this they introduced an unusual integration of infantry, artillery and cavalry to form a structured plan. They were further developing the scope of warfare by bringing 80 ships into Scapa Flow.

On the morning of the second day, Arran put into action a desperate plan to overcome the overwhelming odds. But his men moved more slowly than he had anticipated, and at the same time the guns from the ships opened up to decimate Huntley's pikemen. Obviously Arran was the first to realise his plan was failing and he was in danger of being made prisoner, so wisely he was among the first to flee. But the experience annihilated what little confidence Marie might have had in the reliability of the Scots to fight wars.

She realised then that if she required reliable defence, it could only be through bringing over French troops. To entice them she suggested that they should take over several key Scottish castles, notably Dunbar, Dumbarton, Dumfries and Inchkeith. As a reward it was arranged that Mary, now aged six, would be sent to France, where at least she could live without threats and be educated by her grandparents. She was also to be officially betrothed to the Dauphin. That, of course, would be of considerable prestige for Marie's family of Guise.

The French duly agreed to Marie's suggestion and in return declared they would defend Scotland "as though it were their own country". In fact they had no such intention, for Henri was afraid that any more influence there might drive Philip of Spain into forging an alliance with England.

In 1548 the Scottish Parliament duly ratified the agreement. Poor Marie. Her daughter had grown into a pretty and extremely attractive child. "One of the most perfect creatures the God of nature ever formed" was only one of the many ecstatic opinions expressed about her, and now she must part with her, perhaps for ever.

The French were as good as their word and a month later, in June 1548, 6,000 troops under the command of André de Montalembert duly arrived to keep the forts safe. A month later the King's Galley docked at Dumbarton. On parting with her mother, Mary shed tears, but she had already learnt that royalty do not make scenes in public and she let herself be led on board.

It was a dangerous journey, made the more so by the fear of English intervention, so instead of taking the direct route, despite very stormy weather, the ship sailed west round Land's End. On arrival the French proved no less ecstatic over the little Queen. "It is not possible to hope for more from a Princess on this earth" gushed the French Captain De Beaugne. Henri II was no less enthusiastic: "The little Queen of Scots is the most perfect child I have ever seen". Both Catherine and, perhaps more importantly, Diane de Poitiers had also fallen for the child and her life in the French court was bliss.

It was the start of an idyllic childhood for this unfortunate, star-crossed girl. Henri II and Catherine de Medici had by this time inherited the throne and, to all intents and purposes, the strange relationship remained unaltered. The King continued to insult Catherine with his open and blatant attention to Diane, and Catherine continued to behave as though she did not have a care, apparently accepting the situation without rancour. Now Marie found she no longer had to worry about her daughter, she soon had the country in good order.

Only two years later she felt she should go to France, not so much to see how her daughter was progressing but to try to gain sufficient backing for her regency. She took the wise precaution of insisting that she should be accompanied by the Earls Huntly, Cassillis, Maxwell and several others she suspected might otherwise make trouble in her absence.

Marie had left France as the young bride of James V. Now she was returning to visit her daughter as Dowager Queen and Regent of Scotland. She joined the court at Rouen. Mother and daughter were in heaven over their reunion and Marie had no doubt that her lovely child was developing into a charming, responsible and clever young girl. The King was delighted to see and welcome her as the true leader of the Scottish people; so was the Queen and so was Diane de Poitiers. She was received by the Guise family as their provident daughter. She had proved she could handle highly political problems and responsibilities with skill.

She still took the opportunity to seek the advice of her family on managing her turbulent country. They were still mourning the death of her father, Duke Claude. So her meeting with her brother Francis was the first since he had acceded to the title. He was to carry on the Guise ambitions with unabated ambition. Regardless of any natural brother and sister relationship, it soon became clear however that he was assuming all the autocratic attitude of the head of a great family. And there was still her uncle, the Cardinal of Lorraine, less a churchman than a leading politician, and he too, no doubt, gave her counsel on the government of Scotland.

Marie's mother was the formidable Antoinette, who had 12 children and all the vigour of a person who was to live to be 89. She administered a household run on a scale similar to the royal court and additionally ran the whole of the family's widely-ranged estates. She was immune to the blandishments of the actual King and his mother. Indeed it was her firm belief that her establishment was much the superior.

Considering all the royal intrigues and infidelities, she was probably right. Yet she had a robust approach to the real world bordering on the idiosyncratic. She had a peculiarly-shaped cupboard made for her bedroom. It was designed to become her coffin, so that she could lie in bed and ruminate on the transience of life.

Even though Marie was now in France, she found a major problem which the family were loath to solve. Not only had she paid all the bribes to keep the Scots lairds loyal, she was having to pay for the French soldiers billeted in Scotland. It had reached the stage where she did not have enough left to pay her personal servants, and had to borrow from the Countess of Montrose. But the King kept stalling over paying her agreed allowance. As her debts mounted, so she had to keep reminding him and he would put her off with promises to pay it shortly. He did however bribe the Earl of Arran into officially abdicating his place as Regent by making him Duke of Chatelherault, together with a gift of 12,000 crowns, which Arran took with alacrity, though he took much longer over the actual signing.

Amongst other entertaining interludes during her stay, Marie witnessed the manoeuvrings of the new English Ambassador, Lord Northampton. He was now representing Henry's son Edward VI. Reconciliation was his avowed concern, so almost on arrival he made Henri a member of the Order of the Garter.

It was not long, though, before his real task became apparent. It was to try and reclaim Mary from her engagement to the Dauphin. The King refused. Lord Northampton then moved on to plan B. The Princess Elizabeth was up for marriage again. She, instead of Mary, could marry the Dauphin. Again the King graciously declined, and still Marie had not received her allowance.

After a few weeks, regardless of the justice of her claim, she was becoming a bore. Then, to add to her woe, Francis, Duc de Longueville, her second son by her first marriage, suddenly died. Now, of all the five children she had nurtured, only Mary was still living. So it was with an even heavier heart that, her visit over, Marie once more took up the burden of keeping Scotland ready for when her daughter should return as Queen.

According to routine etiquette, as much as to precaution, Marie had written in advance asking permission, should it become necessary, to take refuge in an English port. And indeed storms did force her ship into Portsmouth Harbour. She was mindful that only four years before, the English had carried out the bloody battle of Pinkie. So it must have been with some surprise when, on landing at Portsmouth, she found every courtesy being extended to her. It was evident that the ambassadorial failure of Lord Northampton had not in the least diminished the English hope.

There was even an invitation to visit London. There she was

greeted by the Princess Elizabeth, dignified by a train of 120 retainers. She was then escorted to Westminster by Lady Jane Grey, Countess of Suffolk. It was arranged for her to lodge with the Archbishop of Canterbury at Lambeth Palace. The City of London provided her food, and it was provided in prodigious quantities. When she eventually met Edward VI, it was remarked that her curtsey was so deep it almost amounted to a genuflection. When the King asked her how she liked England, she replied, ever tactful, "I like it passing well, but of all I have seen here, I am best pleased in its King".

However their conversation in private did not progress quite so smoothly. Edward came quickly to the point: "Yet you would not have me to your son?" Her reply was perfectly candid. If he had asked before all the recent happenings, she might have felt able to give a different answer. It was clear that the King was being no more successful than his ambassador.

By 1554, however, Marie's life was made much easier through her daughter officially coming of age. Marie was now in a position to see that the administration was close to collapse. Her chancellor was Earl Huntly, who was completely inadequate for the job. He could barely write. She could not even rely on her Prime Minister, the Archbishop of St. Andrews. Whenever there was a controversial decision to be made, he feigned illness.

All the time Arran had been Regent, he had relied on the support of the Catholic element within the council. But this was only because his brother held the key clerical post of Archbishop of St. Andrews. Now the Catholic element was openly averse to Marie and opposed her making any changes. Fortunately the Protestants in the council, particularly the younger members, such as Maitland and Lord Lovat, realised that now Mary Tudor had come to the throne, they had no hope of support from England. Furthermore, they had travelled abroad sufficiently to have some comprehension of what Marie had in mind.

They backed her in appointing de Roubay, as replacement for Huntly, and when she went on to appoint Louis de Bouton as Governor of the Orkneys and de Villemort as her comptroller. But when she wanted to appoint yet another Frenchman as her Secretary of State, the council refused. She had to compromise by appointing William Maitland, whom she at least knew she could trust.

At the same time she found many of the church clerks had been to France to finish their education. They too had some conception of what she was trying to do.

Marie next decided to journey around Scotland settling civil and legal disputes. Among the several pieces of advice the old Duke had given her was "to deal in Scotland in a spirit of conciliation, introducing much gentleness and moderation into the administration of justice". She was horrified at the state it was in. Justice was administered by the clan chieftains. Largely ignorant and largely isolated, they effectively were accountable to no one.

She found justice had little meaning. Many cases were brought seeking help or retribution against witches. Usually the unfortunate woman had been arrested and tried through a mixture of local prejudice and envy. Punishment was extreme and administered without mercy. There were instances of women hanged with babes in their arms. But while Marie's husband had found ruthlessness the most effective way of keeping outlying areas under some sort of control, Marie, in contrast, administered the law with fairness and humanity. In cases where her husband would have had the accused hanged, she merely had them imprisoned. Her ability in creating reconciliation and restoring accord enormously increased the people's love and respect for her.

Immediately on her return to Edinburgh, she finished the job by summoning the help of Henry Sinclair, Dean of Glasgow. Together they overhauled the entire justice system, with considerable and lasting success. It was proof of her ability, but only so long as she was left to carry out the wishes of the French lords in her own way.

Unfortunately it was not so successful when the policy emanated from France. While there the Duke had advised her to place the army on a permanent footing. He presumably had in mind Marie's dependency on his troops for her authority. Marie certainly appreciated the point. The official existing arrangement could hardly be considered satisfactory. Whenever a national army was needed, the major lords were supposed to provide a stipulated number of men. With their pronounced sense of independence, this could hardly be described as a reliable and efficient way to mobilise. Few of them would come up with the required numbers within a reasonable time, especially as many were being bribed by the English. Even after the men had eventually been assembled, most of them were untrained. Marie had experienced all this, of course, in the disastrous defeat of Pinkie Cleugh.

Another problem was that whenever the army had been officially stood down, the Lords had a habit of keeping their men in arms, virtually turning their retainers into armies of their own. It seemed obvious that in preparing the way for a national army, these unofficial armed men must be stood down. So, as a start, Marie issued a decree that no lord might have more than 1,000 horsemen and that he should instead make contributions to this new army.

The response was emphatic. The Earl of Angus arrived in Edinburgh with just over 1,000 men in his train. When she reprimanded him, he replied "Greatly would I be rid of them, for they devour all my beef and my bread and much, Madam, would I be beholden to you if you could tell me how to get quit of them". This insolence had its effect, and Marie had to abandon the idea.

Her worst fears were realised four years later, when England was at war with France. Although both queens were Roman Catholics, one owed allegiance to Spain and the other to France, so they were still at enmity. Indeed Marie had even taken in English refugees from Mary's excesses. So Marie thought it was only logical that she should come

to the aid of her family and declare war on England. Her intention
was to capture Wark Castle. Hardly an ambitious target since it was set
on the English bank of the Tweed. However, even this modest attempt
ended in her utter humiliation. The Lords simply refused to obey.
Defending Scotland against attack from England was one thing;
invading England on behalf of a foreign country was another.

In any case, theoretically Marie could not have raised a fully
mercenary army without first asking Parliament for the money, and
they would never have agreed. So in her dilemma she had to raise as
many men as she could from among the border chiefs, even though a
short time before she had been trying to disarm them. However they
were a wild lot and quite prepared to go to war on any account so
long as they could return home at nights. That ruled out Wark Castle.
So Marie's declaration of war became more a gesture than a threat.

Hardly surprisingly, this failure to form a national army also
convinced Marie that the only way she could hope for adequate and
reliable protection was to return to her previous policy and rely on
bringing in French troops.

Edward's pressing wish to marry Mary Queen of Scots had by 1553
become a vain hope. Mary was still only nine and Edward was already
far gone with galloping consumption. During his last years the Earl of
Northumberland had seized power by having himself appointed
Regent. He then persuaded the young king to sign a "device"
amending Henry VIII's will. It decreed that Edward's stepsisters Mary
and Elizabeth Tudor were illegitimate, and that the true inheritor of
the throne was Lady Jane Grey. It was nefarious and completely
contrary to the law. Any legitimacy it could claim was through having
been agreed by Parliament. But this was no less questionable. Lady
Jane's ambitious father the Earl of Suffolk and several of the major
landowners had bought their estate at knockdown prices after the

dissolution of the monasteries. Now they were fearful that should Catholic Mary come to the throne she would insist they return their ill-gotten gains.

Added to this, there was a highly dubious clause in Henry's original will. Directly contrary to the constitution, it excluded his elder sister's Scottish descendants. Only after all these highly questionable genealogical questions had been settled could it be claimed that next in line for the English throne was Lady Jane Grey.

Northumberland, in cahoots with Lady Jane's father, tried to strengthen the claim by having her married to his son. At first everything seemed to be going to plan. The Council were ardent Protestants and had already declared Lady Jane Queen.

Mary Tudor, the successor named in Henry's will, had all this while been living in London. She had discreetly been allowed to follow her faith undisturbed, largely because Charles had made it clear that he would raise strong objections if it were otherwise. So she was only too well aware of Northumberland's plot to exclude her from the throne, and she was prepared to defend her claim.

She had two days warning that her stepbrother was dying and quickly left for her estate in Northumberland. There she could rely on the loyalty of her tenants. Actually she had a six-day bonus, for Northumberland was so anxious to strengthen his position that he withheld the announcement of the King's death. This gave Mary time to form and hold a council, after which she issued her first orders as Queen. It was a letter to the council in London declaring that she was lawful heir to the throne.

She then set out with her household for London. Her cause rapidly gained support in the eastern counties. As she progressed through East Anglia, she acquired more and more followers, which included many Protestants. They rallied not so much for her beliefs as because she had become the icon for resistance against the hated Northumberland.

Her situation further improved when the troops sent to take her prisoner mutinied and crossed over to join her supporters. Finally a naval squadron sent by Northumberland to try and hem her in at Great Yarmouth mutinied. In fact their protest was against their wretched conditions, but it was widely assumed it was in support of Mary.

Poor Jane. The one decision she had made as queen had been wrong – fatally wrong, as things turned out. She had begged that instead of her father-in-law leading the forces, the responsibility should be transferred to her husband, who quickly proved inadequate for the job.

Meantime the Council were alarmed to learn that Mary's cause was being championed by a powerful foreign clique. The adept yet extremely bigoted Roman Catholic Simon Renard was sent by Charles V. Not to be outdone, Henri sent his secretary. Such strong foreign interest against Lady Jane Grey somewhat alarmed the Council, who tried to keep the Frenchman in diplomatic isolation.

Then Northumberland made a tactical mistake. He left London to deal personally with Mary's followers. In his absence the Council discovered that Northumberland had been secretly negotiating with the hated French to back Lady Jane Grey.

He had achieved this astonishing Catholic volte face on two counts. First, Charles V was an arch enemy of France and, since he was backing Mary Tudor, the natural inclination of the French should be to support the contender Mary Queen of Scots. Also they thought they would be able to control her better. A much more subtle reason Northumberland had put forward was that if Mary Tudor was allowed to come to the throne, the Catholic families would almost certainly not be interested in all the trauma of having her removed in favour of another Catholic who was, in effect, a foreigner. But if Lady Jane Grey could stay on as queen, there would be time for the powerful English Catholic families to rally and oust Lady Jane and put Mary Queen of Scots in her place. And this, of course, Northumberland felt confident he could prevent from ever happening. However, when it came to the moment, Mary had the considerable advantage of being actually in the country and taking the initiative. Mary Queen of Scots, on the other hand, was still far away in France, so her claims were little more than theory.

By this time caution had caused most of the Council to melt away to avoid being implicated deeper. Those who could not retire dutifully rescinded their choice of Lady Jane, curtailing her reign to nine days. They hastened to proclaim Mary as sovereign in her stead. And so when in July 1553 Mary re-entered London, she was still unsure of the reception she would receive. As a precaution she had most of her armed supporters masquerading as retainers. She need not have worried, for the citizens of London received her amid widespread rejoicing.

Fate was to become weighted even further against Lady Jane. After obsequious recantations, her father was pardoned, and so was the no less odious Duke of Northumberland, though his subsequent actions soon caused him too to be executed.

Mary was just as reluctant to execute Jane. Then came the ill-fated rebellion by Thomas Wyatt, and Mary showed considerable courage. When the rebels reached the very precincts of the city, her council advised her to flee. She refused and instead made a speech to her people from the Guildhall. She was even prepared to lead the troops herself. It had a dramatic effect. The citizens rallied round, barricading the streets and preventing Wyatt from making the final triumphant stage of his journey.

It was then she realised that, even though Jane had had no part in the rebellion, so long as she remained alive, Mary's throne and, indeed, her life, were in danger. Her execution was a political decision and one she simply could not avoid. On the scaffold Jane, barely 17 years old, proclaimed her loyalty to Mary and with obvious sincerity declared she had never wanted to inherit the crown of England.

Unfortunately Mary also brought with her a whole baggage of complexes. It was hardly surprising, considering her chequered childhood. First there was the way her father had treated her mother, Catherine of Aragon. He had pushed her aside so that he could marry Anne Boleyn. He had only been able to do this by splitting from Rome and appointing himself head of the church of England. The chasm between the two faiths had been widened in Mary's mind as her mother had brought her up according to her deep faith in Roman Catholicism. When Henry, with his fixation on begetting an heir, divorced Catherine, he had ordered Mary to sign an agreement that she was illegitimate. She refused. It went against everything she believed in. Added to this, she had suffered the indignity of having her status as princess reduced to lady-in-waiting to her younger sister Elizabeth. It was an insult, and she was of an age when she was only too conscious of the unfairness of it all.

Matters were not helped by the fact that Elizabeth's mother was beastly to her and even threatened to have her executed. Henry would have had her imprisoned, except that Charles V, who was her first cousin, was making it clear that he was taking considerable interest in her welfare. So Henry merely had her separated from her mother and sent to Hatfield.

When she had first entered London, Mary had made a show of unity by having her sister Elizabeth ride by her side. But it was not long before the dislike that had long existed between them began taking specific form. Mary could not forget that Elizabeth was also a confirmed Protestant, and now that she was bent upon returning the country to the true faith, Elizabeth seemed to be dragging her feet. It was only under extreme duress that she had been persuaded to attend mass at all. Upon these grounds, Mary fully expected her to be complicit in any conspiracy to turn her off the throne or even plot her assassination.

Confirmation came when, unbeknown to both sisters, Northumberland secretly wrote to Henri II in France, suggesting he send letters to the English Catholics urging them to rebel. Following this lead, the English exiles in France planned an invasion to put Elizabeth on the throne. But Henri s letters were intercepted and Henry Dudley, the main perpetrator in England, was identified and executed. There was no proof that Elizabeth had taken any part in the plot. Even so, the faithful Catholic gang pressed for her arrest, and it did indeed reach the stage when she was put in the Tower.

Fortunately there was never quite enough evidence for her to be actually executed. On the contrary, recognising the danger, Elizabeth had become extremely careful to keep clear of any suggestion of conspiracy. She dressed in black and had no truck with pageants or any entertainment, as this was associated with the pagan Renaissance. In actual fact Elizabeth was genuinely loyal, for she held a very strong view that the Lord's anointed, no matter under which faith, was sacrosanct.

Despite this Mary had, unlike both her father and her sister, grown up to be straightforward and without guile. She was loved by everyone in her household and she, in turn, doted over literally scores of godchildren. But she had no sense over the advisability of creating an image or making an impression. Now, at 38, she was short and flabby rather than fat. She had a white complexion with no eyebrows and looked "washed out". She had no dress sense and was dowdy. Her appearance was not improved by her love of jewellery, which she wore lavishly and flashily about her. Yet she had a degree of dignity and "an intimidating eye", though the effect would be lost when occasionally fell into hysterical tantrums.

On coming to the throne, she put duty first. She even gave up those few things that gave her pleasure, particularly hunting. Instead she would get up at dawn and hear mass before starting the day's work, and she could often be found still working on state papers well after midnight.

She unfortunately chose her Council primarily for their Catholic beliefs rather than any political acumen. Most of the members had been part of her entourage tucked away at Framlington or else they had only recently emerged from imprisonment imposed by Northumberland. So they tended to be out of touch with current affairs. Those few still in the council who had been wrong footed over the accession assumed that Mary did not particularly like them. Indeed she did not like any of them and once in private she admitted she could scarcely see anyone around her without seeing someone who had not done her an injury or would fail to do so again if the opportunity presented itself. These deficiencies in advice were magnified since she was quite convinced of the validity of the widely held view that a woman's mind was inferior to that of a man. She said as much when she declared she was "of a sex which cannot becomingly take more than a moderate part in them". So in state matters, and even in domestic ones, she would simply outline what she wanted, based mainly on religious grounds, and leave the detail to others. She took it to the stage where, if her council were in two minds, she did not argue or persuade but merely lost her temper.

In practice she looked for guidance from Stephen Gardiner Bishop of Winchester, whom she made her chancellor. Even more to the point, there was Simon Renard, who had stayed on in England after he had so successfully helped ease Mary onto the throne. Charles had decided that he was a useful man to keep there as his representative. He had soon proved his worth for, although he was still only ambassador, Mary had come to appreciate just how adept he was. Ever looking for a strong arm to lean upon she had come to lean upon him more and more until he came to be widely acknowledged as the most powerful man in the realm.

Contrary to common repute, Mary was a kind woman. She was in fact the most merciful of all the Tudors. Although 480 people had been convicted after the Wyatt rebellion she pardoned 400 of them and, had she been left to her own wishes, it is unlikely that any of them would have been executed. This was in strong contrast to Elizabeth's later ruthless action after her confrontation with the Northern lords. Mary was even prepared to restore forfeited goods and lands. She actually wanted to meet Wyatt's wife and commiserate with her over the way she had been forced to have her husband executed.

Mary also showed surprising tolerance towards the Protestants. An early proclamation hoped that the people would embrace her own religion but that she "mindeth not to compel any of my said subjects thereunto". So it is difficult at this point to reconcile her natural liberalism with the "Bloody Mary" reputation history has given her.

Because the Catholics had been persecuted under Edward VI, her advisers believed her subjects would welcome a return to the old religion. In fact, the people had become so confused through being instructed in first one faith then in another and now back to the first, they did not care particularly which they practised so long as it did not impinge on their daily life.

Charles, however, was wary. He warned her not to push conversion too aggressively or she might seriously alienate opinion against her. So when he learnt that Mary had invited the hard line Catholic Cardinal Pole back from exile in Rome, he was afraid she might exacerbate the situation by appointing him Archbishop of Canterbury. He also knew that Pole was very much against some of his long term schemes. So while the Cardinal was travelling through his Habsburg country, he took the opportunity to confiscate his passport and held him for nearly a year until Mary had established her Council.

Then Mary got herself into real trouble. She announced she was going to marry Philip, the King of Spain.

In fact she had been nobbled.

Back in 1555, Charles V had come to the conclusion that the Austro-Hungarian empire had become too unwieldy. So he decided that before abdicating and retiring to a monastery in Yutse, he would divide the empire between his brother Maximilian, Arch Duke of Austria, and his son Philip. Maximilian's portion was fairly compact, comprising Austria and Hungary, a section of the Balkans, Germany and parts of Italy. Philip's portion comprised Spain and the Netherlands. The Netherlands was still one of the richest nations in Europe, so economically the arrangement may have made sense. However, politically it was clumsy. There is that wedge between them in the shape of France, and at that time France was no ally. So communications had to be either through the volatile states of Italy or down the Channel.

Here again there was a snag. France had control of much of the south coast and the northern side had, until recently, been controlled by the violently protestant Edward. Now, heaven be praised, the English coast was under the control of the far more amenable Mary Tudor. But how could this satisfactory state of affairs be put on a permanent basis?

At this time Charles V was declining into senile dementia to the degree that Mary, who was still Governess of the Netherlands, had in effect taken control in running the Habsburg Empire. Immediately on learning of Edward's death, she wrote to the Queen of England in Charles's name suggesting she should marry Philip of Spain.

At the same time she wrote to Philip, who had been sent to woo the Infanta of Portugal, telling him to break off his advances and sail at once for England. She even tried to arouse such passion as Mary might have and arranged to send her a portrait of Philip. It had proved to be a highly successful ploy when a Holbein painting of Anne of Cleaves had been sent to Henry. The Governess commissioned Titian, another artist known to be highly skilful in the art of flattery, and there was little need for him to be told to depict Philip as young, handsome and athletic. To make sure, she even sent Mary detailed instructions on how she must view the portrait "at a distance and in full light as one cannot recognise a Titian from too close".

Again, it did the trick.

Altogether Mary could have hardly been more amenable to the idea. For one thing the suggestion came from her dear and reliable Mary of Hungary, whom she had known since she had been a child, when she had played an important part in the negotiations over Henry's divorce from her mother Katherine. She had also met Charles V personally when he had come over to England thirty years before, when it was thought he might marry her. Then the Governess had cunningly arranged for her letter to be delivered through the hands of Simon Renard, so that it carried his blessing too.

A note of warning, however, was given by Cardinal Gardiner. Marriage to Philip was unlikely to have the approval of the people. With typical petulance, instead of accepting it as advice based upon observation, she accused him of being disloyal and putting the wishes of her subjects before her own.

Largely under Gardiner's influence, Parliament issued a similar warning. To them she was no less abrupt, making the cutting reply that "Parliament was not accustomed to use such language to the Kings of England nor was it suitable or respectful that it should do so".

Parliament, however, had an instinctive aversion to a foreigner being put into such a major position and feared it would lead to disaster. It agreed to the marriage eventually, but made some stringent stipulations. Philip must not interfere in politics in any way. He was not to have any authority, nor could he appoint foreigners to any office. He was not to be crowned. Finally any children that might stem from the marriage would be heirs to the throne of England alone. If there were no issue, neither Philip nor his heir, Don Carlos, could lay claim to the throne. It would go instead to "the next successor by right and law".

Even though Philip more or less lived up to Holbein's portrait, both parties understood that the union was purely a matter of providing an heir. He was in effect a stud, for he was 27 and she was 37, but he was a stud of international status, for he eventually married four queens or princesses. He was a competent stud too, for altogether he fathered ten children. But in so far as Mary was concerned, he initially appeared to be far from impatient to meet his intended. He kept postponing sailing for England, for so long in fact that Charles had to reprimand him and make it plain that he was to look to his conjugal duties and not spend his efforts dallying with other ladies.

However, once Philip had arrived, he played his part to the full. He overcame his natural aloofness and disdain and immediately embraced the Queen, not to mention all the Queen's ladies "so as not to break the customs of the country, which is a good one". He never failed to show consideration and respect for his wife.

For her part, though she may not have been in love, she certainly respected him and was genuinely fond of him. True to character, she set her heart on being a loyal and steadfast spouse.

Philip's court, however, failed to find popularity among the ordinary people. One wrote home: "They rob us in Town and on the road and we Spanish move among the English as if they were animals, trying not to notice them and they do the same for us". Indeed the English pointedly referred to "The Queen's husband".

All those constrictions the Government had placed upon Philip still allowed him to take charge of the wedding ceremony. As a result, it was a great deal more impressive than her coronation. The conditions also allowed him to organise the palace administration. Under Mary's indifference it had become lax, but Philip soon had it working with a great deal more efficiency.

But his most important contribution was less obvious. He pursued one of the few good policies that Northumberland had initiated; the development of foreign trade. English internal trade had already undergone a revolution due to the demise of agriculture following Henry's dissolution of the monasteries. Wool had taken its place. Unlike crops, wool had durability, so it was easy to export. Consequently it had rapidly become the staple growth and success of English trade.

The foreign credit had in turn stimulated imports. A whole line of new commodities came into vogue. With the improvement in the refining process, sugar imports increased. There were advances in the processing of tobacco and in the metal industries. All over Europe the traditional medieval markets determined by land routes were being overtaken by international sea trading ports, with Antwerp the most prominent. Mary had even used this advantage to introduce controls forbidding Hanseatic merchants from entering English seas, thereby granting English merchants a monopoly in trading wool between England and Antwerp.

The struggle for the seas really dates back to 1453, a time when cartographers were still putting Jerusalem as the centre of the world. Pope Alexander VI had blithely divided the world beyond Europe into two. He allocated the East Indies, Brazil and the whole of Africa south of the Canaries to Portugal. The other half he gave to Spain. England had nothing, and had remained content, for at that time most of the trade was conducted within the Mediterranean area.

But now the Americas were becoming of major importance and the heart of European trade was shifting so that England's position was becoming central.

Due to the fairly benign conditions of an inland sea, most European sailors considered navigation to be little more than hugging the coastline, backed by a degree of instinct and guesswork. Courtesy of the newly-invented printing press, navigation was undergoing a profound change. Every mariner could refer to Martin Cortes's book

The Art of Navigation and Mercator's map projection. England, with its long and ragged coastline, often battered by Atlantic storms, had bred generations of conditioned English sailors. They developed storm-weathering ships, so that now they were able to extend their routes as far afield as Barbados, the South American coast and beyond. Commerce had followed close behind. Within the first year of Mary's reign, a company had been formed to trade with the Guinea Coast. It was soon overtaken by disaster but it had shown the way for the slave trade, which was soon to prosper mightily.

Mary gave a royal charter which, along with a letter from Philip, persuaded the Tsar of Russia to give trading rights to the English Muscovy Company. This was in itself innovative, for it was the first chartered joint stock company. Up to then the capital, as well as profits in any speculation, were, if successful, returned to the investors once the enterprise had been completed. Under this new arrangement, several merchants and wealthy individuals could, through a Government charter, buy joint stock and invest it long term, taking a proportion of the profits on the same principle as interest.

But in other ways Philip's influence was disastrous. The first sign came when he invited Cardinal Carranza of Toledo over from Spain. He had been Primate and had played an enthusiastic part in setting up the infamous Spanish Inquisition. Once in England, his bigotry soon drew him into close collusion with Simon Renard and Bonner, Bishop of London. Almost certainly it was Philip who gave them encouragement. Recently he had been urging the Inquisition in Spain to ever greater excesses. In the near future he was to replace the amenable Margaret of Parma as Governess of the Netherlands with the notoriously blood thirsty Duke of Alba.

In England, the bigots found their opportunity with the long-drawn-out problem of the restitution of all those former church lands confiscated by Henry. The Pope, in his Vatican aloofness, wanted them to be returned to the church. But one only had to be in England to realise it would be madness to try and wrest the lands back from their newly-enriched and highly influential owners. So Cardinal Pole had entered into negotiations with the Pope and it was agreed the estate situation would be allowed to stay as it was. To compensate, Parliament would reinstate the Heresy Act. This brought Roman Catholicism back as the recognised faith of the nation.

For the next few months little more happened than the imprisonment of the more resistant Protestant bishops. But then the Council ordered that the prisoner bishops should be executed. The burnings of the Oxford Martyrs in 1555 marked the highlight of the Marian Protestant prosecution.

The more conservative Bishops, such as Gardiner and Pole, were not enthusiastic over such a drastic policy, but they did nothing more than look upon "Bloody" Bonner, the burning Bishop of London, as "a useful instrument for disagreeable work rather than a desirable colleague".

Sympathy for the Protestants became widespread when the wives of Protestant priests were being hounded out of their homes; later because the burnings were being extended to artisans and even humble working people, people with whom the ordinary man could associate himself.

It has been suggested that Mary went along with this ruthless policy, partly because she had genuinely fallen in love with Philip, perhaps even more so because she knew he was not in love with her. This may account for the fact that in the last years of her life, after she realised he had abandoned her, she reverted to her original concern for people. She would "dress down" as an ordinary woman and go about her estates, succouring the poor.

When in 1494 the Habsburg and Valois forces had first proudly marched into battle, both sides had failed to appreciate the recent enormous increase in the cost of war. At that period the major toll had been the cost in human life and that, of course, was infinitely cheap. Otherwise there had been little more than such costs as armour, which the knights paid for themselves, and woodworking the bows, which the archers usually whittled for themselves. But recently gunpowder had come into general use. It increased the costs of war immeasurably. The precision mechanism of the musket could only be made by specialist metalworkers and was very expensive. So, too, was gunpowder, and even the matches to light the fuses. Added to this, it all needed preparation, which included living expenses now that the men required training.

This traditional spat had been taken up by Charles V and Henri II and in 1557 Henri was ignominiously retreating from the Italian border. Philip had been supporting his father Charles V with subsidiary battles in Northern France, and this was the reason why he had abandoned his newly wed wife. But now was the moment to bring in more forces.

So, after a two-year absence, Philip suddenly reappeared in London and became the attentive husband again. Mary did not require much persuading. However the Council, and Cardinal Pole in particular, were strongly against such an idea. Then in 1557 the French settled it by making what they hoped would be a preventative move, landing at Scarborough and capturing the castle. There was a further touch of bravado when Henri, on receiving the Mary's declaration of war, roared with laughter and said "What a pass things have come to when a woman declares war on France".

But he laughed too soon. Top among Philip's priorities was to oust the French from their occupation of St. Quentin. The British forces duly arrived on the Continent and went directly to help the Spanish, who were already on the verge of relieving the citadel. In fact the Spanish forces would have had no trouble in defeating the severely-weakened place on their own.

In fact the English contingent brought the whole enterprise close to disaster. The Earl of Pembroke, who was leading the English force, was late, and it was etiquette not to go into battle without one's allies. But once arrived, the English forces redeemed themselves and after a two-week siege, St. Quentin was freed. The Spanish claimed that all in all it was truly a victory of God. Indeed Philip was so astonished at his success that instead of seizing his main chance and advancing on a largely undefended Paris, he spent the time mopping up surrounding villages.

The Duke of Guise, still in Italy, had seen the crisis and force-marched his troops back to Paris. He thus, in a few days, converted an ignominious retreat into a heroic rescue of the capital. He was greeted by a King so relieved at his arrival that he embraced him with such fervour "that he seemed unable to detach himself from his neck." Even better, the Duke of Montmorency, in charge of the French forces in the north, also took advantage of Philip's hesitation. He was able to regroup his forces and successfully counter attacked, regaining St. Quentin. The tables had now been completely turned.

Henri could not wait to follow up his success. He took a gamble and ordered Guise to go further and attack the English garrison in Calais. This outpost had for long been used by the English as a convenient trading post for the Continent, and in due course they had commandeered it. For more than a century, this had rankled with the French. However, for the moment the English garrison felt reassured by the exhausted state of the French army. Not only that, but winter had come and mud made all military manoeuvres virtually impossible. So the garrison had, in effect, been stood down. The French attack took them completely by surprise. Even so the English forces could have defended Calais longer had the Spanish, who were nearby at Gravelines, come to help. But they did not and the Fort fell after only a few days, in January 1557, leaving considerable bitterness between the allies.

Mary was humiliated by the defeat. Her misery was not helped when the French started a malicious rumour that Philip was now asking the Pope for a divorce. She made no attempt to recapture Calais and within the year she was dead. Poor Mary; she died in November 1558 in the full knowledge that after five years on the throne all her good intentions had come to nothing. She was not deceived, and realised she had in practice lost Calais. She had failed to produce an heir, and all her efforts to guide the country back to the true faith had been thwarted.

Armagil Ward, Clerk to Mary's Council, wrote a disturbing account: "The poverty of the Crown, real exhausted notability, poor and decayed, want of good captains and soldiers, people out of order, justice not executed, all things dear, excess in meat, drink and apparel, divisions among ourselves, wars with France and Scotland. The French king bestriding the realm having one foot in Calais and the other in Scotland. Steadfast enemy but no steadfast friendship abroad".

Now she was having to leave the country in the hands of her sister. It was so awful that she could not even bear to mention Elizabeth by name, and in her will she simply left it to "her legal successor".

But the war was dragging on and both and Charles and Henri had been meeting their costs through traditional methods, increasing such taxes as they had under their personal control. This had its limitations. Henri's most lucrative tax was on land, but it had reached the stage of diminishing returns. Landowners were living under such high taxation that their estates were running at a loss. The only way of avoiding tax would have been to sell, but the law forbade this. The only solution left was simply to disappear. Incredibly, Henri kept his money in a chest and his expenditure was controlled simply because it could only be opened by using three keys. Normally the King had one; the other two were held by the Treasurer and the Comptroller. However in these times of extremes the King had managed to get possession of all three, and now his chest was empty. His debts amounted to 40m livres, his annual income was five million and there was rampant inflation.

Then he thought he had found respite in the new breed of bankers. They did not seek immediate collateral but were prepared to make loans in anticipation of the money the King could expect to raise from future taxes. It meant that for the moment the King only had to find money for the interest. But even this had its limits, and in due course Henri could not find anyone to make him any more loans, even at 16 per cent.

Charles also had frightening debts amounting to 50m ducats. Before long, following the same line for raising money, the interest was soon taking up a third of his income. His response was to purloin the family silver and gold accumulated by the nobles and give them worthless IOUs in exchange. Again this procedure had its limitations. In the final months he was writing "I find myself under an absolute impossibility of continuing the war. I have already spent 1,200,000 ducats which I raised from Spain two or three months ago and I have need of another million in the coming months of March. They have sent me from Spain Doctor de Lasco to assure me that they cannot do anything more for me. The situation seems to me so very grave that under pain of losing everything, I must come to some sort of an arrangement. I am waiting with a very active impatience for news, but on no account whatever must these negotiations (for an armistice) be broken off".

Henri was no less pressed: "Do what you can to give us peace." A little later he was to write "I would gladly suffer death which I would consider happy and I would die content if I could see a good peace." Consequently, in this supposed year of triumph, both Spain and the Spanish Netherlands went bankrupt and announced they would pay only 5 per cent on their debts. Indeed most of Europe was close to bankruptcy.

So it was with considerable relief to all when the powers agreed in April 1559 to negotiate a peace treaty to be called the treaty of Cateau Cambresis.

PART II

1559-1568
THE REGIMENT MUSTERS

Cateau-Cambresis was a truly international treaty. If all the Dutch, German and Italian states are included, it altogether involved 18 countries. Even so, the French were annoyed that, while England was represented at the negotiations, Mary, as Queen in absentia from her realm, had not been invited. The treaty in effect set out international law which was observed more or less for the next hundred years. But at the negotiating table it was only France and Spain which really counted and it left both very much as they had been before. Henri II was allowed to retain Savoy and Piedmont, which he had been occupying for the past 80 years, along with two areas within buffer zones; Metz provided a bulwark against Germany and Calais against England. Otherwise he had to surrender virtually everything he had so painfully gained.

Catherine and most of the nobles were horrified at how much Henri had surrendered. It was so disastrous that it was widely rumoured that he must have been influenced by Diane. Spain retained control of the states it had occupied in Italy and, while this was not agreeable for the French, it provided a roundabout land corridor with the Netherlands.

At first Philip felt it his duty to put his weight behind his erstwhile ally. But Elizabeth looked upon her late sister's loss of Calais as an unfinished national interlude and was determined to take this opportunity to put it right. He soon grew tired of Elizabeth's persistent carping over Calais. The other leaders also became fed up with her, so that she was in danger of losing everything. In the end she was forced to accept a compromise. The French were to lease the city for the next eight years. While this provided a face-saving formula, everyone realised that possession is nine tenths of the law and when the term was completed, there was every likelihood France would find some way of keeping the city for good. Elizabeth did, however, have an unexpected bonus clause when France agreed in future not to attack England.

Although Cateau-Cambresis had been largely brought about through the foolishness of men, when it was finalised in 1559 it was implemented largely by women. Its effect was to bring peace for the next forty years. It also saw the emergence of the new generation of Knox's monstrous regiment.

Soon after the death of Marie of Guise, Mary sailed to Scotland and claimed her inheritance.

It so happened that at about this time Philip handed the government of the Netherlands over to his stepsister Margaret of Parma.

In a bizarre twist of fate, Henri was killed in a jousting accident which ironically formed part of the sumptuous celebrations he was holding in an effort to cover the humiliation of the treaty's terms. He was succeeded by Catherine's eldest son, Francis II. Since he was a minor the power was partly, and later completely, delegated to Catherine.

Most of all, Europe's hierarchy were intrigued by Elizabeth. She was 25 but she had lived her past 10 formative years as a virtual, sometimes an actual, prisoner. Little was known about the way she had developed. She had been brought up a Protestant, but she had conformed to the Catholic faith and had been known to attend mass. However that had been under the threat of execution, so it did not necessarily carry any conviction.

Early in her life she had learnt not to express an opinion. Even the few who had met her were ignorant of her real thoughts. They reported that she dressed soberly in black and without any adornments. She did not express interest in music or dancing. This was calculated, for such frivolities tended to be associated with the Renaissance, and the Renaissance had become tainted with the hated Protestant movement.

Elizabeth was undoubtedly of strong character. While still only 16 she had been subjected to intense and threatening interrogation over the unorthodox behaviour of her guardian's husband. Her interrogator reported admiringly "She hath a very good wit and nothing is gotten of her but by great policy". Similarly she refused to say anything incriminating against her companions under suspicion, Mrs Ashley and her treasurer Thomas Parry. When she reached 20 she had undergone much more serious interrogation on suspicion of being involved in the Wyatt rebellion.

Her upbringing had not been conducive to a stable character. She had lost her mother at the age of three. Of course she had no clear memories of her, but throughout the rest of her childhood she was constantly reminded of her shame as the daughter of an adulteress who had been executed for treason. Her relationships lacked any stability. Her father had sometimes loved her, calling her his 'little princess'. He had even thought about christening her Mary in an effort to obliterate her elder sister. Then, when he married Jane Seymour, Elizabeth was declared a bastard, so that any children Jane might have would take precedence. Relations with her elder sister were just as confusing and bitter. In later life when she was at liberty to speak her mind, she was, hardly surprisingly, quite unsparing in her criticism.

Academically she owed a lot to her father's enlightened Renaissance outlook. Henry had read and been impressed by Vives and Hyde, who had recently written major philosophical works. She became an outstanding pupil. When she was 16, her tutor, Roger Ashcam, found her excellent at Latin and Greek and cleverer than other educated girls of her age. In fact this happened to coincide with the time when Henry wished her to supplant Mary. He had therefore made sure she had the better education. But she was also fortunate in having the love of the last in her line of stepmothers, Katherine Parr, who took a personal interest in her education. But it was particularly the example of how Katherine had acted as a clever and effective regent while Henry was away at the wars that gave her the confidence to face the political future. Indeed Katherine's influence was even greater than the example of Mary of Hungary.

Altogether, when the time came she had little or no compunction over taking up the reins of power. She was high minded and combined courtesy with dignity: "The constitution of her mind is exempt from female weakness and she is endued within a masculine power of application". When in November 1558 Elizabeth emerged from her obscurity, she was 25 and riding a wave of public goodwill. Just as her sister had been considered an icon against all the excesses of Northumberland, so now Elizabeth was hailed as a merciful alternative to her sister's stern Catholicism. The woman literally burst upon the nation and Europe. Her personality immediately reached out and won the hearts of her citizens. While her sister's coronation had been a drab affair and barely noticed, Elizabeth had a splendid procession. She allocated an eighth of her annual income, some 16,000, towards the celebrations. Customs officers were told to commandeer any crimson silk coming into the country for regal use. She herself wore a mantle of 23 yards of gold and silver tissue. The tails and harnesses of the horses matched the red of her hair.

She exchanged repartee along the route. With typical instinct for the popular touch, in the midst of all this splendour she kept in her hand a sprig of rosemary given to her by a poor woman along the route. When the crowds shouted "God bless your Majesty", she responded "God bless you all, my good people" and the people loved her for it.

Now that at last she was her own mistress, she threw off all the drabness that had been a pall over her recent living. She showed her true love of music, dancing and the theatre. She wore highly-coloured dresses and bedecked herself with jewellery. She soon made it clear she wanted the tedium and tensions of kingship to be kept entirely from her day-to-day living. A courtier wrote "nothing is treated earnestly and though all things may go wrong he who invents most ways of wasting time is regarded as worthy of honour".

Elizabeth was also highly conscious of her feminism in what was traditionally a man's world. While she herself saw it as no disadvantage, she was sufficiently level-headed to take prejudice into consideration when negotiating with men who did not. During her coronation she responded to people's salutations almost apologetically: "You may well have a greater prince, but you shall never have a more loving prince". It was to colour her policy throughout her reign.

In her famous speech at Tilbury she referred to herself as a "weak and feeble woman" and even shortly before she died, she upbraided the Venetians for failing to send a resident ambassador, "for my sex cannot diminish my prestige". In private life she enjoyed the company of other intellectual women such as Lady Mary Sidney and Cecil's wife, Mildred who wrote over 30 books. In council she would act on a woman's intuition, even in the face of the strict logical reasoning of her male advisers. But she particularly won the genuine admiration of men. With her fluency in classical languages, she held the admiration of the scholars; with her courage, she won the loyalty of her servicemen, and with her love of living she won the love of her court.

Certainly she had her shortcomings. Undoubtedly the major one was indecision. She would go completely against her word. She would promise her commanders a precise number of men or ships and then reduce them, often without giving notice. Her Secretary of State wrote: "She was at all times uncertain and ready to stays and revocation. This irresolution doth weary and kill her ministers, destroy her actions and overcome all good designs and counsels". She would cancel instructions, tear up documents she had just signed and act contrary to all the logical reasoning of her advisers to a degree that seemed positively wanton.

Alternatively she would do nothing. She gave no direct answers, made no specific statements and kept silent on controversial issues. When asked hard questions, she would generalise. Cecil, her chief adviser, wrote: "It driveth me up the wall". Even by the end of her reign it was never clear to what degree this behaviour was deliberate. It might have been to keep her advisers and her court on their toes. Others believed she tended to be swayed by the last person to whom she had been speaking. Some said that while she was quick to understand a situation, she gave far more weight to the obvious risks than to the inherent danger of not doing anything.

Certainly during the time Cecil was ill and unable to advise, her policy especially towards the Netherlands, was completely scatterbrained. If her indecision was indeed an act, then she often pursued it to a dangerous degree. Several times it caused her to miss golden opportunities, and there were occasions when she put the country in considerable danger. She always economised on supplies and the number of men asked by her commanders. After her death Walter Raleigh said "Her Majesty did all by halves and by petty invasions taught the Spanish how to defend himself and to see his own weaknesses". But she was astute in choosing people of ability to surround her and, in turn, she backed this with loyalty through thick and thin. At a time when her sister was regarding her with the gravest suspicion, she had recognised the honesty and ability of her surveyor or estate manager, William Cecil. Directly she became Queen she made him her Secretary and charged him: "This judgement I have of you, that you will not be corrupted by any manner of gift and that you will be faithful to the state, and that without respect of my private will, you will give me that council which you think best and if you shall know anything necessary to be declared to me of secrecy, you shall show it to myself only. And assure yourself I will not fail to keep taciturnity therein and therefore herewith I charge you".

For the best part of 40 years, despite numerous court intrigues, she and Cecil kept almost entirely to this simple agreement and in due course elevated him to become Lord Burghley. Other examples of her astute choice of advisers included Sir Thomas Gresham, a top financier, who not only arranged for her to be kept in funds but also regulated trade on her behalf. The third was a later appointment, Sir Francis Walsingham, a farmer, who also proved a formidable and highly effective head of security. Over the years he succeeded in protecting her not only from court intrigues but from increasingly determined enemies abroad.

She inherited a council of 40, which was much too large. She kept 10 of them, mainly because they had been serving her sister with reluctance. She chose only nine replacements. Several of them were elderly intellectuals. While still ambitious for power, they held no realistic intention of bettering themselves by having her turned off the throne. A number had benefited from the dissolution of the monastery lands and therefore held strong anti-Catholic sentiments. This meant they were also anti-Spanish, anti-French and anti-Scottish. In fact they were truly English.

Of all those leaders abroad, the one most anxious to influence the new queen was Philip of Spain. In fact he had started wooing her while his wife was dying. It was a desperate attempt to ensure the English Channel remained open for him. Even if he did not have Elizabeth's affection, he had sufficient grounds to expect her goodwill. While Mary, under the stern regard of Renard, had been seriously thinking of having Elizabeth executed for treason, Philip had persuaded her to be lenient. It was largely due to his persuasion that Mary had not specifically excluded Elizabeth in her will as her successor. But then, with infuriating complacency, he declared that he did not wish to marry Elizabeth but duty forced him to do so; hardly the way to win a lady's affection.

In any case Elizabeth had other ideas, and so did her councillors. They put forward the convoluted argument that should she accept the Pope's dispensation to marry her sister's husband, it would automatically infer that Henry's marriage to Catherine of Aragon had also remained legally binding. This would mean Elizabeth was a bastard. But Philip forlornly hoped that if she turned to Catholicism, the Pope would look leniently upon the marriage and forgive all.

She did indeed need his support, and not only in regard to the feeble position England held during the protracted negotiations of the Cateau-Cambresis treaty. Philip's likely support of England was the main thing that restrained France from occupying Scotland completely. He also knew that Elizabeth realised her only hope of regaining Calais would be through his support, so she set about tarrying by artifice. She managed to convey the impression that she might yet say yes. Indeed this had some immediate advantages. Philip learnt his marital hopes were about to be put into jeopardy when Pope Pius IV decided to declare her illegitimate and excommunicate her. This would probably turn the powerful English Catholic families against her, and just at that parlous moment which attends any sovereign who has recently inherited a throne. Above all, it would scupper any hopes he might still have of becoming King of England. So he did Elizabeth, as well as himself, another favour by persuading the Pope to abandon the idea.

Eventually Elizabeth could pretend no longer and told Philip that she owed her position to her people and they would never stand for her marrying a Spaniard. He must be content with her promise not to let her judgement be swayed by the prejudices of her people.

As soon as Elizabeth had become Queen, her adviser Cecil had presented her with a list of matters which needed her immediate attention. Top of the list was Scotland, which soon lived up to its reputation as "a thistle in her side", although, more accurately, the problem lay in France, for there lay the Scottish powerhouse.

Elizabeth's council was urging her to give the Scottish Protestants military support and take advantage of that very moment when the French were too involved in civil war to invade.

Elizabeth was not so sure. In any case she was hard up, and realised war had become an expensive indulgence. Fortunately, Cecil was in agreement. He too appreciated the expense. He also pointed out that the English forces were still in disarray following Mary's escapades and that an attack on Scotland would almost certainly bring France into open war. As it was, the Scottish Protestants were enjoying a revival simply on the assumption that they would benefit from Elizabeth's accession. Naturally the French were seriously alarmed, and Marie received instructions from Henri to tighten up on discipline - in other words, to persecute the Protestants.

The drawback was that the French were completely ignorant over problems which were so essentially Scottish. They simply assumed Scotland could be governed as though it was a province of France. Marie too was of this persuasion, but in a more practical way. She always tried to introduce the changes gradually and carry public opinion along with her. Also she realised that she still depended on the Protestant lords for her support. The Guise thought she was too sweet-tempered and were urging her to be more aggressive. Marie told them: "It will never do to make any compulsory acts on the subject of religion", and warned that if she did as they proposed, it would lead to riots. However the French insisted, and with considerable misgivings Marie complied.

She was most certainly right to be apprehensive. She decided the best way to carry out Henri's campaign was to issue instructions that mass must be attended daily. This was studiously ignored, so she summoned the leading Protestant lords to Stirling to explain themselves. Instead they sent a delegation to protest. They purposely included Sir Hugh Campbell and the Earl of Glencairn, since they knew Marie distrusted both of them after she had discovered they had been on Henry's pension roll. Nevertheless, with her usual good manners, she told them that, regardless of their protests, she was determined to stop their preachers "even if they be so eloquent as St. Paul". The delegation reminded her that it was not so long ago she had promised to be fair and equal-handed over any disputes.

Unfortunately this provoked her into making the indiscreet remark: "Princes ought not to be urged with their promises further than suits their convenience to observe them". One of the delegates quickly replied "Then, Madam, if you are resolved to keep no faith with your subjects you must not be surprised if we renounce the obedience which otherwise we should consider as your due". The remark pulled Marie up short, and she had to admit she had lost her temper. None the less it defined her policy, even though she offered to withdraw the proclamation on condition that they would disperse the Congregationalists protesters already gathering at Perth. The delegates refused, and Perth duly erupted. Congregationalists broke into the monasteries and desecrated the tombs of the Scottish Kings.

Marie interpreted this as an act of civil war. Mindful of the treachery of the lords in preventing her from raising a Scottish army, the only way Marie could see towards exerting discipline on behalf of the absent Queen of Scotland was to call on the French to provide troops. It meant that for the first time the Catholic faction was openly accepting the authority of France.

It was a fatal mistake. When the French troops duly landed at Leith the Congregationalists felt this proved Marie no longer had faith in their land. It was another move towards occupation. England thought the same, and so it became the first twist in what was to become a descending spiral of international distrust between France, England and the two leading factions in Scotland.

It was unfortunate that Marie found herself in this position at just about the same time that John Knox was making himself felt after 12 years in exile. He had just published his pamphlet "The First Blast of the Trumpet against the Monstrous Regiment of Women". Since Elizabeth had taken umbrage against both the pamphlet and its author, Knox quickly came to rue his words, saying "The blast hath blown from me all my English friends".

Nor had Knox improved his chances when he had sought permission to visit England on his way back from exile. He had written less like someone asking a favour than as a messenger of God who assumed no queen would dare bar his path. Not that the two would ever have been likely to agree over anything. Elizabeth was never very far from accepting Catholicism, whereas Knox was furiously intolerant of it. On reaching Scotland, he had found that since his deportation, the Congregationalists had moved far along the path linking faith with politics. Only two years earlier the Lords had signed the Band of the Lords of the Congregations. They comprised many of the leading Scottish lords who were horrified when Mary married the Dauphin. They had passed the Band with the avowed intention of driving Catholics out of the country. It was, in effect, the first of five wake-up calls whereby the Congregationalists reaffirmed their intentions with growing confidence. However Knox set himself to fire the situation, putting behind him the inconvenient fact that it was largely through Marie's intervention that he had been freed as a galley slave.

Soon he was largely responsible for the conversion of several major political figures, including Maitland To his credit and under his guidance, the scope of the Parliamentary acts extended beyond faith and, for instance, the Book of Discipline, accepted in January 1561, covered education for all and for the relief of the poor. In this Knox was, in fact, bringing Scotland out of medieval politics and into a modern age. Under the peculiar circumstances then prevailing, these laws were being passed by Parliament but not sanctioned by the crown.

The unrest, caused through the difference in faith, was by no means being confined to Scotland. Most of Europe was now undergoing the schisms that England had resolved during the reign of Henry VIII. Protestantism, established by Luther in 1517, was becoming a formidable power throughout Europe. Its principles were directly rooted in the Renaissance, with its accent on looking for guidance from the ancient Greeks and Romans.

The Renaissance had been started by the Italian poet Petrarch back in 1330, but it was not until the sixteenth century that it was influencing the very fabric of Europe. The basic concept was to refuse to accept hidebound learning without question. Initially this was applied to classical learning, and was consequently largely retrospective. It merely encouraged the scholar to refer to original ancient Latin and Greek literature. Then the discovery of the papers of Pythagoras in 1554 suggested that the principle need not be confined just to literature but could be applied to almost every form of culture.

Throughout the "dark" ages, the church had exercised iron control over everyday living. All forms of art were clearly defined and had to be scrupulously followed.

Music was heard only during services, and it had to be plainsong, so that the words could be clearly distinguishable. The Renaissance, however, popularised the harmonic with its more dramatic and sensuous effect. As a result music started being played outside church and purely on its own merit, such as a part of nonsecular processions and concerts with large and orchestras.

Similarly portraiture and graphic art had previously been seen mainly in the stained glass windows and murals in the churches. The biblical figures were symbolic and idealistic rather than natural. The saints must have their halos and the Virgin Mary must be given prominence. This was to be done by painting her clothes blue, for blue was used sparingly, being the most expensive colour on the artist's palette. The Renaissance, in contrast, encouraged portraiture, and princes began exchanging portraits under much the same concept as visiting cards.

The church had even laid its dead hand on medicine. The human body must be as complete as possible so as to be ready for the resurrection, so the only cadavers available for medical study were those of criminals and suicides who were considered beyond redemption. As that did not provide a sufficient supply, human anatomy instruction was mostly carried out on pigs. Without the opportunity for accurate dissection, medical practice remained largely based on mythology.

The influence of the Renaissance moved on into architecture. For a while the Italian architect Filippo Brunelleschi had been pondering the problem of constructing the 138 ft. spanned cupola of Florence cathedral. He found the solution through studying ancient Roman buildings.

During the 15th century the Renaissance crossed the Alps and was hailed by Henri II of France and Charles V, but they had not realised just how far its tentacles would extend.

For centuries the authority of the priests had depended on the illiteracy of peasants, artisans and even the squires. Unable to interpret the Latin bible for themselves they relied on the priests for enlightenment. It was the younger generation of priests in Germany and Switzerland, such as Tyndall, Luther, Calvin and Knox, who applied Renaissance principles to their faith. Much of Luther's doctoring was to strip all the dogma and dictums accumulated over many successions of Popes.

The result was a fundamentally different creed. There was the question of the divinity of the Virgin Mary. Even more controversial was the transsubstantiation of the host. The Protestants refused to believe that at each Communion service there was a miracle and that the wine and bread transformed into the actual body and blood of Christ. They considered it no more than symbolism in memoriam. Another fundamental difference was the belief that redemption was assured through heartfelt faith rather than the performance of irksome rituals ordered as penance for sins confessed.

Thanks to Martin Luther, the bible and prayer book were translated into native languages. The newly-invented printing press enabled tens of thousands of Christian congregations to read and interpret the bible and prayer book for themselves. Almost as influential was Fox's Book of Martyrs, heavily biased against the Catholics since by far the majority of those selected had been burnt by Mary quite recently.

Even, so the New Learning might never have taken hold except for the degeneration of the clergy, not just in Scotland but throughout Europe.

These revelations not only completely removed the credibility of the priests who, by using a mixture of threats and mysticism, had more or less been able to make the laity do whatever they wished. Worse, the priests had come to finance their extravagant living by imposing outrageous charges for performing such offices as christenings, marriages and interments. To make sure no lapse should reduce their income, they held that these ceremonies were essential if the person was not to suffer eternal hellfire.

The church also had their own courts for punishing any offence against church law. They broadened its scope as widely as they could, and their fines became out of all proportion to the offences. This combination had become so effective that they were able to imply justification for their blatantly luxurious mode of living.

These ills had been felt most acutely by the lowly, so that Protestantism first took hold among the peasants and artisans. But it quickly percolated upwards, finding acceptance among the squires and lesser gentry. Eventually it would find favour among the nobles and princes. Not that the sovereigns had any particular reason to find fault with Protestantism in itself. Luther had declared specifically that princes were not to be deposed because of their faith. Rather he recognised two powers to which obedience is owed, the Kingdom of God and the world under the magistrates, by which he meant the law as administered by the sovereign. He added the significant point that only the magistrates rightly held the power of compulsion. This ruled out the power of the priests, their confessional boxes and their courts.

In brief, the Sovereigns had no reason to fear that change of religion might lead inexorably to a change in customs, laws, in obedience and finally to a change in the state itself. They did, though, have several practical reasons for concern. Several sovereigns had only recently wrested from the Pope the right to nominate priests and furthermore insist upon their appointment. It was a privilege that offered excellent opportunities for patronage. Nor were they particularly happy that the priests should lose their infallibility. All these threats of hellfire were an excellent way of ensuring discipline among a largely illiterate peasant congregation.

Finally, the priests were often the only people in the parish who could read, write and undertake much of the secretarial side of local administration. They were prepared to undertake this work because it also included gathering taxes, and these were then split between church and state. Altogether the church acted as policeman, government administrator and tax collector. Latterly it had descended into the scandalous. It was quite usual for the so-called celibates to be living openly with mistresses.

Despite the pressure from her Council, Elizabeth initially limited her recognition of the Scottish Congregationalists to sending messages of goodwill and moral support. This was not the sort of response they had been looking for, but they themselves were very vague about their aims. Cecil tried to get some sense out of them. Would they please set out their objectives? What opposition did they expect? How did they think England could be of help? But the recipients were not particularly enraptured by the missive, because it implied that the Scots were helpless without English support and Cecil did not help matters by incorporating a lot of Poloniusal advice.

Their reply was virtually irrelevant and had obviously been influenced by Knox. It gave much attention to the need to uphold the faith. It was pure rhetoric, and not even new rhetoric, except for begging sufficient finance to hire at least 1,000 foot and 3,000 horse. If the English did not provide them, they threatened to go it alone.

After that, even Elizabeth realised that honeyed words were not enough. She sent Sir Ralph Sadler to Trent, officially to settle some border differences. In fact he took a large bag of money with him, for Elizabeth had commissioned him to get in touch with the Congregationalists "wherein such discretion and secrecy is to be used as no part of your doings may impair the treaties of peace lately concluded betwixt us and Scotland".

So it was highly embarrassing when Lord Ossulston, one of the Scottish lords, was caught in possession of a handsome portion. There was no doubt over the provider; the money was all in English crowns. When Marie challenged her, Elizabeth reverted to what became her stock denial whenever she was cornered. She pointed out there was no order with the royal seal and, as everyone knew, all her orders had to carry such a seal. She could only imagine that it was one of her ministers working without her authority, "Some of whom might possibly have been fools enough to hold misjudging conferences with the Scotch". However, she continued, she would look into the matter and punish any of her subjects who had engaged in such hostile action.

Then, with supreme impudence, she wrote to Marie complaining that it had come to her ears that she was spreading wicked rumours that it was she who was stirring up trouble in Scotland. Marie replied with studied courtesy pointing out that the source for the rumours were the actual recipients of Elizabeth's largesse and they were talking about it quite openly. Even though Elizabeth was sending money to Scotland for her own advantage she was typically anxious for a bargain. She made it clear that the 3,000 was just a loan. Then she shilly-shallied, keeping the Congregationalists waiting. Only after they had become desperate did she fulfil her obligations with an addendum. Once those four major Scottish fortifications namely Dunbar, Dumbarton, Dumfries and Inchkeith, had been freed from French control, they were to be handed over to her.

All this time Elizabeth and Cecil were trying to persuade the Council against actually deciding on war. It was difficult. Thomas Gresham was sending warnings from the Netherlands that there were 4,500 Spanish troops massing in Zealand. As he was at pains to point out, since there was no existing war for them to go to, it was his belief that they were being assembled ready to take over Marie's stronghold at Leith.

However, these reports could well have been engineered in part by Cecil. He appreciated the difference between going to war on behalf of a country and merely ensuring the threatened country had adequate defence. His only problem was that Elizabeth was resisting even this part measure, but he had already discovered that the best way to persuade the young queen was to have her representatives abroad send his suggestions as though they were their own. Even so, Elizabeth was reluctant to act.

Then in December came news that the Duke of Guise was sending his brother the Duke of Elbeuf with a fleet. Cecil was not to know their intention was no more than to relieve Marie of her post and replace her with a stronger character. Naturally he assumed there were hostile intentions. While Elizabeth was still dithering, he took it upon himself to order Admiral Wynter to sail with several ships laden with arms for the Congregationalists. On reaching Scotland, it was to be made out that the winds had blown the ships into the Firth of Forth accidentally.

As Cecil had anticipated, directly Elizabeth learned about the move, she forbade it. One of her very real fears was that it might provoke Philip to come to the assistance of the Scottish Catholics and himself make a "protective" invasion. Cecil was so sure he was right that he gambled his career on it. He wrote to the Queen professing his profound loyalty but declaring that if she refused the advice of both himself and her council to back the project with ground troops, he would have to ask to become her gardener instead. Elizabeth knew when she was cornered and approved the move. Of course she changed her mind, but by then Wynter was beyond recall.

The situation was somewhat calmed when the winds providentially blew the Duke of Elbeuf back to France. But it had come dangerously close to a major confrontation.

And so it came about that Marie in her Leith stronghold, keeping watch for her brother, suddenly saw instead the English fleet anchored just off shore. It meant she was now cut off from all Catholic support.

In considerable trepidation she sent to Admiral Wynter asking whether his intentions were friendly. He said he was on his way to deliver supplies to Berwick and had strayed off course through "chasing pirates"! It was not a convincing story, and Marie asked him, if this was so, how come he had two French ships in tow? He explained that the French garrison had fired on him. This was even more unconvincing. Certainly the garrison had fired, but that was because they had mistaken Wynter for Elbeuf and had been firing a salute.

In October 1559, Marie had another setback. The Earl of Arran suddenly announced that he had changed faith yet again. Though his record was quite despicable in every way, his heritage was so noble that he still remained a political rallying point.

This latest of his conversions was due to a far darker manipulation arranged by Cecil. Some months before, Cecil had come to the conclusion that, with their Regent deprived of much of her power and their Queen absent abroad, the Scots had reached a stage where they might be prepared to think of an alternative head of state; one the English could control.

The young Earl of Arran – he who had been put forward as suitor for the baby Mary – had by this time succeeded to his father's title, his father having been further dignified as the Duke of Chatelherault. During the intervening years young Arran had joined the army. He was evidently following in the muddy footsteps of his father, for he had deserted his regiment and been forced to flee to France. There he had been appointed Commander of the Kings Scots Guards, and there was even talk of him marrying the daughter of the King's mistress, Diane. But before this could happen, he came under suspicion of having an unhealthy bias towards the Huguenots. So once again he had to flee, this time to Geneva.

The bait with which Cecil now lured him back to England was to suggest he might marry Elizabeth. Not only would such a marriage unite England and Scotland but, as a Protestant, young Arran would have the backing of the Congregationalists. It was rumoured that on his arrival Elizabeth had indeed met him in the garden at Hampton Court and, as was her wont, flirted with him most convincingly. More certainly, he had stayed at Cecil's London house and Cecil had even loaned him 200,000 crowns which – surprisingly – he eventually repaid.

Elizabeth decided not to marry him. Probably she never intended to; perhaps she had detected the early signs of the dementia that was soon to overtake him.

But Cecil's reasons were far darker than mere caprice. He had realised that, unaware of Elizabeth's decision, the Scots still believed that the marriage was on. So with true cunning, he had Arran disguised and, under the name of Monsieur Beaufort, smuggled back into Scotland. This certainly caused widespread repercussions, for it was immediately after his return that he had persuaded his father to revert yet again to Protestantism.

Marie's position was now so insecure that in 1559 the Congregationalists entered Edinburgh and announced her "suspension" as Regent. Knox made sure it was announced with great éclat, heralded by trumpet calls and a proclamation from Edinburgh Market Cross. The crucial factor behind his decision was the landing of the French forces, but he cunningly spun this into a declaration that her dismissal was on orders from the King of France. True to plan, Arran was acclaimed to take her place.

Now finding herself in a sort of political limbo, Marie continued to fight as best she could for the peace of Scotland. First she needed still more help from the French. But by this time the situation there had changed from serious to critical. Far from the King supplying more forces, the fresh demands of the civil war meant he required all the men he could muster. Indeed he would have liked to have withdrawn those he had already posted to Scotland. So instead of the reinforcements Marie had been hoping for, she found herself palmed off with the arrival of The Bishop of Valence, which showed how completely out of touch the French were with the Scottish people. The Bishop had been instructed to convert the leading Congregationalists to Catholicism. What a hope!

Not only was Marie deprived of power, she was also seriously ill with dropsy. She struggled on for a few months trying to carry out the orders from France, but eventually died in April 1560. Even though she had tried so hard for the good of Scotland and suffered such pain, the Congregationalists continued to be spiteful. They declared that because she had been given Catholic last rites, they could not release her corpse. It was four months before they allowed the body to be taken back for burial in her native France.

But there were many who were generous in their eulogies. Throckmorton spoke of "her queenly mind" and said: "She hath the heart of a man of war". But it was left to Bishop Spottiswood to sum up her character with full justice: "She was a lady of honourable conditions, of singular judgement, full of humility, a great lover of justice, helpful to the poor, especially those whom she knew to be indigent but for her. In her court she kept a wonderful gravity tolerating no licentiousness. A great dexterity she had in government which appeared in decomposing the tumults in the North and in pacifying the isles which, by her wisdom, were reduced to perfect obedience. As to those wars which afflicted the kingdom in her last days, they had not fallen out at all if affairs had been carried according to her mind, but in all matters she must needs attend responses from the French court."

While Elizabeth had problems over Scotland, she had just as many in England. The nation had become as fed up with extreme Catholicism under Mary as it had with Protestantism under Edward VI. Consequently, when it came to the theological niceties separating the faiths, most people were quite indifferent. So, in truth, was Elizabeth. While her upbringing had been definitely Protestant, she personally rather liked the symbolism of Catholicism and preferred that priests should not marry. She also believed that politically the Catholics were motivated by national rather than Popish interest. These were the factors that largely determined her home policy. She made all this clear when at the swearing in of loyalty she refused to let "Bloody" Bishop Bonner kiss her hand.

During the months while she was finding her feet, she managed the delicate situation by not doing anything controversial. She had the title of "Supreme Head" of the church, inherited from Henry, moderated to "Supreme Governor", and she shortened her list of impressive Protestant titles by substituting "etc". She also omitted to make the obvious appointment of Throckmorton to her Council, because she considered him "too exuberant a Protestant".

However, after three or four months it had become clear to everyone that she was following a middle course. One of her most revealing remarks was "There is one Jesus Christ. The rest is a dispute over trifles", and on another occasion she famously remarked that she had no window into men's souls.

The average number of people executed on religious grounds was reduced to about four a year compared to the 56 during the reign of Mary. Inevitably she disappointed the more serious adherents of both faiths. But neither did they feel unduly threatened. While she made it clear that her authority was paramount, the Catholics realised she was acting as their barrier against the strongly anti-Catholic Parliament. This became all the stronger when Renard's secretary revealed all the anti-Protestant plans that lay in the Spanish Embassy's files. Parliament's immediate reaction was to pass the Act of Uniformity and emphasise the break with Rome. It confirmed Elizabeth as head of the Church of England. In fact it went much further than Elizabeth would have liked. She wanted the services unchanged, but the act reverted towards Protestant extremism, keeping the Edward VI prayer book and prohibiting all forms of mass. It required that everyone in authority should take an oath confirming their loyalty, on pain of losing office. It also demanded a shilling fine for not attending church on Sunday.

In practice, Elizabeth had it diluted, and the fine was only applied spasmodically. In fact the repression of Catholicism was so minimal that it was quite difficult to buy an English translation of the bible. When one was found, it usually did not even include the amendments that had been incorporated during the reign of Edward. As a result, the Catholics appreciated that their situation was not so very burdensome. They were certainly not going to risk the freedom they already had. Reason also showed that even if they did install Mary Queen of Scots, she would bring with her a lot of hated French courtiers and hangers-on - not to mention troops.

Another problem facing Elizabeth was her finances. Her sister had left a debt of 130,000, largely through an inheritance from the extravagance of Henry VIII. He had lived an opulent lifestyle and, more particularly, he had conducted the costly wars against both Scotland and France. By dint of making economies, selling off monopolies and borrowing just about as much as the City was willing to lend her, Elizabeth managed to pay off these personal debts within two years. Part of this can be ascribed to Elizabeth's cavalier attitude to Philip and his shipping. She challenged the tenacity with which Philip still recognised the Pope's allocation of much of the New World. Using her own particular interpretation of the Treaty of Cateau-Cambresis, she winked as her sea dogs, notably Drake and Hawkins, conducted piratical attacks. These had the additional advantage of irritating Philip to the degree that it diverted him from carrying out any aggressive escapades he might have in mind.

There remained, however, the national economy. When Henry

VIII had found that even the sale of monasteries was not paying for all his needs, he started issuing coins with cheaper metal mixed in with the silver. This had encouraged counterfeiters to shave the edge of the old full-value coins. So long as this was done with discretion, it was not noticeable. These pure silver shavings could then be sold as profit. Mary had let the practice continue virtually unchecked, so that shortly before her death it was estimated that 58 per cent of the coinage had been "abused" in this way.

The problem could no longer be ignored, so Elizabeth asked Sir Thomas Gresham how she could stabilise the national economy. He defined four points: The first was to restore purity to the coinage. Consequently Elizabeth called in all the coins and at the same time announced its debasement by 25 per cent. However, she also said she "would sustain the burden". Typically, her apparent generosity was not, in fact, so very noble. The total sum in current circulation was 7m. The £1m debased coinage was bought in below its true value and converted into 670,000 in the new currency. In this way the government was able to make 50,000 over the re-minting. The edges of the new coins were bevelled so as to make shaving impossible.

Gresham also set about repairing England's low financial reputation on the continent. He started by repressing the steelyard merchants. They were mainly Dutch and Germans who were not so much concerned with steel as wool and cloth. They enjoyed considerable tax privileges, which gave them an advantage over the London merchants. They had their own London colony, complete with churches and houses, near Upper Thames Street. The second move was to grant a few licences, and his last recommendation was that the state must borrow as little as possible from overseas. He also managed to have the exchange rate adjusted from 16 to 22 Flemish shillings to the pound and urged the queen to keep good credit with the English merchants. Fortunately this coincided with a notable increase in both population and employment, which helped to overcome the inflation.

Everyone had been enchanted by little Mary, despite an unfortunate introduction to Catherine de Medici. Catherine had come into the nursery unannounced, and the little girl asked whether she realised she was in the presence of the Queen of Scotland. Catherine responded rather tartly by asking if she realised she was in the presence of the Queen of France.

The agreement had already affianced Mary to the Dauphin and it was taken for granted that marriage would follow in due course. To everyone's delight, the two became immediate friends and soon were inseparable. It was a genuine relationship that was to last for the rest of their lives. As a matter of course, Mary was brought up as French. But Marie felt it unwise that she should lose her Scottishness completely, so when she arrived, she had in her train four other children, all, as it happened, called Mary. To supplement this, Lady Fleming was appointed as her nurse.

Unfortunately, in this particular matter, things did not quite work out that way. One of Janet Fleming's undoubted attractions was her vivacity. She made no secret of the fact that she was both proud and honoured that the child she was bearing was the King's. For once the battle lines between Catherine and Diane were forgotten under the threat of this mutual enemy, and Janet Fleming was promptly returned to Scotland.

Mary had an idyllic childhood with the Royal Family, surrounded by every sort of amusement and luxury. She proved quick and anxious to learn, acquiring Latin, Italian, Spanish and some Greek. She had good handwriting and was able to draw, sing and play the lute. Her accomplishment was shown when she was eleven, when she wrote and delivered a speech to the King in Latin.

At twelve, the Guise took her away from court to learn statecraft under the guidance of her highly-experienced uncle the Cardinal of Lorraine. At the same time she absorbed much about administration from her grandmother, the formidable Antoinette de Guise.

At 16, Mary was due to be married to the Dauphin. Marie had delegated her mother, the Duchess Antoinette, to represent the bride's interests in the marriage settlement. Certainly this ensured a reasonable balance between the interests of the bride and groom. What it did not provide, however, was a reasonable balance between the nations of France and Scotland. Unsurprisingly, it was heavily weighted in favour of the French. Indeed it was so weighted that it was decided to draw it up in four parts, and only the last part was publicly signed and revealed. In this the Dauphin was recognised as the King of Scotland, and when he became King of France the two countries would be united and the citizens given combined citizenship. Also the French were to ensure Mary's first male offspring would be heir to the thrones of both Scotland and France. If Mary had only daughters, the eldest would be recognised as heir to the Scottish throne. All this was normal and perfectly acceptable to the Scots.

Of the three secret parts of the marriage agreement, the first stated that if Mary died without heir, Scotland and Mary's sovereignty would be made over to the French throne. The second agreement assigned all the Scottish revenue to the King of France and his successors until Scotland had fully reimbursed France with the money already spent on Scottish defence. The third was the most pernicious. It simply countermanded any agreements Mary might sign in the future. These latter three sections were signed by Mary and kept secret even from the Scots Commissioners. So in effect, the first section was entirely cosmetic and was automatically made invalid by the third.

The first was simply to screen the fact that Scotland had been transferred into a dominion of France. Mary was being advised by the two uncles she loved and respected for most of her life. It is not clear whether she was, at the age of 16, following their advice blindly, or realised she was entering into a gross deception. At that time the French looked upon Scotland as a province which ought to be glad to have such a sophisticated government looking after it. Considering the behaviour of the Scottish chiefs, the reasoning seemed valid.

All these negotiations were struck by ill omen when the nine Scottish commissioners, who had come to arrange the marriage contract, were suddenly taken by illness and four of them died. The Scots, of course, spoke of poison. It was without grounds, because some of the party were unaffected. Despite all this, the wedding was magnificent. It was held, of course, at Notre Dame. Throughout the ceremony the Duke of Guise circulated among the guests, making sure they had a good view of the ceremony and fully appreciated all the expense. Quantities of gold and silver coins were scattered among the crowd. The only thing which was not quite perfect occurred during the banquet, when the Queen found the crown so heavy a lord in waiting had to hold it above her head. This was an obvious omen that she would not be able to sustain her royal position.

Although Francis had by this time reached the age of maturity (if, in fact, he ever did mature), Mary was very fond of him, even if she did not actually love him. He responded extravagantly in his devotion and would follow her advice even when it was contrary to his mother's wishes.

Mary had been married barely a year when in 1559 the death of Henri brought her husband to the throne as Francis II and she became Queen of France. Her father-in-law's death had come suddenly. He had decided to turn the marriage of his daughter Elizabeth, Mary's sister-in-law, into a most lavish affair, hoping it would help divert attention from the débâcle of the Cateau-Cambresis agreement. Jousting had been one of his favourite pastimes, and it made up the final day's entertainment.

Friday 23rd June was a day dreaded by Catherine, as a few nights before she had dreamt that it would end in tragedy for her husband. Now the day was over, and he was still safe. But in the last joust he had been defeated by the Captain of the Guard, so he insisted on one further round so that he could claim his revenge. Catherine begged him not to continue, but he just laughed off her protests. At the critical moment of contact, the Captain's lance broke and a large splinter happened to catch a weak part of the King's visor. It entered his eye and came out by his ear.

Catherine was beside herself. She sat distraught by his bedside throughout the four days in which he lay in agony before he died. Her grief was so great that her attendants thought she would become dangerously ill. For the rest of her life she dressed in black, with her magnificent jewels alone indicating her status. Even in old age, she would remember the anniversary of that fateful day and light candles for his soul. But it was typical that even in these hours, during all the time she kept her bedside watch, she still had a mind to practical matters. She proved herself to be stern but not vengeful. She ordered Diane to relinquish the crown jewels and all the other gifts the King had given her, but she allowed her to keep all the estates she had amassed. This was largely because Diane's daughter had married one of the powerful Guise family, so that in due course half the property would end up in the Guise estates. Though Catherine despised them for fawning on Diane, she was anxious at this juncture not to offend them.

Francis II was both intellectually and physically weak almost to the extent of being an invalid. This was due, it was said, to all the potions Catherine had taken in her anxiety to become pregnant. He was pale and short, bordering on stunted, with the physique of a boy rather than a man. While not actually deformed, he was swollen rather than fat. Nor was he any more prepossessing in character.

He tried to make up for his shortcomings with a love of hunting and exercise which bordered on the fanatical, yet he was timid and in constant fear for his personal safety. Presumably for the same reasons, he assumed an air of great importance and indulged in the extremes of fashion, making himself a ludicrous figure. In short, he was a pretty repugnant individual. Catherine had not had him educated beyond immediate and complete obedience to her. He did not know anything about state affairs, nor even what to do. Nor did he care; he never hesitated to put hunting before any state business.

At 15, Francis was still a minor and must have a Regent, and the law did not allow the Regent to be a woman. So the leading families let no time pass before manoeuvring for influential positions. Indeed their machinations boded such ill that Catherine had to call them to order, pointing out that their plotting was undermining the very stability of the country.

In fact the Guises were in such a strong position their success was a foregone conclusion. They swayed the Parliament. They met in secret before the first council and arranged between themselves to push through a highly controversial, indeed illegal, motion. They claimed that the six months that lay before the King's majority was so short a time that there really was no need for a Regent. Since Catherine was not eligible, everyone realised the Guises would, in effect, be ruling France.

Mary's relationship with Catherine was unusual for mother-in-law and daughter. The daughter held all the prestige and required all the deference for being queen, but the mother-in-law had all the experience. Mary and Catherine were not at that time particularly well acquainted, for Mary had spent most of her adult life in the house of Guise. Now ambassadors usually found them sitting side by side, Mary at Catherine's right hand. But they never let it be clear who was really in command.

Both were, to their mutual disadvantage, snobs. Mary always had it in mind that Catherine was no more than the daughter of a merchant, while Catherine was never rid of an overwhelming awe of true royalty. Of course Mary knew that her husband was subjected to his mother's influence, no matter how subtly it may have been camouflaged. On occasions she herself had to try and counter her mother-in-law's advice in order to impart the wishes of her family.

Despite this conflict, Mary never had the slightest cause to complain about Catherine. She learnt a lot about persuasiveness and, indeed, intrigue; "never make enemies because friends are less suspicious of your motive". While she could always depend on her for advice, she never felt her mother in law was trying to impose her ideas. Indeed Catherine made a point of invariably deferring to whatever Mary or the King eventually decided.

Mary certainly appreciated all this. Writing to her mother, she declared that should Catherine by any chance die it would be "the greatest misfortune that could happen to this poor country and to all of us". The nearest Catherine came to actually criticising Mary was to say that she was "always pushing the wheel of trouble". And so Mary became as reliable and effective a conduit as the Guise family could have hoped for, and this state of affairs looked set for as long as anyone could foresee.

Urged on by her family, Mary now took every opportunity to lay claim to the throne of England. Accordingly, the day after Elizabeth's coronation, the Dauphin and Dauphine were proclaimed King and Queen of England and Ireland. The royal coat of arms was incorporated into Mary's shield and the great seal referred to the King and Queen of France, Scotland, England and Ireland. All this might seem fine when seen from France, but it all ricocheted back on Marie.

By this time Elizabeth had come to realise that her previous attempts at providing verbal support and supplying money to the Scottish Protestants had proved useless, but still she remained hesitant over actually invading Scotland, so she instructed the Duke of Norfolk to advance to the border. Once there he was met by a Scottish contingent consisting of the Congregationalists the Earl of Arran and Lord Henry, and in 1560 they negotiated the Treaty of Berwick.

Since Catherine was at this time engrossed over a conspiracy at Amboise and Marie was by now seriously ill, there was no one representing Mary, so it was hardly surprising that the agreement had singular advantages for the English.

Fugitives from justice on either side were to be returned within 20 days. That was fair enough. But it also stipulated by mutual agreement that the two sides should not help one another's enemies, and the fully appreciated that this meant the French.

Still Elizabeth was hesitant. Then she learnt that Mary had excelled herself in her programme of insults; she had invited the English ambassador to dinner and served the meal on platters which carried the French insignia quartered with those of Scotland. That in itself was perfectly acceptable, but they were also quartered with the arms of England. This implied that Mary was defying Elizabeth's sovereignty, and since it was made to the Ambassador, it was a direct insult to Elizabeth personally.

When Elizabeth heard about this, she was furious. "These insolent attempts are but the abuse of the House of Guise who have the chief governance of the crown of France during the minority of the King and Queen". All the advice her Council had given her combined with the warnings from her foreign ambassadors, and even the threat of action by Philip was as nothing compared to this personal insult. It had the desired effect, and in 1559 she was spurred into declaring the "War of the Insignia". She ordered the Duke of Norfolk to cross the border, where he immediately joined up with the Congregationalist forces. The combined troops then went on to lay siege to the French forces holed up in Leith. The Scots proved to be as feeble as ever, and the English were little better. Among several administrative bungles, one attack had to be called off because the scaling ladders did not reach the top of the city walls. By the end, the Scottish and English forces were soundly trounced.

Philip, much to Elizabeth's relief, had shown no sign of supporting the Scots Catholics. For one thing he was still hoping she might agree to marry him. So he merely scolded her for going ahead without asking his advice. In fact Philip was just as worried as Elizabeth that the French might land in Scotland. He even hinted, through the Dutch ambassador in Paris, that if asked he would send Spanish troops to take over the strongholds the French still held in Scotland.

Elizabeth paid no attention. She now found herself in a strong position. Once the forces in the Congregationalist-English alliance became organised they provided a formidable challenge to the Scottish Catholics. This was all the more acute, as the death of Marie had left them completely ineffective. At the same time it had become clear that, due to internal problems, the French were most unlikely to come to their support. Indeed it was not long before they were sending out feelers to negotiate a truce. So Elizabeth sent Cecil up north to negotiate a treaty which she felt confident would be far more advantageous than the Treaty of Berwick.

The Berwick Treaty had been between England and Protestant Scotland. The new Treaty of Edinburgh was far more significant, for it included delegates representing Mary Queen of Scots and the King of France. Negotiations were started in July 1560. The terms were highly favourable for England, especially when compared to the grovelling attitude that had been necessary during the Cateau-Cambresis negotiations barely less than a year before. Now the whole of Europe realised that here was a Queen to be taken seriously.

While Mary had stayed in France throughout the Edinburgh negotiations, she had given her delegates full authority to initial the treaty, but when she saw the clause by which she was not only to disclaim the English crown for herself but also for her progeny, even after Elizabeth's death, she baulked. Mary had every reason to claim the Crown of England. It was another problem inherited from Henry

VIII's will, or rather his controversial divorces. It was particularly potent because it had all become a matter of faith. The Pope had refused to annul Henry's marriage to Catherine of Aragon, therefore Elizabeth's mother, Anne Boleyn, as Henry's second wife, was not legally married. This made Elizabeth, in the eyes of all Catholics, illegitimate.

There was another highly questionable clause in Henry's will. He decreed that his elder sister Margaret, who had married James IV, and all her progeny should be disqualified from the English throne. Although the clause had been passed by Parliament, it was doubtful if it was legal. These two highly debatable questions could therefore be interpreted as meaning Margaret's living descendant was the true heir to the throne - Mary Queen of Scots. But Mary was still in France. Indeed the high-handed behaviour of her family was already beginning to have long-range repercussions. The Bourbons had been incensed when the Guise seized the regency. Strictly, according to the law, the head of a Regency Council in France had to be the next male adult in line for the throne. As all four of Catherine's boys were under age, this led to Antoine de Bourbon. He was more generally known as the King of Navarre, a title he had gained through marriage. He did indeed have a kingdom, but nearly all of it had been annexed by Spain. It remained Antoine's overriding ambition to regain the kingdom for his wife. Consequently he did not feel the Regency was all that important. However, his young brother Louis was much more ambitious. He persuaded Antoine to go to Court and stake his claim, even though it would only last a few months. But on arrival Catherine persuaded him not to pursue it further. Louis was furious. He allied himself with a willing conspirator, a minor noble, La Renaudie. Using the melodramatic alias of "The Silent Chief" he set about plotting against the Guise. His idea was to take the King and his mother prisoner while they were staying at the Palace at Blois. He would keep them safe, but the Duke of Guise and his brother the Cardinal of Lorraine would be forced to give up their offices. If they refused, Antoine was quite prepared for them to be murdered.

The coup required bands of armed men. The Huguenots sent out 500 recruiting sergeants. Their work was not all that difficult. The country was flooded with soldiers who had returned from Italy and the Guises had by this time made it clear they were not going to pay them. So as not to arouse suspicion, these men were being gradually infiltrated into the area. This still involved a lot of people, which made it almost impossible to keep it secret. Indeed there were so many rumours that the court decided to move to Amboise, which could be more easily defended. The conspirators moved with them. When one of them was caught with 10 trunks filled with arms, the mounting fear changed into panic. Those that were caught were executed.

Shielded by his alias, Louis managed to escape detection, though he was under considerable suspicion. Cunningly, Catherine appointed him to be head of the King's bodyguard. While this was a very prestigious appointment, it also meant he had to be in constant attendance on the King, which gave him no opportunity for any further conspiracy. His plot had obviously required a lot of money which Antoine did not have. This immediately fell on Elizabeth. Cecil strongly denied any such thing and pointed out that the plot was only to be expected, since the Guise had so much power. It was indeed a perfectly credible point, for half of the Huguenots were more consumed with hatred for the Guises than with any principles concerning the succession.

Not appreciating his good fortune, young Louis tried his luck with another attempt which also failed. This time the Guise manipulated the evidence and had Louis put on trial, found guilty and condemned to death. But the Guise had been thoroughly alarmed at the size of the conspiracy and just how unpopular they had become among the ordinary people. Fearing the next conspiracy might well prove more successful, they turned to the only person they felt could help: Catherine. She made it clear that she would help, but only if she held real power.

Hardly had they agreed than Francis suffered an ear infection and unexpectedly died. Along with him died the Guise family's influence over the crown; or so it might be thought. However, it was noticed that among all the people calling to make their condolence, the Spanish ambassador had been closeted with Mary far longer than was normal for the customary commiserations. It was generally assumed that even then they had been discussing the possibility of her marriage with Don Carlos.

Aware that Catherine did not want this, the Guises tried to mislead her. The Cardinal of Lorraine, apparently off his own bat, suggested Mary should marry the Archduke of Austria. There was no doubt that Mary was being pressed by the Guise family to marry, and almost certainly they really wanted her to marry Don Carlos.

The very idea that anyone should marry the heir to the Spanish throne arouses amazement at the dedication with which these princesses were prepared to fulfil their royal obligations.

If Francis had been physically unattractive and with a personality not much better, he was a paragon compared to Don Carlos, who was positively repulsive. He had a twisted face and misshapen legs, and one shoulder was higher than the other. He was epileptic and had a severe stutter. His character was equally unpleasant. He had hit his head falling downstairs while chasing a scullery maid. As a result he had undergone a trepanning operation and while it had relieved the pain, it had left him with fits of homicidal mania. One of his main pleasures was torturing animals.

Philip must have been aware that his son's mental stability was deteriorating to the degree that any marriage would inevitably be annulled soon after, so he let it be known he was not prepared to let him marry anyone. He gave as an excuse that whatever his choice, either Elizabeth or Catherine or both would be offended. So Mary was now 19 and still had to make up her mind on whom she would marry and whether she would sail to Scotland to claim her heritage.

Naturally Elizabeth was curious about it all and sent the Earl of Bedford to Paris, ostensibly to convey her condolences, in fact to report back on the actual situation. Another person with an ulterior motive was the Countess of Lennox. She was ambitious for her son, Earl Darnley. He was a Catholic and the English Catholics considered him the proper heir to Mary Tudor, so the Countess had high hopes and made him the messenger of her condolences. But to her chagrin, they merely exchanged pleasantries and parted. There was no spark between them – not yet.

From the far side of the Channel, it was difficult for Mary to judge the subtle changes that had come about following her mother's death. Now that England had become Protestant, the Congregationalists were gaining more confidence. They were coming to look upon England rather than France for protection. Indeed Mary's welcome would by no means be assured. Some reports suggested that many Catholics preferred the Countess of Lennox, since she had no French monarchist appendage and was less likely to clash with the Protestant Parliament.

Nor was there any guarantee that Mary would receive support from the Catholics of England. Many were thought to prefer the claims of her aunt, Lady Margaret Douglas. Then there was John Knox. Needless to say, he would make Mary's return as unwelcome as he could. He said he would never accept her until she converted to Calvinism.

It was enough to drive Mary to distraction. At one point she confided to the English ambassador: "My subjects in Scotland do their duty in nothing, nor have they performed their part in one thing that belongeth to them. I am their Queen, as so they call me, but they use me not so – they must be taught to know their duties".

Despite all this, John Leslie, the Bishop of Ross and head of the Scottish Catholic church, arrived in Paris. He suggested she should take advantage of the fact that Lord James Stewart, her half-brother and one of the leading Scottish Protestants, was also in France. It provided an excellent opportunity to have him arrested. If she did this, the Bishop would make sure that on landing at Aberdeen she would have 20,000 Catholic men at her command. Of course he had no guarantee, and Mary wisely declined the offer. She had questioned every Frenchmen who had recently returned from Scotland and they had told her she would be wise to listen to Lord James for advice.

Then came Lord James himself, closely followed by Maitland and the other Protestant nobles. They all thought it would be advantageous to have a young, malleable girl as Queen. Not only could they manipulate her, but she had a strong claim to the highly desirable English throne.

Lord James invited her to Scotland, on condition that she embraced the Protestant faith. She refused. Instead she asked him to be her adviser and said that, should he agree to renounce Protestantism, she could promise him a Cardinal's hat. Lord James preferred the probable alternative of being made Earl Moray, with all the income that came with it. Eventually it was agreed she could hold mass, but only in private.

On his way back, unknown to her, Lord James stopped off at Paris and told the English ambassador and the Cardinal of Lorraine everything they had discussed. He also stopped off in London and had intimate discussions with Cecil. To be fair, his intention was probably more to keep in with Elizabeth than to damage Mary but it also indicated a worrying degree of ambiguity.

Then, in what might be interpreted as something of a warning, the Scottish Parliament passed a "Protestant Confession of Faith". It forbade the celebration of the mass in Scotland. To Mary, this was throwing down a gauntlet. Even at this late stage Mary could have decided to stay in France. As The Duchess of Touraine, she would be assured of a handsome income and a comfortable life. As the Queen Dowager, she would additionally have a place in court, and she could expect to make a good marriage. Alternatively she could face the unknown and uncomfortable life by taking her place as Queen of Scotland, a position that had become extra risky, since she could no longer be certain of support from the French army.

The Guise family, ever seeking to extend their sphere of influence, had no such worries and made it clear she must claim her heritage. They pointed out that it was her duty to help strengthen the spread of Catholicism, and suggested that if she refused, the faith might actually die out. Of course their real reason was the opportunity of gathering yet more territory under their control.

At last Mary made her fateful decision and wrote to the Scots saying she was willing to return and would not lay down any conditions or force of arms. Her greatest desire was to return to her kingdom. At the same time, to show she really meant it, she asked for a list of possible candidates to be her treasurer and controller; also for a copy of the royal accounts, right from the death of her mother.

When Elizabeth had repelled Philip's advances, the Spanish problem of keeping the channel open between Spain and the Netherlands remained unsolved. The obvious solution would be to persuade Elizabeth to marry some other member of the Habsburg family. And so in 1563 it came about that Elizabeth was receiving the emissary of Charles, the Arch Duke of Austria, ostensibly conveying his congratulations. But it was a little late for that and really it was to size up the chances. Elizabeth considered this a far more serious proposition. Such a match would indeed provide England with a formidable bulwark and dissuade France from placing troops in Scotland to launch a combined attack. It was clear. There must be an engagement, and the longer it could be extended the longer it would shield the country. Then if Elizabeth were to refuse the offer, Catherine might get her way and have the Archduke affianced to Mary Queen of Scots. This combination would create a formidable threat to England.

However, Catherine de Medici had other ideas. The Archduke was virtually the traditional enemy of her husband's family, and she dearly wanted to dash his hopes. First she tried to spoil the engagement by trying to engineer a marriage between Mary and Lord Courtnay, the Duke of Devonshire. Since the Duke could also lay some claim to the English throne, they would, combined, present a formidable rival to Elizabeth. However Lord Courtnay inconsiderately died while still in exile in Padua.

Catherine then instructed her ambassador in London to do everything he could to encourage Elizabeth's unofficial and more intimate person-to-person romance with Robert Dudley. It was another spoiling ploy. Elizabeth realised this and found it amusing, since she had no more intention of actually marrying Dudley than she had of marrying the Archduke. She was happy to let the situation bubble for as long as possible, and in effect it bubbled, although not always at boiling point, for close on thirty years.

Elizabeth might have been officially engaged, but that did not prevent her from quite blatantly showing interest in other beaux. They included Eric XIV of Sweden. This courtship was rather strange, for his cause was pleaded by his brother, the King of Finland, who tried to impress everyone at the English court by "scattering money among the ladies in waiting like a drunken sailor".

King Eric, from afar, also did his best to impress, and wrote her long love letters in Latin. He became incensed at the thought that

Dudley might be winning and challenged him to a duel, but he seems to have had some hesitation in coming over to carry out his threat.

Elizabeth even considered the King of France, which delighted Catherine no end, but at 15, he was half her age. Officially she told the ambassador how honoured she was, but she fell back on the excuse she had given Philip; that her people would only accept her marrying an Englishman. Shortly after her coronation, she had declared that she would remain a virgin. In fact she was playing a carefully balanced game. She was able to take full advantage of the changing social behaviour in this era. The traditional view still prevailed that virginity, with its repressed sexuality, was akin to the Madonna. It implied dignity and was something to be admired. Socially this gave the unmarried woman status above the married.

Elizabeth made much play of this and followed the custom of keeping her hair loose. But recently the Renaissance had altered the concept. Courtship could now promise fulfilment which both parties knew would never be actually reached. It made courtship almost a parlour game, and it was a game Elizabeth greatly enjoyed playing; "She enjoyed being desired without being possessed". Psychiatrists claim that a woman who has been subjected to violence – and surely having your mother executed qualifies as that – subsequently has difficulty in sexual relations.

Elizabeth was also frightened of pain. On one occasion when she was advised to have a tooth pulled, she was so reluctant that the Bishop of Winchester volunteered to have a tooth pulled to show her it was not all that painful. So the pain of childbirth, not to mention the real possibility of death, may also have been a reason for her reluctance. In any case, if engagement could be used as a political ploy, she certainly played it to the full. Yet her flirtations were usually genuine. When years later, she heard of the death of some of her former beaux, she was genuinely heartbroken. On hearing Anjou's death, she cried for three weeks. After her death, Dudley's last letter was found in a box beside her bed.

She had grown up with Dudley and together they had been prisoners in the Tower. He was charming and good looking. The problem was that he was already married. There was talk of divorce. Cecil was extremely worried, for it would cause widespread disaffection among the Catholics.

By 1561 Cecil felt it had become so serious that he tried to distract the Queen's attention by virtually inventing a Catholic conspiracy as a warning. The romance was only seriously disrupted by the death of Dudley's wife, Amy Robsart. The situation was complicated because it was no ordinary death. Amy had sent all her servants to a local fair. When they returned they found her in the empty house lying at the bottom of the stairs with her neck broken. It is almost certain it was not murder, but inevitably rumours became rife. The Spanish Ambassador, for one, wrote to the Governess of the Netherlands saying he thought it was obviously murder and that Elizabeth might be sent to the Tower. Elizabeth accepted that it was too dangerous to continue the liaison, and Dudley left Court. Towards the end of her life she was to put the relationship in context: "I have always loved his virtues but the aspiration to greatness and honour which is within me could not suffer him as a companion and a husband".

It was in December 1560 that Francis II suffered a severe ear infection, so bad that it was clear he was dying. His brother Charles was only 10, so there could be none of the fudging of the Regency that had occurred on the ascendancy of Francis. Yet the Guises were more than ready to try their luck again. They had for some days been calling in their supporters and building up a major force in Paris ready to threaten Parliament. However Catherine had by this time acquired sufficient experience to thwart them. The first thing she did was to close all but one of the entrances to the Palace, so that she could make sure there were no back-stairs conspiracies.

Although she was genuinely devastated by grief, she watched developments carefully. Taking advantage of a moment when the dying king seemed to be rallying, she left his bedside and summoned Antoine de Bourbon. In front of the Guises, she accused him and his family, as Huguenots, of inciting rebellion.

Antoine showed that he had not become any more courageous than before. He was fearful of sharing the fate of his brother Louis, who was now in prison and under threat of execution. With this fear of losing his head literally, he lost it metaphorically, and with a little prompting offered to give his claim for the Regency to Catherine. Catherine made him put this in writing and rewarded him with the prospect that when her second son Charles became King he would appoint him Lieutenant General.

This filled the Guises with alarm, for it was they who had engineered the false evidence linking Louis with the Amboise conspiracy. Now they were all living on a knife edge. So long as the king survived beyond the date of Louis's execution they would be all right, but if the King died first, Antoine, in his new post, would have his brother freed and both would undoubtedly seek revenge on the Guises.

Catherine then carried out her masterstroke. She went to the dying king and persuaded him to sign a document quite falsely claiming that it was he who had caused Louis to be imprisoned. As a result Catherine now had both the Bourbons and the Guises in her power. To make it clear to all, she suggested these two deadly rivals should embrace one another. They did so, giving every impression of sincerity.

The day after the King died, the Guises came to offer their condolences. They followed what they could be sure would meet with Catherine's approval; they admitted their errors, but claimed they had made them at the behest of the late king. Whenever they hesitated or it looked as though there might be a hitch, Catherine solemnly nodded and said "It is true. It is true".

Philip was also racked with fear over the Guise family. He realised that, given the chance, they were quite capable of ousting Catherine and her succession of sons. In that case, next in line for the throne would be the Protestant King of Navarre. So the Guises hoped to take the throne for themselves. To this end they would back Mary Queen of Scots to oust Elizabeth, then the Guise would control the English Channel.

All in all, Philip decided he preferred the devil he knew and, much to Catherine's relief, wrote a letter to the leading figures in France, including the Guises, thanking them for supporting the Queen Mother over the accession and urging them to continue to do so. This time it was she who called the council meeting to proclaim the new King. The boy also closely followed his mother's script and declared in front of the assembled princes, cardinals and dukes that they must do whatever his mother told them.

She then challenged anyone present to object, as she knew full well nobody dared. But while she had the agreement of all those around her, there was no concealing the fact that the law stipulated that the Regent must be the next male adult in line for the throne. It could not on any account be a woman.

With her usual persuasiveness, she persuaded Parliament to agree to ignore the technical detail. The official law would be modified on condition her correspondence should be read and all instructions should be given in the presence and with the approval of the regent. And so Catherine was able to write triumphantly to her daughter in Spain: "Although I am compelled to have the King of Navarre next to me because the laws of this kingdom provide, when the King is a child, that the prince of the blood should be next to the mother, nevertheless he is obedient to me and has no commands to give except what I permit him to give". Then, as she had promised, she had Antoine appointed Lieutenant General and the Guises hastily left court.

Now that she held the reins of power, a trait of character emerged that was to persist throughout the rest of Catherine's life; her obsession with her children. For as long as she could, she kept them strictly in hand. The Venetian Ambassador wrote: "She is so respected and revered by her children that up to now no one of them has ventured even to lift an eyebrow without her advice."

As they grew up she continued her hold over them. It was so far reaching that even when her daughter Elizabeth, now married to the King of Spain, opened a letter from her mother, she found herself trembling for fear of being scolded. So it is hardly surprising that from the earliest days Catherine took every precaution against any interference with the young King. She had her bed made up in his bedroom and she appointed an Italian, Count de Retz, as Charles' chief attendant. His job was to report back everything that happened while she was absent.

It was soon shown that her caution had every justification. She had given Charles a copy of a Huguenot book, "Psalms of Marot", and told him he must not show it to anyone, but he showed it to his tutor, who took it from him, saying a man should not obey a woman. When Catherine got to hear of it, she sacked him. But it did not stop there. The Guises got to hear about it and to them it confirmed their fears that the boy King was being brought up too close to the Huguenot Creed. So they detailed the Duke of Nimes to visit the lad and spirit him away to Lorraine or Savoy, where they could hold him in their virtual mini realm.

The Duke tried to frighten him by telling him he was in great danger and should immediately accompany him to safety; the King refused. In any case Catherine had suspected some plot and had taken the precaution of hiding two of her waiting women behind the tapestry. Unfortunately there was insufficient evidence to fulfil the real object of Catherine's precautions and incriminate the Guises.

Catherine's insistence on the welfare of her children now became a basic component in both her foreign policy and home government. It meant she appraised matters almost entirely from a personal point of view. It was presumably her idea that the young King should send sprigs of lily of the valley to all the inhabitants of Paris. A nice idea and well intentioned, but it all went wrong. Most of the people mistakenly drank the water and fell ill, so her son became widely known as "the cursed King".

Her foreign policy was dominated by the fear of invasion by Spain. Should this happen, Philip would almost certainly depose Charles and his younger brothers and rob them of their inheritance. He had quite openly declared that he was merely waiting for the ideal opportunity to invade France. Catherine considered, with complete logic, that this opportunity would most likely present itself should France fall into civil war, which something that must be avoided at all costs.

But circumstances were against her. It also happened that Catherine was living through a major upheaval in the structure of French society. Almost unnoticed at the time, the conspiracy of Amboise had marked a watershed. On the surface, the conspiracy over the Regency had taken the conventional form of intrigue between the Montmorencys and the Guises. For many years the sovereign had taken precaution against any possible conspiracies against the crown by encouraging the leading families to reside at court. Consequently, any tendency for palace intrigue had focused on inter-family rivalry for the favour of the King. So Amboise was, to all superficial appearances, just the leading families shuffling and manoeuvring for the Regency.

But the conspiracy really marked the redrawing of the traditional lines. Protestantism was making its mark and family loyalties were being replaced by internal divisions drawn between religious creeds. Protestantism had been introduced into France by Calvin, who was himself French. He had gone to Geneva, where he had developed a creed of Lutherism mixed with Erasmus. There was an administrative difference too. Luther was the intellectual, Calvin the general. It was Calvin who realised in the 1530s that it was comparatively easy to smuggle priests over the inland borders between Switzerland and France. His followers in France were given the name Huguenots, since they held their early prayer meetings outside the gate of St. Hugo at Tours.

As a native, Calvin had a sure touch in spreading the creed among the French. He was enormously helped by the behaviour of the church. The priests were even more scandalous than in Scotland. For instance, Charles Broomer had been made titular head of a monastery at the age of 12 and at 21 he was made a cardinal. Pope Pius IV was his uncle. As usual, the protest started among the peasants but soon reached modest country gentry. The cult spread quickly, until the King decreed that anyone thought to be a heretic was to be banned from holding any municipal or judicial office.

Despite this, within seven years there were 40 Protestant churches in France and three years later, the number had astonishingly grown to 2,150. It took a powerful hold within the leading families, the Valois, the Bourbons and in particular, the Montmorencys. François had been the first in the family to be converted. He was followed the next year by Gaspard. Not only was Gaspard the head of the family; he was the much respected Admiral of France. He became such an ardent supporter that he was holding meetings in his house openly, which became a scandal. Finally there was Odet de Coligny, who was converted four years after that. He was Cardinal Bishop of Beauvais, yet somehow he managed to avoid being excommunicated, so that he became known as the "Protestant Cardinal."

The full weight of the Bourbons came over to the Huguenot side with Louis, the head of the family. With him he brought not only political clout but military experience, as the younger members of the family were military men with cavalry experience. Calvin was not particularly happy over this, as they threatened to take over authority within the movement. Indeed they virtually became a military movement with lay "protectors" in each region. He would have preferred that power should remain with the preachers. More acceptable were the bankers who were educating the Huguenots in financial acumen.

The Guise family, however, remained totally Catholic. Then, protected by Mary's influence, they unofficially intensified the persecution and within months had martyred 200 Huguenots. The degree of persecution can be gauged when compared to the dozen or so who had been burnt throughout the 12-year reign of Henry II. But it had no effect. The bands of armed Huguenots were so strong that they were able to snatch their compatriots on their way to execution. In Rouen they tore down the gibbets, despite the presence of some 5,000 troops.

Now Catherine had to deal with the old families at loggerheads, sometimes divided according to faith rather than blood loyalties. Both faiths had become sufficiently strong to make a full-blown civil war a real possibility. Over the coming years Catherine made the mistake of overestimating the strength of the Huguenots and was prepared to make unnecessary concessions, just as the Guise mistakenly favoured force, believing that the Catholics were strong enough to eliminate the Huguenots. Consequently when the civil wars did break out, they were particularly tragic. Normally in such instances one side comprises a party in opposition to a king or existing government. In this case, however, the antagonists simply held different beliefs, often within the same family.

The first battle, the battle of Dreux, came about by accident. Conde, leading the Huguenots, had failed to arrange advance scouts, so that when they caught up with their enemy both parties were caught completely by surprise. For two hours the two armies looked at one another, unable to believe the moment had actually arrived when they must fight their friends and relations. A cavalryman among the Huguenots wrote: "I had a dozen friends from the other side of whom each one was as dear to me as a brother, so much so that when they asked from their officer to speak to us the two separate lines of those in purple and those in white were mixed and when the time came to separate, many of us had tears in our eyes".

Traditionally the King had been the personification of the Catholic Church in France. But although Catherine had been brought up a Catholic she was, in fact, quite ambivalent over the Huguenots, and so were her children. From the start she made it clear that she had no truck with the Guise policy of persecuting the Huguenots. Indeed the man she had recently appointed as her adviser and Chancellor, Michel l'Hopital, told Parliament that the King's first duty was to protect the welfare of his subjects and that this included freedom to follow the faith of their choice. So instead of Catherine and the monarchy forming one side of the conflict, the monarchy was in the middle, desperately trying to establish a truce.

L'Hopital was a shrewd choice, for he was above all fair in his judgement. He was largely responsible for navigating Catherine's ideas through government to eventual fruition. He made several edicts by which he tried to reform the administration of the state. The first was fines for any governor or royal official who accepted "gifts by taxation". He went on to manage everything from the unification of weights and measures to stopping the magistrates from passing the actual payment of taxes downwards until it finally ended with the poor. Although he was a Catholic, he did much to protect the Huguenots from the clutches of the inquisition and he passed the Edict of Nantes, which gave them much more freedom. Catherine was to keep him in power for the next eight years.

However he was never able to harness the really serious political flaw in Catherine's character. This was because it directly stemmed, ironically, from her very considerable powers of negotiation. These were not just astonishing, they sometimes bordered on the miraculous. The formidable Duke of Alva said she "displayed in her manner of handling the subject with more tact and skill than I have ever found in any person under any circumstances". On numerous occasions she patched up bitter quarrels. On one occasion she even persuaded Pope Nuncio to listen to a Protestant sermon, although, significantly, his attitude remained intact. Similarly she apparently brought about a conciliation between Gaspard of the Montmorencys and the Dowager Duchess of Guise, who had previously accused him, not without good reason, of murdering her husband. Catherine persuaded them to participate in a "kiss of peace". It was a double act, for Catherine also persuaded the Marshal Montmorency to express his great esteem for the Cardinal of Lorraine while the Cardinal firmly declared he now realised that Montmorency's attack on him in Paris had been prompted "by the highest sense of duty to the King".

Unfortunately she had one failing which frequently brought her negotiations to collapse. It was her complete inability to understand the meaning of faith or why anyone should think it so important. This was particularly significant with the civil wars, over which she spent most of her energies trying to iron out religious differences. The Venetian ambassador wrote "I do not believe that HM understands what the word 'dogma' means". Right up till the end of her life, she still did not understand that while political policies can be traded, faith is a matter of conscience. As a result, although many worthies may have been convinced by her reasoning and subtlety, once they had returned to their families and tried to reason with their colleagues, the prejudices and enmities re-emerged as strong as ever.

Catherine tried to reconcile the two faiths by arranging the colloqy at Poissey, and was completely confounded when, after she had wheedled and cajoled, she achieved what appeared to be a triumph, only for both parties subsequently to renege. Consequently her long term policy took the form of a see-saw; she would show favour to the group that seemed weakest. As a result they would believe they enjoyed her favour and would start taking liberties. Upon this, Catherine would make the next edict or agreement so that it favoured the other side, which would then make the same mistake.

The English Ambassador put a more personal interpretation upon it: "The Queen Mother is not assured of the loyalty of either. She hopes, by her uncertain dealings, to nourish their enmity to her gain without profit to either and so proceed giving countenance sometimes to the Guises and otherwise to the Montmorencys. And although the principal affairs of the realm be dealt with in the body of the council, yet is not propounded which is meant nor that executed which is there determined but every man's opinion heard, she makes her profit thereof and resolves what she thinks to serve her turn".

Over the years this policy led her to negotiate a long string of pacifications, edicts and other forms of agreement, nearly all of which would barely last the week. Historians have classified the active hostilities into three civil wars, though it is often hard to spot when one finished and the next began. They lasted from 1562 to 1563 and from 1567 to 1568, with only a short interlude, since within the year the conflict continued to rumble on. The see-saw effect also governed Catherine's foreign policy. It became even more erratic, since the crucial factor was usually the welfare of her children, frequently centred on their marriage prospects.

Certainly Philip was very concerned over the direction in which things were moving. While he may not have appreciated just how strong the Huguenots were in France, he did realise that if they were to start befriending the dissidents in his Netherlands, he would have a major problem on his hands. He had already pointed out that his claim as protector of Catholicism would justify an attack on France. Now his ambassador in Paris was warning Catherine she must govern the country differently. The message was astonishingly stark and ominous: "...for the King, my master, is afraid that his objects are clear enough and in the end he and his party will not find any other remedy for the dangerous situation except killing you and your son".

Catherine pretended his blatant threat had had the desired effect and that she was badly frightened. She was almost certainly feigning, for on several occasions she showed considerable courage in the face of danger. After all, what else could she do? In either direction lay disaster. If she failed to carry out Philip's wishes, he threatened to assassinate her. Yet to carry them out would inevitably lead to civil war, weakening the country sufficiently to encourage him to launch an invasion. So she made a feeble effort to pacify him by adding a supplement to the Amboise settlement with an edict tightening control over the Huguenots.

Elizabeth was not at all happy. If Catherine really was going to put down the Huguenots, the Guises would then come into power and they would ally France with Spain. She naturally wanted to know whether it was Catherine or the Guises who now really held power. Another question puzzling her was the real strength of the Huguenot movement. So she sent the Duke of Bedford to the French court, nominally to convey her congratulations to King Charles on ascending the throne. In practice she instructed Bedford to make contact with the Huguenot rebels. Within a month the Duke was sending back optimistic reports: "It is more probable that there will be a lack of (Huguenot) ministers to distribute the truth than of places in which worshippers to receive it".

The English ambassador, Throckmorton, had already been urging Elizabeth to send financial help to the Huguenots or else, he claimed, they could be crushed into extinction, so he advised Elizabeth to invade Brittany and Normandy. But back at home Elizabeth was more impressed by the Spanish ambassador and initially, upon his advice, she decided against this. In any case England had neither the troops nor the money to carry it through. She doubted the Huguenots were strong enough to create resistance that was sufficiently robust and that they would need a lot more support.

So the Huguenots secretly sent an envoy asking for cash. They even suggested ways in which she might give subtle help to Catherine in her struggle against the Guises. But Catherine had other ideas. She suspected Elizabeth was up to her tricks and wrote her a strong letter. She sent an even stronger message via the French ambassador in language so plain that she did not think it worthy of her pen to write it. Elizabeth replied "People talk of me often like hungers who divide the skin of the wolf before they have him... but I am not so reckless that the security of my government puts me so much to sleep that I do not make provision in advance for any accident which can wake me up. I am not of those people who open their mouth and wait for God to send them something to eat. Yet God forbid that I should not use the good means which God has given me to prevent and prepare for my troubles, which is what I hope that you yourself, as my very good sister, would wish me to do".

Elizabeth had no intention of supporting the Huguenots openly and she was certainly not going to do anything that might make it seem she was the European leader of Protestantism, so the money and artillery and ammunition were sent out in the utmost secrecy. At the same time she was reassuring Catherine that she would "never maintain any subject in rebellion against his sovereign".

Almost immediately, Elizabeth blatantly proved the lie to all her protestations. The citizens of Le Havre were almost entirely Huguenot and had made it a citadel of their own, but they were anxious to consolidate their position, so they turned to Elizabeth for help. She immediately recognised that this could be a stepping stone to regaining her beloved Calais. Suspecting the worst, Catherine sent Marshal de Vielleville to thank Elizabeth for her congratulations to the King - and ask her advice. He, too had a concealed task. It was to find out what preparations Elizabeth was making to help the Huguenots reinforce Le Havre (in fact it was 10 ships and 6,000 troops).

Within a month, Bedford had signed a secret treaty with Vidame de Chartres, the City's commander. It was arranged that directly the English ships appeared off the coast, the key defences were to be put in British hands and when the English troops landed, the Huguenots would withdraw. Then the combined English and Huguenot force would advance on Calais. Once the city had been captured, it was agreed that the Huguenots would exchange it with the English for Le Havre. When the English finally arrived in 1562 there was dismay when Elizabeth made it clear that her troops were to be used only for garrison work and were to concentrate on reinforcing the fortifications. When it came actually to fighting, other things went wrong too, and though the Huguenots captured Dieppe, they almost at once had to retreat back to Le Havre.

The Huguenots hoped to save the situation by sending an envoy to Elizabeth carrying a sheet of parchment blank except for their signatures. They begged her to save the situation by sending 10,000 more men and some money. The parchment turned into the Treaty of Hampton Court, in which the Calais-Le Havre exchange was confirmed, and Elizabeth duly gave them 40,000 crowns.

For Frenchmen to hold part of France in defiance of the King was one thing, but to then voluntarily hand it over to the hated English was something quite different. It provoked Catherine into action and what is more it provoked the Guises, who up to then had been prevaricating against her in every possible way. She appointed the very able Duke as commander. Bankruptcy never troubled her and so, without hope of being able to pay for them, she placed an order for 116 new cannon mounted "so that we can give the town a durious battery". Within a few days the Duke had won the Battle of Dreux. Elizabeth was still prepared to fight on, and she offered to pay the Huguenots handsomely so that they could bring in German mercenaries. But without reference to her, the Huguenots made an independent peace with Catherine.

Elizabeth now found her troops on their own besieged in the city. She raged at the Huguenots, but all they could say in mitigation was that she should not spoil the universal benefits brought about by their surrender. England was, as Throckmorton expressed it, "left to blow the coal". Even so, Elizabeth kept the troops walled up till the summer, when plague so decimated the garrison that she was forced to bring the rest home.

Catherine behaved in a surprisingly magnanimous way. She could easily have camped without the walls, laid siege and massacred the troops. Instead she waited, to the extent that after all the delay Elizabeth could still withdraw the bedraggled remnants of her forces back to England without harassment.

The subsequent treaty of Troyes was negotiated by the ambassador in Paris. In it the English agreed to renounce any claims on Calais. Predictably this was unacceptable to Elizabeth, so she sent out Throckmorton, telling him he must get a better deal. It proved not to be a good idea. The French remembered he had previously been a negotiator for the Huguenots and promptly put him in prison.

Catherine emerged from the engagement with considerable good fortune. Brief though the war had been, the Huguenots lost Conde and Montmorency, both of whom Catherine had been finding rather tiresome. Another casualty was her adversary in temporary alliance, the Duke of Guise.

In allowing the English forces to retire from Le Havre, Catherine had other very good reasons. She had just discovered the Guise plans for the marriage of Mary. This rearranged all the factors. They accepted that Phillip was not going to allow anyone to marry Don Carlos, so instead they planned to oust Elizabeth directly and make Mary Queen of England. They hoped that this on its own would so impress Philip that the prospect of such a grand alliance would make him change his mind. As a final stage, with the combined strength of Scotland, England and Spain and with the Guises at the summit, it would be easy to send Catherine and her pack of sons running.

Catherine fully realised this and her counterplot was as devious as anything she had ever devised. The Duke of Guise knew that Catherine was hoping Mary would marry one of her sons, so to conceal their plan, they told her they did not like the idea of Mary marrying Don Carlos after all. The Cardinal of Lorraine then laid a red herring by approaching Charles to allow Mary to marry the Archduke of Austria. What they did not know was that Catherine already had the Archduke in mind to marry one of her daughters. Nor did they know that she knew they were secretly canvassing Mary's case with the King of Spain. To prevent any chance of their guessing the truth.

Catherine first pretended to agree with their subterfuge and said that she was amenable for Mary to marry the Archduke rather than Don Carlos. At the same time she instructed her daughter to do all she could in the Spanish court to counter the Guise campaign. But Catherine realised that in the long term, her only reliable bulwark against the Guise plot was for Elizabeth to remain safely alive in England. She was prepared to do everything she could to prevent such a calamity and even warned her over a plot she had unearthed.

The situation brought about a strange chemistry in the rivalry between these two queens. It was a sort of love-hate attitude. Their countries were traditional enemies, but now they were being brought together through necessity. Both were afraid Philip and his allies would succeed in turning them off their respective thrones.

In August 1561, Mary set sail from France for Scotland and took the usual precaution of writing to Elizabeth for permission to enter an English harbour should her ship have to take refuge from a storm. Elizabeth replied by asking whether she had ratified the Treaty of Edinburgh yet. Mary gave the diplomatic reply that bad health and the necessary preparations for the voyage had not allowed her sufficient time to give it her attention. Elizabeth's response was to refuse permission. It was an insult, and it surprised not only Mary but even Elizabeth's advisers.

But Elizabeth had more reason than mere pique. Secretly, she was seriously considering kidnapping Mary. In any case, the longer it took for Mary to reach Scotland the more time it left in which the Scottish Protestant opposition movement could grow in strength. Mary, in contrast, gracefully apologised to the English ambassador for troubling him about her passport, tactfully pointing out that she now realised that, since she had not needed one when she had sailed to France, there was no reason to have one for her return. In practice, though this considerably increased the already hazardous voyage, for she would now have to brave any storms she might encounter.

Her confidence could not have been much raised when the Cardinal of Lorraine suggested that for safety she should leave her jewels in France. Mary rather tersely pointed out that if the journey was safe enough for her, then it was safe enough for the jewels. The day came and Mary was heartbroken at leaving her beloved France. So long as the shoreline remained in sight she kept murmuring "Adieu, France, Adieu, je pense ne vous revoir jamais plus".

As events turned out, there were no storms. Elizabeth's ships did come out, but typically they had not been given any specific instructions. They made their presence evident, but not really knowing what to do they saluted Mary's galley, inspected the others and, to show they were not to be trifled with, detained one of the party, Lord Eglinton, though they released him a few days later. And now she was landing at Leith in thick fog. Knox, never missing an opportunity, declared it was a portent of "sorrow, dolour, darkness and impiety".

Just as her mother had been, Mary was charmingly polite and agreeable. She was greeted with a chorus of psalm singers, whom she duly complimented on their performance, ignoring the fact that they had sung badly out of tune. She was escorted to Edinburgh by the Earl of Argyll, Lord Erskine and her half-brother Lord James. The people greeting her on her way were loud in their admiration for the beautiful young girl riding in such a stately manner. She in turn quickly saw that the reports she had received from French travellers had been right; it was indeed an infertile land. It was quite evident that the poor were miserably poor, for they were dressed in rags. The horses were scrawny and malnourished compared to those in France. The road was in bad condition and while there were no inns, significantly there was no shortage of hostelries. She found Holyrood bereft of any comfort. The Palace had been burnt down by the English 17 years before, so it was little more than an abbey with a tower. Her mother had tried, not very convincingly, to make the drawbridge and gratings over the windows look more domestic. The place was cold and the furnishings primitive. The Scots, of course, thought the place was magnificent.

Mary had arrived with the impression that the Scottish Protestants were still in much the same position as the Huguenots were in France;

nothing more than a large vocal group. But during the 14 months since her mother's death and led by the turbulent Knox, they had gained a lot of ground. Even in August 1560, as her mother was dying, they had passed a "Protestant Confession of Faith" which completely outlawed Catholicism, along with the saying of mass. This had so disheartened the Catholics that they had, in effect, retired from public life, leaving the Congregationalists in undisputed power. Even the aggressive Philip advised her to temporise over Protestantism.

Mary soon realised the wisdom of this. On her first Sunday in Edinburgh she had followed her agreement to the letter and attended mass at the Chapel Royal rather than in a public church. None the less, at the chapel entrance she was confronted by Patrick Lindsay with a group of fellow protesters calling for the idolatrous priest to be put to death. Her servants had the altar candles snatched from their hands and thrown onto the ground. During the mass, tension had become so high and the priest was shaking so much that he could hardly lift the host at the elevation.

For the first time Mary realised just how great an obstacle her faith was going to be if she was to gain real love among the Scottish people. Fortunately, like the other women in power, and contrary to her family advice, she felt that religious faith was a matter of individual choice, so she went out of her way to be fair to the Protestants. The very next day she made an order designed to bring peace between the faiths. There was to be no change in the existing situation. She would not threaten anyone and no one was to threaten her or anyone in her household. This rather questions as to what degree she had really been influenced by her family. She recognised that though "The Book of Discipline", introduced in 1561, was very harsh in its wide jurisdiction over personal morals and conduct, it also went far to encourage education and relief of the poor. However the country had never properly recovered since her grandmother, Margaret, wife of James IV, had bankrupted the state. Mary was not much better off, for she had to rely on Parliament for her funds.

There was still discussion as to whether all the Catholics' wealth and property should be handed over to the new Protestant Kirk, which would leave the old Catholic priests without compensation or pension. But the motion had not been passed by the Lords and instead it was passed to Mary for her decision. Far from favouring the Catholic priests, she had the total wealth split. Two thirds of the revenue was to remain with the existing holders for their lifetime. The remaining third was to be split between the Government and the reformed church. She also gave the church £10,000 of her own money - her entire income for a year.

Her magnanimity had made her popular among both faiths. She showed extraordinary tolerance with Knox and his outrageous and hurtful declarations. She invited him to meet her and tried to reason with him, a task that was almost impossible with such a bigot. She explained she was quite prepared to accept the differences between them but upbraided him for his tirades against her as his sovereign. She even invited him to come and tell her anything she did that he disliked. At one meeting she resorted to tears, which discomforted Knox considerably. So he agreed to modify his outbursts - though that did not last not long.

Scotland was too poor even to have its own coinage, and was having to use English currency, so one of the first things Mary tried to do was switch the country from using English to French coinage, but there was insufficient cash flow to make the change without undue hardship.

After she had been in Scotland 45 days, Elizabeth's permission to take refuge in an English port arrived. It seemed rather pointless, for although Mary's tactful response had softened Elizabeth a little, her official line was not to any attempt any reconciliation. On the contrary, when Sir Peter Mewtas, as Elizabeth's representative had officially welcomed her on behalf of England, he had immediately followed on by asking yet again if she had ratified the Treaty of Edinburgh. Mary replied that she had not. She explained that the situation had changed so much after the death of her husband that they should appoint new commissioners to scrutinise it again.

Despite this, Elizabeth had at one point hinted that she was ready to alter the controversial clause. While Mary herself was still precluded, it would have allowed her heirs to become eligible to the English throne after Elizabeth's death. Elizabeth wisely refused to agree to anything more because she had seen the problems that had surrounded her sister when she had been the adult successor in waiting. In any case Parliament would never have agreed to anything allowing Mary direct access to the throne.

One of the first things Mary had to do on her arrival was to choose her advisers. Some considered her tolerance a weakness, but within the year she had taken the brave step of largely divorcing herself from her Catholic councillors; in her council of 16 only four were Catholics.

Having been brought up in a close-knit and happy family, she almost inevitably turned to her half-brother James Stewart one of her main advisers. He was 30 and of a serious disposition, and was one of the new generation of nobles with a sense of national responsibility. William Maitland, aged 33, was another, a sophisticated and astute diplomat with integrity. He had been secretary for her mother. Otherwise Mary found herself among a set of lords belonging to a generation brought up without male mentors since their fathers and uncles had been killed at Flodden, Solway Moss or Pinkie Cleugh. Their upbringing had been poverty and indiscipline. Consequently, as her mother had so sadly found, they were wide open to bribery and had no sense of patriotism. Added to which a network of clan intermarriages and traditional feuds provided constantly-shifting hates and loyalties.

The leading Catholic lords were Huntly and Atholl in the North, Bothwell in the Borders and Lennox in the south west. They were an ill assorted and non cohesive bunch. In contrast, though barely 20, Mary was quickly proving herself to be clever, politically astute and, like her mother, a strong character who could also be diplomatic. She showed "both a great wisdom for her years, modesty and also of great judgement in the wise handling of herself and her matters which increase with her years cannot but turn greatly to her commendation, reputation, honour and great benefit of her and her country.... her behaviour to be such and her wisdom and modest dignity so great in that she think herself not too wise, but is content to be ruled by good counsel and wise men".

Melville considered her "so princely, so honourably" that she showed up the young Elizabeth, who was already proving to be headstrong and stubborn. Mary was quick thinking and courageous, though sometimes the two qualities could be at odds, leading her into taking decisions which on reflection were unwise. She had learned from her mother-in-law the art of intrigue, and enjoyed indulging in it, although she lacked the strong self-interest necessary if it was to be practised successfully. She could speak Latin, English, Spanish, Italian and Greek as well as French. She was fond of hunting and was an excellent horsewoman. She played the lute and virginals and enjoyed dancing. Again, unlike Elizabeth, she was not the least ostentatious, but dressed quietly and with discretion.

Her genuine lack of self-aggrandisement was shown when Charles IX offered her the great honour of becoming a Princess of the Royal Blood. She replied that nothing could be more honourable than the rank of her husband. She was fond of her personal servants, who in return adored her. She enjoyed their companionship and shared their joys and woes, confident in their loyalty. She was unusually tall, and she was attractive rather than pretty, with auburn hair and heavily-lidded eyes which gave her a degree of allure.

After a few months in Edinburgh, it was time for Mary to make her presence felt throughout the land so, in August 1562, she set out on a fact-finding tour. She first went to Linlithgow, then on to Perth, where she collapsed through sheer exhaustion. But she recovered quickly and carried on to Dundee and St. Andrews. Each Sunday throughout the progress she would confirm her authority and hear mass and each time there were vociferous protests. But this was of minor importance compared to the way the character of the tour changed when she reached the north east: Inverness, Spynie and Strathbogie. This was the land of the Earl of Huntly, who had a history of such deep treachery; "no man will trust him in word or deed". His sons were no less retrograde. Sir John, his eldest, had escaped while under arrest for severely wounding Lord Ogilvie in an Edinburgh street brawl. Mary bluntly told Lady Huntly that she would not pardon her son until he gave himself up. He did and was held at Stirling, but he escaped again.

Father and son next materialised with 10,000 horsemen and they started shadowing the Queen's train. John had high hopes that he could capture and marry her. She was finally forced into battle at Aberdeen and defeated them. She was helped not a little when Huntly suffered a massive, if timely, heart attack. It must be one of very few instances of a person dying on the battlefield through natural causes.

While the threat from the Huntly family had been increasing, that from England was receding. Up until then Elizabeth had been following much the same aggressive policy as had Henry VIII and Edward VI; every move by Scottish forces had been interpreted as a hostile move against England and had to be opposed by threats or actual force.

But now Mary was actually established in her realm, Elizabeth's attitude underwent a subtle change. She evidently felt the danger no longer lay in French forces gaining a foothold. Her interest was now focused on the woman herself and in particular her claims to the English throne.

The crucial point lay in the degree of success Mary might have if she called on the English Catholic families to rebel. From a political point of view, Mary had every reason to look upon Elizabeth as a usurper. At the same time she realised it was wise to remain on affable relations. For one thing, if she were to marry, the chances of her progeny ascending the English throne would largely depend on Elizabeth's consent. For another Elizabeth was a bulwark against the almost fanatical hatred in which the English Parliament held her. Mary was convinced she could best ensure Elizabeth's favour once they met face to face. She attached such importance to this that despite having to deal with an unreliable rabble of peers, she felt it more important for Maitland to go to London to plead for such a meeting. "We are both on one Isle, both of one language, both the nearest that each other hath and both queens", was the message from her that he took with him. He also took the gift of a ring, together with a poem. Elizabeth dutifully responded by sending another ring which, on receipt, Mary fulsomely declared to be "marvellously esteemed often times looked upon and many times kissed".

But Maitland was also to see the Spanish Ambassador, for she felt he might persuade Philip to change his mind over marriage with his son. She even threatened Philip, telling him that if he would not let her marry Don Carlos, she would agree to marry the King of France.

Mary's overtures may have been further prompted by Elizabeth falling seriously ill with smallpox. It was a situation which caused everyone to reflect soberly upon the English succession. Several parties emerged, canvassing for potential incumbents. Mary was dismayed to learn that among the English Catholics, the preference was not, as she had presumed, for herself but for Lady Lennox. More than ever Mary needed to mend her fences with Elizabeth. Despite the gift and surviving the smallpox, Elizabeth was still wary of a meeting. Much of her reluctance may have been due to the fear that if they were seen together she would lay herself open to personal comparison. Not only was Elizabeth the older, even if only by six years, but Mary was obviously the prettier. It was something Elizabeth's vanity could not accept. Also Mary might raise the question of marriage, and at this point in history, the Queens were in rivalry for the few eligible males on the European scene.

On the positive side Elizabeth realised that such a meeting might make it possible to persuade Mary to sign the Treaty of Edinburgh. So with reluctance, she did eventually agree. The meeting was to be held in York. Anxious to make an impression, Elizabeth even commissioned a celebratory masque which, she insisted, should be complimentary to England and Scotland in equal measure. But early that summer it rained so much that the roads became impassable and the meeting had to be postponed.

Then came news that the Guises had fired on a Protestant prayer meeting, plunging France into civil war. Elizabeth said she feared Spain was going to take advantage of the turmoil and invade France. In that case, England would have to take emergency action, so she must stay in London. Although it was a possibility, it seemed a pretty lame excuse, for no one considered such a development to be likely. Mary wept with frustration.

Having established her policy of lighting fires of discontent actually in Scotland and France, Elizabeth realised that Spain required a different approach. Philip and the Inquisition were exercising such ruthless control that it was smothering any significant Protestant opposition, but Elizabeth was quick to realise that instead of lighting fires in his realm, she could achieve much the same results if they were outside the Spanish boundaries. To this end she, typically, chose to interpret the treaty of Cateau-Cambresis in a way peculiar to her own convenience. The official agreement allowed a belligerent nation to stop and confiscate a ship so long as it was to prevent war materials from reaching an enemy state. Even if there was no war being waged at that moment, it was an arrangement that was only too easy to fudge and only too difficult to prove in its abuse. Elizabeth decided that it allowed her to turn a blind eye to her unofficial pirates, notably Hawkins and later Drake.

This brings into the story the other major figure to appear on the European scene after Cateau-Cambresis. After Mary of Hungary had retired as Governess of the Netherlands and before he appointed a successor, Philip had a try at leading the country himself. He proved completely incompetent. Of course, he was undertaking a difficult task. Fundamentally the cause of the Dutch problem lay in the very composition of the country. It was made up of 17 provinces speaking several dialects. For instance the northern areas, including Holland and Zealand, spoke Dutch and tended to be Germanic in outlook and followed after Calvin. The southern regions were richer and more densely populated. They spoke French and were predominantly Catholic. They all jealously guarded their traditions of municipal and provincial self-government and when it came to matters of trade and tariffs, they were deeply divided. The situation was now worse, because wages were not rising in step with inflation and the decline in the cloth industry was causing considerable hardship. Altogether there was a degree of unrest, particularly among the peasants.

Officially all these states were governed by the Estates General, which was in turn largely under the influence of the hereditary nobles, led by William of Orange and the Counts Horne and Edmond. As a start of his period of control in 1568, Philip introduced an army of spies, not something to be expected from a so-called mother country. Unsurprisingly, this was deeply resented. Then, as a precaution against a threatening situation on the border with France, he brought in 3,000 Spanish troops. The Dutch did not consider them an army for their defence, but as an army of occupation, and protested so vigorously that he had to withdraw them.

Far from understanding his mistake, Philip became firmly convinced that the Dutch were untrustworthy. From then on he treated them as enemies. Then his Holiness the Pope put in his oar, and told Philip that he strongly disapproved of the lenient way the heretics were being treated. Philip decided that the solution was to establish an Ecclesiastical Council made up of three archbishops and 15 bishops. This in itself was acceptable to the Dutch, but then they learnt that the Council was to be superior to their own Estates General. The Calvinists again jumped to the wrong conclusion and assumed the council was to be another form of the Spanish inquisition. Their fears were increased when Philip promoted the much-hated Bishop Antoine Granville as one of the Archbishops.

It was into this highly-explosive situation that in 1559 Margaret of Parma took up her post as Governess. Born in 1522, she was the illegitimate daughter of Charles V and a Flemish girl. She had married Alessandro de Medici, Duke of Florence, but within a year he had been murdered. She then married Ottavio Farnese, Duke of Parma, and had a son, Alexander. She was now 32 and it looked as though she could be as successful as her two predecessors, though if looks were considered literally, she was rather unprepossessing, with hair on her upper lip and taking unusually long strides. Anxious to be as able as her predecessors, she no doubt carefully studied how her aunt had managed whilst she had been Governor. But no matter how able she might be, Philip made her task almost impossible and her governorship was dogged by misfortune. First of all she was handicapped by the fundamental problems of communication. Passage down the Channel was threatened from both sides. Spain was a thousand miles away and the time between dispatching a message and expecting a reply was a matter of months.

This was aggravated since Philip proved to be a hopeless administrator. He might well have a rule that all correspondence was to be answered within 24 hours, but an answer did not necessarily mean a decision, and this often took him weeks. Then he was ill advised to tell Margaret to ignore the opinions of everyone except Granville or the Walloon nobility. His instructions were contradictory. She was to get all Dutch elements working together under his aegis, but at the same time she "must express notions rather than instructions". The upshot was that whenever circumstances forced her to take an immediate decision, he would in due course countermand it. This not only sapped her confidence but undermined her authority among the Dutch.

To cap it all, Philip appointed the much-hated Cardinal Granville as Margaret's chief adviser. William of Orange, together with other princes, wrote to Philip protesting that their influence was being diluted to an unacceptable degree. Margaret, who favoured conciliation, added her warning. She wrote that it was her belief that if, as seemed quite possible, the French chose this moment to invade, they would probably receive overwhelming support from the people. Philip and his advisers felt she was over-dramatising situations, for after all she herself was half Belgian.

So Margaret had to withstand mounting pressure for several more months. However, the nobles brought things to a head, warning her that the States General would not reassemble until Philip had sacked Cardinal Granville. Margaret had no alternative but to be conciliatory. She agreed, and dispatched her secretary to Madrid. Surprisingly Philip agreed. Showing unusual consideration for another person, he did not actually sack Granville but merely suggested he should go on indefinite leave to visit his ageing mother, and indeed that he should altogether spend more time with his family. He also wrote to the Dutch nobles confirming his decision, and they obligingly started attending the meetings of the Estates again.

All this time Margaret's problems were much the same as had confronted her predecessor Governess Mary, except this time they were being exacerbated by Elizabeth. For some time now her sea dogs had been raiding the Spanish and Dutch shipping. Soon she realised they were not only being successful in irritating Philip but were proving highly profitable in their own right. Margaret, on the receiving end, found they were doing so much damage that she put in an official complaint. Having exhausted her efforts negotiating with Thomas Gresham, the English ambassador at her court, she sent a personal envoy with a long list of assaults for which she considered Elizabeth responsible.

But she had more to add. Some of the Dutch had set sail with a number of ships under the leadership of Count de la Mark, a retrograde known as the Wild Boar of the Ardennes. They turned up at Dover, where they were joined by 18 ships manned by several thousand more Dutch refugees, so she was happy to give the Beggars, as they now called themselves, unofficial recognition. Elizabeth not only allowed them to stay but posted Admiral Wynter, along with four ships and two barques, at their disposal.

Soon they were collaborating with the Huguenot privateers and, working from the French ports, they effectively controlled the Normandy coast, notably Le Havre and La Rochelle. The English ports proved very convenient in providing refuge from storms or for shaking off Spanish ships in hot pursuit. Another advantage was that the prevailing winds quite often blew Spanish ships willy-nilly into the English coast, where the Beggars would finish them off. Altogether it was quite a formidable force that roved the sea, taking every opportunity to harass Spanish shipping. Within four months the Beggars had captured 300 vessels.

Additionally there were several perfectly legitimate trading agreements dating from the time of Mary. For instance, the English Navigation Act grossly favoured English shipping. It imposed duties on the import into England of such items as saddles, gloves, daggers, pins etc, all of which were made in the Netherlands. Elizabeth feared that if she rejected Margaret's complaint outright, Margaret might retaliate by imposing duties on English cloth. However she took a chance and typically gave vague answers, declaring that all the piracy had been carried on without her knowledge. Indeed she would punish any of her adventurers who even suggested such action. Her condemnation was so strong that it suggested she was protesting too much. Indeed Elizabeth continued her policy unabated. So Margaret conjured up an imaginary outbreak of the plague as an excuse to place an embargo on the English exports of wool.

Wool had become the staple export of England and cloth-weaving a major part of the livelihood of the peasantry, so that by this time cloth was amounting to 70–80 per cent of England's foreign trade. Margaret well knew that any disruption would impoverish large numbers of English peasants. Elizabeth sent Dr Valentine Dale to protest and hinted that the English could find alternative markets. Indeed the English merchants had foreseen this possibility and had already chosen Bremen as an alternative, so Elizabeth felt it safe to raise the stakes further. She put her own embargo on the sale of English cloth to the Netherlands. Ten days later Margaret responded by prohibiting goods of any nationality being transported by English ships within Netherlands waters. This ruled out Bremen.

The problem for Margaret was that Antwerp trade was no less important for the Netherlands than it was for England. The embargo was seriously damaging the port which handled three quarters of Spain's wool exports and four fifths of the ships plying the trade routes with Spain. The port had additionally become the European centre for banking. So whilst the move was very inconvenient for England, any major disruption in Antwerp trade also disrupted both the Dutch and Spanish economy.

Cardinal Granville advised Margaret that the embargoes would hurt England more than Spain. Elizabeth thought differently, and made it a question of who blinked first. Fortunately for England, the situation was not so dire as it might have been. Although Bremen was now ruled out, the Countess of Friesland had been watching developments. She negotiated with some of the English traders to open business in the port of Emden. It was not so convenient as Antwerp, but it did not entail any major diversion and it was beyond Philip's jurisdiction. Also it did not have the associated facilities for dressing and dying cloth. Without these added values, the price for crude cloth was so low that it meant England still suffered considerable loss of revenue.

Early the next year the Countess reached an agreement with the Merchant Adventurers and by May, they had already marketed 75,000 pieces of cloth through Emden. This indeed brought England merciful relief, and stocks that had been building up alarmingly could now be released.

If Philip was complaining over the marauding of his ships, it was nothing to what he was to experience when Elizabeth, no longer having the fear of retaliation, decided to intensify her raids on his shipping. The first indication Elizabeth had that she was winning came when Philip replaced his austere ambassador in London with Guzman de Silva. He was far more amenable, and it soon became clear his appointment had been made with a view to restoring trade.

Then she received a hint that Margaret would be prepared to start trading immediately, pre-empting discussions that had already been arranged. Once Elizabeth knew she was close to winning, she realised that agreeing to any immediate redress would allow Margaret to regain much of her bargaining power, so, although it was causing even greater unemployment at home, Elizabeth protracted the negotiations for as long as she could. By December Margaret had become so desperate that she was prepared to accept the terms without question. So the embargo was finally lifted, leaving things very much as they had been before.

But while Margaret had brought enmity with England to a conclusion, the Dutch population were becoming increasingly resentful against Spanish rule. This now surfaced through the magistrates who were relied upon for maintaining day to day discipline within the country. A large number of them were simply refusing to implement the anti-heresy laws Philip was insisting upon. William of Orange aggravated the situation when he made a rousing speech in the Brussels Council calling for liberty of conscience. This made Philip increasingly concerned over the Huguenots in the Netherlands. He had recently seen in France how they had taken advantage of the smallest degree of leniency to threaten to renew the civil war. Consequently Philip felt his Netherlands policy was no longer just a matter of faith but had become one of political necessity.

By mid-April he was in daily council, working out details in case it should come to war. He confirmed his determination in a letter to the Pope. He was hoping to settle matters peacefully. If, however, the only way the Pope's demands could be met was through military action, then he would have no hesitation in applying it. He instructed Margaret to rescind the amnesty and to raise troops in Germany. Matters had reached the stage where Margaret had felt bound to let Count Egmond go on a mission to Madrid to urge Philip to give more power back to the nobles. He returned in jubilation, having, as he thought, won considerable concessions. It might have been diplomacy or it might have been duplicity, but when Margaret opened the sealed letters he brought back they told a completely different story. "My intention", Philip wrote, "is neither to resolve the Count's demands at present, nor disabuse him about them...... If we refused outright we would never see the end of him". In fact Philip had not budged a bit: "In the question of religion, what most concerns me and what I can least permit is any change, and I should count it as nothing to lose a hundred thousand lives - if I had them". While he agreed the administration should be changed, he gave no intimation as to how. He agreed to a conference to reconcile the heresy laws and, according to William's request, nominated those who were to attend. They included a majority of staunch Catholics who were at loggerheads with William. Philip also specified that the deliberations must not be held in public.

His letter was received by both Margaret and the Dutch in utter consternation As though this was not sufficiently depressing, the general feeling was that Philip had tricked Egmont deliberately. Margaret realised that feelings were so strong that she sought some sort of conciliation by temporally suspending the execution of several heretics which Philip had demanded. This decision was received by the Madrid advisers in a vein typical of those isolated from the actual situation. They told Philip: "There is little hope that Madame will do it, judging by her letters, since she is dominated by the gentlemen in those states".

Margaret at last persuaded Philip that if his authority was to survive, he must visit the Netherlands in person. But then the inevitable procrastination set in. Eventually, in November, he sent instead another letter to Margaret. Initially he seemed to be taking a conciliatory line. A general pardon would be issued. But then he became as adamant as ever, qualifying the amnesty by saying it was to be extended only to those who had not been arrested on religious grounds. On second thoughts, Philip decided that even this concession was too much and retracted the offer altogether.

By this time the country was almost in open revolt. Once again

Margaret sent one of the Dutch nobles, but it was too late. The nobles rose in "iconoclastic fury" against the new restrictions Margaret had been forced to impose on them. There were strong protests in all the provinces. Eventually Orange, Egmont, Horne and the other grandees presented Margaret with an ultimatum: if greater toleration was not allowed, they would resign from the Council of State. They, and into the vacuum stepped the lesser nobles who normally ran the country at local level. But they were no less adamant. Two of them arrived at the head of some 300 armed men and presented Margaret with a "Compromise Bond". She was to demand that Philip modify the laws repressing the Calvinists. Margaret's defence was hardly helped when one of her entourage sneered at the delegation, describing them to their faces as "beggars". It was a term which in time they were to adopt as a mark of pride. But at that moment it considerably embarrassed Margaret. She knew that they knew she was powerless to refuse their demands. Without them the administration would disintegrate completely. The situation was so serious that for once she took the initiative and there and then issued an order modifying the heresy laws.

Philip now decided it was time to squash the Dutch resistance once and for all. He sent 20,000 troops. Obviously it was easy to send them direct by sea, but Philip could not resist embarrassing Catherine in all her difficulties, so instead, he ordered them to be taken from his force in Italy. Alva would join them in Flanders.

He then asked Catherine for permission to march the men through France. She was aghast. Beyond the burden on the population along the way, all Huguenots within France would assume it was a trick against them and the country would be in uproar. She and Philip took offence. Throughout the next few months, preachers in the Netherlands were encouraging the Protestants to riot. They were so effective that over 400 Catholic churches were sacked. Margaret was sending a whole sheaf of letters to Madrid reporting "defilements, abominations, sacrileges".

The situation then took an international turn. Though Margaret did not know it, it was entirely through pique over Philip's presumption that he could march his troops through France. Catherine appointed the prominent Huguenot Conde as Governor of Picardy. A Huguenot in control of an area so close to the Netherlands border could be construed as a direct threat. Considering how unpopular Philip was among the French, Margaret had strong reasons for believing that they were about to back the Huguenots actively. Indeed, the Dutch were encouraging them by intimating that if they made any inroads into the Netherlands, they would be rewarded by being allowed to keep some of the land.

It reached a stage when Margaret could wait no longer for permission from Spain, let alone did she have time to expect reinforcements. The only hope for peace was to issue a general amnesty. To an extent this steadied the situation and persuaded William of Orange and the other nobles to cooperate once again. At the same time, and with their approval, she ordered in supplementary mercenary forces from Germany. Calm was restored.

Margaret now felt justified in writing to Philip that there was no need for the German mercenaries to be kept, nor for any further action. Indeed, she strongly advised him to leave well alone. But it was too late. The day Philip received her letter was the day Alva was embarking for Brussels. It took only a few weeks for Margaret to recognise that Alva's heavy hand was completely wrong. She now knew the Dutch sufficiently well to realise that they would resist in one way or another. They would never be cowed. In 1567, after a few months witnessing his ruthlessness, Margaret resigned and Alva was left to carry out his bloody repression without restraint.

In the meantime, everyone was speculating about who Mary would choose to marry. She went through the ritual of receiving all the hopefuls, most of whom had already been spurned by Elizabeth, such as the King of Sweden and the King of Denmark. Elizabeth too was taking a close interest in Mary, and Mary was just as concerned that Elizabeth should approve her eventual choice. Besides being a powerful neighbour, Elizabeth's disapproval could preclude any possibility of her progeny ever succeeding to the English throne. So Mary asked Elizabeth directly to recommend someone.

The choice astounded everyone. It was her former beau Robert Dudley, whom she had hastily discarded when his wife Amy Robsart had died in extraordinary, if not outright suspicious, circumstances. Indeed, to help make him more acceptable Elizabeth created him Earl of Leicester. However the degree of seriousness she attached to the appointment became questionable when, during the ceremony, she was noticed tickling his neck.

Mary, however, did not consider Dudley sufficiently exalted to be the husband of the former Queen of France. In any case, it would hardly have been appropriate for her to take on Elizabeth's cast-offs. So Maitland, still in London, tactfully replied that unless the union would guarantee the throne of England, Mary would be reluctant to deprive Elizabeth of such a "prized" man. It may well have occurred to Elizabeth how advantageous it would be if she could "bounce" Mary out of her high ideals and into marrying some nondescript individual.

Indeed, this may have been the reason why she made the apparently innocuous request that Mary should end the exile of Darnley. He had been expelled along with his father, who had, expressly against James's orders, fortified Dumbarton Castle. He had then gone on to fight with the English. Elizabeth was also well aware of the ambitions of Darnley's mother, the Countess of Lennox, who, despite the failure of the meeting in France, still held high hopes. Mary agreed to the request, but when he arrived even this second attempt at match-making apparently failed. The only result was that Darnley caught measles.

And then it happened. She went to his bedside, appointed herself his nurse and fell hopelessly in love. And from that moment, Mary's life changed. Up until then her main preoccupation as Queen of Scotland had been to persuade the two faiths to live in harmony, and she had met with considerable success. But as from this moment the troubles were all the making of her heart. There was no denial that Darnley was good looking and some of the attraction may have been because he was one of the few men taller than she was. He was 6ft 3 and Mary was 6 ft. Her love may have been all the more ardent because it was unlikely that Francis II had been capable of consummating their marriage. Mary herself said she thought Darnley the "lustiest and best proportioned long man that she had ever seen". He was however of inferior stock, and such a marriage would undoubtedly damage her status. But even if all Mary's loyal supporters were not utterly dismayed at the engagement, they soon became so. His doting mother had spoilt the child so that he had become utterly self-centred. He was vain and stupid, and had a bad temper besides. Like so many vain people, he was also a coward. He was quite capable of hitting someone, so long as it was a subordinate who he knew would not dare hit back. Once, when he was expecting Mary to make him Earl of Ross, it was all his attendants could do to prevent him from stabbing the messenger, because the message informed him that he had only been made Duke of Albany.

A large proportion of the people were quite open in their disapproval of the match. Mary interpreted this as being against her, rather than just a protest against Darnley. But these was mere domestic opinions and she was so in love she attached little importance to them.

She did, though, take the precaution of sounding out opinion abroad. Both Charles V and Philip definitely approved. Elizabeth, true to form, did not actually give her approval; she merely appeared to give it by not raising any objection. She did write to Mary advising her not to sack those of her old advisers who were among the protesters.

But then Elizabeth's council sensed danger. Further inquiry showed that Darnley had a rather tortuous, if distant, claim to the English throne. Also his Catholicism was open to question, since he had been known to attend Protestant sermons. But more particularly, they feared Darnley's English birth would strengthen Mary's case among those English Catholics who were still neutral. Mary was therefore surprised that when she heard from Elizabeth it was to learn of her extreme displeasure over her preference for Darnley over Dudley. She even demanded his "return". Elizabeth went even further, and clapped Lady Lennox into the Tower. Certainly Lady Lennox was a trouble maker and over the years had spent a lot of time in the Tower. She had openly declared both Tudor sisters to be bastards, and she was supposed to have been one of the people who had pressed to have Elizabeth executed.

Mary was not only surprised but utterly dismayed at Elizabeth's response, and even had the marriage postponed in the hope that she might be able to persuade Elizabeth to change her mind.

The marriage eventually took place on May 29th 1565 in Holyrood Chapel Royal. Mary wore a black robe, being still in mourning for her first husband. She decreed that the hated Darnley was to be styled "King of this our Kingdom" and that all documents should be jointly signed Mary and Henry. When it was formally announced by the Heralds, instead of the nobles shouting out the customary "Amen" they kept an ominous silence. Many of the Lords, particularly her half-brother Lord Henry and the Earl of Argyll, who hated the whole Lennox family, showed their displeasure in a rather peculiar way. They did not want their action to be interpreted as treason, so their men never actually fought the Queen's men. Whenever it looked as though there might be real confrontation, their forces melted away. It soon became known as the "chase about".

Mary, however, missed the point. She still interpreted it as a revolt against her rather than a protest against the increasing importance she was according her husband. The dissidents were expecting financial support from Elizabeth, but officially she did not oblige. The Venetian Ambassador in London however felt fairly sure she had given Lord James 2,000 ducats and that to make sure its origin could not be traced, "she did not take it as customary from the treasury but from the funds on deposit from the reserves in the Court of Ward." The rebels judged it insufficient to stage a substantial protest and Lord James, among others, felt it more prudent to take refuge in England. Elizabeth suggested sending a delegation to bring about reconciliation. Mary felt this was blatant interference, and replied that she would be happy to receive any delegation so long as discussions were restricted to Anglo-Scottish relations. She would not, however, tolerate interference over the rebels "whom she meant to chastise".

Elizabeth was annoyed. She told the Spanish Ambassador "God forbid that I should help disobedient subjects unless I see good reason why they should not suffer without a hearing". In this way she was typically both distancing herself from helping the rebels and at the same time insisting that should be fairly treated. The astute Ambassador reported "It appears to one that her desire to throw all the blame on the King of Scotland and exonerate the Queen is an indication that she is taking the same course as she did when she helped the heretics in France on the pretext that she did it to free the King who she claimed was being coerced".

Elizabeth now played a pantomime that pleased her much. She called upon Lord James, now in London, to appear before her. To make sure Mary received a full report, she called the whole council to be present. She also made sure that the French and Spanish ambassadors were there as well. Her intention was to warn them that interference by other countries would not be tolerated. She made great show of admonishing Lord James for his wickedness in rebelling against his Queen. Thereupon Lord James, obviously on cue and barely able to keep a straight face, went on bended knee, pretending to be overcome with despair at her displeasure.

But it was not long before Mary herself was beginning to see the flaws in Darnley's character. He was becoming tedious, making persistent demands to be given the Crown Matrimonial, so that he would become King absolute should she die. Not that it was within her power to give it to him anyway, as it could only be granted by Parliament. He began ignoring his responsibilities and lived only for pleasure. He was so often out hunting when he should have been attending to state business that an iron stamp had to be made of his signature. Worse, he had become a drunkard, and in his cups would slight the Queen. He even started insulting her in public.

One of the first signs of her disillusionment was the withdrawal of all the silver coins on which their names were linked. Nor was she still angrily dismissing out of hand any suggestion that she might have to divorce him. Darnley's cronies, however, were urging him to greater aspirations. Soon they were hinting that he would make a good replacement for the present incumbent of the throne. He came to believe this himself. He even wrote to the Pope and Philip. After deprecating his wife, calling her a fickle Catholic, he assured them that he was the more worthy person to wear the crown.

His persistent failure to get his way caused him to look around to see who might be supporting his wife's obstinacy. David Riccio was a bass singer who had arrived in Scotland in the train of the Savoy ambassador. Mary found him an amusing conversationalist and enjoyed reminiscing with him over things continental. After a while she made him her French secretary, but it soon transpired that he was in fact much more. After Maitland, as Secretary of State had lost her confidence over his failure to persuade the Spanish ambassador to change Philip's mind over Don Carlos, she appointed Riccio in his place. Hardly surprisingly, Maitland thereupon joined the growing band of active dissidents in exile. Before long Darnley's toadies were hinting that Riccio was cuckolding him with the Queen. It reached the stage where Darnley conspired with others to murder him.

Then Darnley broadened the plot. On witnessing Riccio's murder, Mary might miscarry, leading to a slow death. She would be put in prison and he would take the crown.

The murder was carried out in the most crude and brutal manner. On the fateful evening the conspirators foregathered in Darnley's rooms, which were exactly beneath those of the Queen. They then went up by a private staircase to where Riccio was having supper with her. She tried to protect him, but she was threatened with a gun. They dragged him out of the room. Mary ran to the window and screamed for help, and when the men in a nearby hostelry turned out to help, the conspirators held the gun against her and forced her to reassure them that all was well. In an attempt to share the guilt, they between them stabbed Riccio altogether 50 times.

Despite the horror of the crime being committed almost before her eyes, Mary still retained her wits. Darnley did not. He rushed to the Queen and asked her forgiveness. She rightly guessed that he was the weakest link among the conspirators, so she persuaded him that his co-conspirators were probably going to murder him next. Darnley believed her story, and was thankful when Mary, with the help of her equity and one of her pages, pretended that the shock had brought on labour pains. It caused sufficient diversion for Darnley to escape from the palace and get out of Edinburgh.

Mary had now successfully split Darnley from his fellow conspirators. But she still believed the assassins had intended to murder her too. She knew she could rely on her French domestic staff to help her escape the same way and, although heavily pregnant, she rode the 15 miles to the safety of Dunbar Castle. When the rebels learned that Darnley had become a turncoat, they lost all hope of success. At the same time Mary was able to call on her loyal lords and, accompanied by 4,000 men, she returned to Edinburgh in triumph.

Mary was shown a bond Riccio's murderers had signed and saw that it included her husband's name. Yet she did not do anything about it immediately. She was pregnant and dared not do anything that might compromise the child's legitimacy. After she had given birth to James, she did her utmost to confirm this fact in public. She took advantage of being in a room full of people to tell Darnley: "My lord, God has given you and me a son begotten by none but you... this is your son and no other man's son. I am desirous that all here with ladies and others bear witness". If verbal testimony were sufficient, she could hardly have made it with more clarity.

At Christmas she played her trump card. She pardoned all the conspirators with one exception; Darnley himself. By Twelfth Night, a group of lords, led by the Earl of Bothwell, had come as far as laying plans for Darnley's murder. By this time Mary had come to dislike her husband so much that she could no longer stay in the same house, and he was staying in Kirk o'Feld. This made it much easier for the conspirators to lay their plan without fear of harming the Queen.

At two o'clock on a morning in February 1567, Bothwell blew up the house. He nearly killed himself in the process but entirely failed to kill Darnley, who had evidently heard something suspicious. Since it had become the fashion at that time to dispose of enemies by way of setting fire to their houses, he took the obvious precaution of running out in his nightgown into the garden. He was crossing the garden when someone caught and strangled him. The next day everyone in Scotland knew that the murderer was Bothwell, and within two weeks everyone in London knew it too. But what no one knew was how much, if at all, Mary had known it was going to happen. Probably she had no idea. This was shown when she appointed a number of nobles to investigate, completely unaware that they were themselves the conspirators. If they followed her instructions as she had asked, they would be assisting one another to the gallows. Instead they were in an ideal position for covering their tracks. They knew where all the evidence lay and they knew all those minions who could implicate them. They methodically set about disposing of them all.

Both Elizabeth and Catherine were highly suspicious over Mary's complicity. In their eyes, to murder a crowned sovereign, no matter how objectionable, was simply not done. Elizabeth wrote her a stern letter. Instead of starting "My Dear Sister" she began "Madam. My ears have been so astounded and my heart so frightened to hear of the horrible and abominable murder of your husband and my own cousin, that I have scarcely spirit to write yet I cannot conceal that I grieve more for you than for him. I should not do the office of a faithful cousin and friend if I did not urge you to preserve your honour, rather than look through your fingers at revenge on those who had done you that pleasure as most people say. I counsel you so to take this matter to heart, that you may show the world what a noble Princess and loyal woman you are. I write thus vehemently not that I doubt but for affection".

Even so, Elizabeth felt such a rebuke was insufficient. Indeed, she felt so strongly about it that she wrote to Catherine suggesting that they should place some sort of embargo on trade with Scotland. However Catherine had the civil wars on her hands, and never replied. Bothwell had been a leading figure at court. Indeed among all the fickleness around, he had been the person most consistently loyal.

Certainly he had his faults. He too was vain, but he was no coward and could be forceful. He had a strange ancestry. His family had followed much the same path as the Habsburgs by marrying royalty. Unfortunately, while the Habsburg wives were princess heiresses, bringing handsome diaries with them, the Bothwells chose the widows of kings who had already provided heirs and had become impoverished. One ancestor had been associated with the widow of James I. His father Patrick had tried to court Marie.

After some initial efforts to find the conspirators, Mary seems to have given up. Even when the Council had at last come round to apprehending Bothwell, he was not only allowed to stay free but actually attended the meeting when arrangements were being made for his trial. The chief witness for the prosecution was Lennox, and he arrived in fear and trembling, even though he had the legally acceptable six supporters. When Bothwell arrived he was accompanied by 4,000 men. Lennox did not dare even attend the court and Bothwell was acquitted.

Elizabeth wrote to Mary suggesting that there should be a retrial at which Lennox should give evidence without threat. But Mary did nothing.

In French law a King did not reach his majority and rule in his own right until he had reached his fourteenth year. Although Charles IX had only just celebrated his 13th birthday, Catherine could wait no longer. She wanted to act quickly while the country was enjoying one of its rare moments of peace. So in 1564 she declared that although in the eyes of the law he would not become king until he was fourteen, there was no real difference between celebrating at the start of this fourteenth year rather than at the end. Since everyone realised she would continue controlling him anyway, no one raised any particular objection.

She had him declare his majority before Parliament in Rouen.

Even so Catherine was not fully satisfied that the ceremony had sufficiently generated the desired response among the populace. It was a genuinely important point. Traditionally the people looked upon the crown as something mystic, decreed by God and therefore beyond reproach and requiring unqualified loyalty. But everyone knew Charles was still completely under the control of his mother, as well as rumours that he had strong leanings toward heresy.

Like Elizabeth, Catherine recognised the importance of the people seeing their prince in all his magnificence. As it happened, Catherine had for some time felt many of the local governments needed shaking up, so she decided that both objectives could be combined in a royal progress. To ensure it was seen by as many people as possible, it was to cover 3,000 kilometres and last 14 months. No place outside Paris would be able to accommodate so many people, so the logistics had to be conceived on the scale of a military campaign. Besides the King and his immediate circle, there would have to be thousands of attendants. There were all the courtiers and hangers on, all their servants and the secretaries and administrators. It would require hundreds of carts. There had to be transport for their domestic needs, their bedding and accommodation, food and furniture.

These were just the basic needs. There also had to be magnificence; everything required to prepare and stage banquets, the stabling and upkeep of horses, hounds, and falcons for hunting; the dresses, scenery and musicians for masques. Most important of all, to counter the rumours spread by the Huguenots, the cavalcade had to include all the furniture and trappings of a place of worship. As many people as possible must see the King at traditional Catholic mass.

Nor did Catherine lose sight of the original concept. At every place where the caravan stopped, she had done her homework. She knew all the local cliques and was aware of local complaints and dissatisfaction even before they had been placed before her. She issued strict warnings wherever she thought the local leaders were falling short in their duties.

The progress was to take 16 months, ending at Bayonne with a splendid meeting between Spain and France. Catherine was looking forward to the occasion when "the merchant's daughter" would be cavorting with the most prestigious King in Europe. However, Philip did not attach such importance to the event. He excused himself, declaring that he could not be seen consorting with Catherine's party when it included a number of well-known Huguenots. He sent the Duke of Alva in his place. This did not unduly dismay Catherine. If nothing else, the occasion provided a good opportunity to see her daughter.

A great deal of money was spent. It ended with a pageant on the River Bidassoa, where the King sat in a barge which was disguised as a fortress. A giant whale emerged and was attacked by fishermen. After that an equally large tortoise surfaced. On its back were six tritons blowing trumpets. Finally Neptune surfaced in his chariot, pulled by three sea horses.

The result of all this magnificence? Absolutely nil.

The trouble was that the two sides wanted to sort out different problems. When Philip had been instructing Alva, he told him to concentrate on his long-standing complaint that Catherine was not persecuting the Huguenots with sufficient energy, while Catherine, as usual, was set on match making. She still hoped her daughter Margot could be married to Don Carlos, added to which she now wanted her son Anjou to marry the Princess of Portugal.

In fact Catherine had already made a creditable effort to appease Philip's demands. Back in 1562 she had had the idea of transporting the more troublesome Huguenots to populate a colony to be started in Florida. Admittedly it was in close proximity to the Spanish colonies, but Philip had not protested. However the settlers did. Within two years they were suffering a major famine, with another four years later.

This had led to a revolt against Catherine's officials. To stay alive, the colonists began making piratical raids on Spanish shipping. The final provocation came when they started fortifying their encampment.

Catherine sent out some ships to restore order, but the Spanish had also had enough and they followed the French ships with eight of their own. Once they had reached Florida there was a sea battle, and the French were defeated. But it was the way the Spanish victors treated the French that caused outrage. They murdered the entire force and, because the colony included Huguenot priests, tried to justify their action by putting inscriptions above the corpses: "Hung not as Frenchmen but as Lutherans".

Catherine tried to appease Philip further by issuing a supplement to the Amboise agreement which tightened the controls over the Huguenots. It left him unimpressed. After she had allowed sufficient time for Alva to have briefed Philip, there was still no response, so she told the Spanish that they must announce the engagement before she would carry out her part of the promise. Unfortunately Philip did not take her promise. Even more unfortunately, the Huguenots did. Their reaction was to plan another attempt at kidnapping the King, this time while he was in his palace at Meaux. But Catherine inevitably got to hear of it, so she immediately set out with the King for the safety of Paris. Although their plans were only half ready, the Huguenots attacked the train. They were repulsed and in lieu they took revenge by raiding Catherine's château of St. Maur.

There they left a sinister sign. They found Catherine's dog had just had seven puppies, so they killed the mother and the male puppies. The message was clear; the two bitch puppies spared represented Catherine's two daughters, Elizabeth and Margot.

While Catherine was impervious to threats against herself, any threat to her children drew an immediate response. She at once negotiated a truce with the Huguenots, but it was to little avail. Killings continued on both sides, the only difference being that they were unofficial. So it was hardly surprising when civil war broke out again officially.

Darnley's murder left Bothwell free to do more or less as he wished, and his next move was awaited by the whole of Scotland.

They did not have to wait long. In April 1567 Bothwell invited all those prominent lords who were sympathetic to him to a drinking session at Ainslie's Tavern. When they were deep in their cups, he persuaded them to sign a bond recommending that Mary should marry him. It was an impressive document, for among the signatories were eight bishops, nine earls and seven lords.

Mary was on her way back after visiting her son. With this spurious authority, Bothwell set out to intercept her and pressed her to come with him to Dunbar Castle. She had no reason to be concerned, for he had been a loyal servant to her mother and herself and had become a close friend. She had attended his wedding. However, once at Dunbar he probably in effect raped her. Whatever the facts, she was now morally compromised.

He then showed her the bond, with the names of all those who declared they would support their marriage. Of course he did not tell her that next morning they had nearly all rescinded this. He convinced her. And so she entered Edinburgh, but with Bothwell holding the reins of her horse as though confirming that she was his chatelaine.

In April 1567 they went through the marriage service, a Protestant ceremony. Normally Mary would never have agreed to such a thing, which just shows how confused she had become. Bothwell took her to the austere castle of Northwick, where he kept her incommunicado with anyone who could give her advice. He stood over her while she wrote to Elizabeth and Catherine. True enough, she pointed out that Bothwell had been acquitted of murder and that a number of lords had urged her to marry him. In any case she felt she desperately needed a consort. But her letters were considered too detailed and logical to have been written spontaneously.

Bothwell quickly took charge of state affairs and managed them with surprising ability. He insisted on regular attendance at the Privy Council. He had laws passed against bringing false money into the country. Another law reaffirmed that Protestantism remained the official religion, but that Catholicism was to be tolerated. They were all Acts Mary might have introduced, had she been concentrating more on Government business.

Despite all the denials, both Elizabeth and Catherine remained quite certain that Mary had knowingly married the murderer of her husband. Assassination was all very well, but the law, in those days, was particularly harsh on a wife's infidelity. If a husband caught his wife being unfaithful it was considered perfectly justifiable for him to throw her out into the street. Mary's behaviour was completely beyond the pale.

Elizabeth wrote again, and this time she did not mince her words: "Madam, to be plain with you, our grief hath not been small that in this your marriage no slender consideration has been had that, as we perceive manifestly no good friend you have in the whole world can like thereof and, if we should otherwise write or say, we should abuse you. For how could a worse choice be made for your honour than in such haste to marry a subject who, besides other notorious lacks, public fame hath charged with the murder of your late husband, besides the touching of yourself in some part, though we trust in that have another lawful wife alive, whereby neither by God's law nor man's yourself can be his lawful wife nor any children betwixt you legitimate".

Even at this late stage, most of her lords would have still been prepared to accept Mary as their Queen, if only she would disassociate herself from Bothwell. But Mary, now pregnant again, was just as anxious that the second in line to the throne should be as indisputably legitimate as was James. She held to this principle even though she knew that the alternative was civil war. So on a day in June 1567, both sides were drawn up at Carberry Hill ready for battle. The French Ambassador made a dramatic move for peace. He rode between the lines and promised her peace if only she would abandon Bothwell. Mary pointed out, and with good reason, that only a short while before, most of those on the opposing side had signed the marriage bond. At least Bothwell had remained consistently loyal to her. He, in turn, tried to redeem the critical situation. He suggested the matter should be decided in single combat and challenged Earl Morton, who was leading the rebels. However Mary forbade it.

All this while, her troops had been melting away. Mary realised the futility of it all and to save any spilling of blood she offered no more resistance and gave herself up. Her only condition was that Bothwell be allowed to go free.

She kissed him goodbye, and he left with the intention of raising more troops. However he failed, and fled to Norway. Which was rash, because he had at one time jilted one of the Norwegian princesses. Through bad luck, he fell into the hands of the King, who kept him prisoner in the hope that he could raise a ransom. The King then forgot him, and when years later he died, he was still chained to a dungeon pillar.

That evening of the battle that never was, Mary was persuaded that the hostile lords really would affirm their loyalty if she disowned Bothwell. While not precisely agreeing, she hoped she could persuade Elizabeth to defer a final decision, so she accepted their invitation to join them to return to Edinburgh. There she was assured that the whole question could be put under review. But immediately she entered their camp she realised she had been tricked. Instead of the cheers she had expected, she was received with jeers.

Certainly the lords kept their word and allowed her to return to Edinburgh, but all along the way she was shocked to find that her ordinary subjects were as cruel as the soldiers. Bespattered with mud and with tears of disillusionment pouring down her cheeks, she entered Edinburgh to the cries of "Burn the whore!" It was clear that she was returning not as a Queen; she was a prisoner. She lost her regal self-possession and shouted back at them.

She was taken to one of the Lords' houses, and by the next morning she had suffered complete mental collapse. She appeared at the window, obviously distraught, her clothes torn open, the upper part of her almost bare, her hair hanging down her face. She told the people she was being kept prisoner.

The crowd was shocked at her appearance and their moral outrage started turning to pity. The Lords holding her feared the change would lead to an attempt at rescue, so they hurriedly spirited her away to the Castle of Lochleven. Set on an island in the lake, it was considered escape proof. With her last hope gone, and under considerable duress, Mary signed her abdication. Catherine and Elizabeth immediately saw their chance and both demanded to take charge of the young King James. Lord James thwarted them by having himself appointed Regent. He also thwarted their avarice after the royal jewels. He gave his wife first choice and only then put the rest up for sale. Both Elizabeth and Catherine had coveted them for many years and both claimed close relationship as reason for being given next choice.

Unaware of this avarice, Mary had letters smuggled out to both ladies. She described her miserable conditions and begged for some help. Some hope. Despite honeyed words in the past, Elizabeth had not the least intention of actually helping Mary. In accordance with her usual policy of compromise, she also refused to recognise the revolutionaries.

She sent Throckmorton to assess the situation. He was to tell the Scots that they must first prove Bothwell guilty and have him and his associates punished, then Mary must divorce him, upon which she should be restored to the throne and appoint lay officers who would act on the advice of her council.

On his arrival the rebels refused to let Throckmorton see the Queen on her own, but he made the mistake of showing the Scots his instructions. Elizabeth was furious and recalled him. Back in London, he tried to justify his work by reporting that Mary was in extreme danger. It was only his presence, demonstrating Elizabeth's concern of course, that had saved Mary's life. Then he made matter worse by giving it as his opinion that Elizabeth could take advantage of the situation by getting control of young James and acknowledging him as heir to the throne of England. This, Elizabeth considered, was seriously overstepping his remit, and she flew into a temper, ordering him back to Scotland. She told him he was to have nothing to do with the rebels, to refuse to talk to them and not accept any gifts of gold or silver, even if they were supposed to have come from Mary. He was to make it clear that the Queen of England did not recognise Mary's abdication, nor did she recognise the regency.

Both countries withdrew their ambassadors and all communication between the two nations ceased. Lochleven was owned by Sir William Douglas, whose brother was Lord James. But his other brother, George, who was also living in the castle, was won over by Mary's charms, and so was Willie, the young orphan of the family. The two together arranged for a boat to rescue her. She lay on the bottom covered with a peasant's cloak and safely reached the shore and freedom.

Her supporters were soon flocking to her standard. The inevitable outcome was another battle which duly took place at Langside, near Glasgow. Initially the Royalists were winning, but then the Commander-in-Chief of Mary's army failed to follow through. Mary, who had been watching the battle from a hilltop, once again showed courage. She mounted her horse and rode down to her troops and was ready to lead them herself into another charge. But her officers were quarrelling among themselves. They completely ignored her demands that they should engage the enemy again. It left her no option but to flee. Unfortunately the ways to both Dumbarton and the coast were blocked by Congregationalist forces, so that she was forced to go south. She rested at Terregles Castle where she was told she still had sufficient loyal forces to keep her enemies at bay for forty days. It left plenty of time to arrange for a French ship to take her across the Channel.

Unfortunately Catherine was, as usual, at loggerheads with the Guises **who were** particularly anxious to help. Her grandmother, the Duchess Annette, disowned her out of disgust over the Bothwell marriage.

The alternative was England. Elizabeth had refused Mary military help but had offered sanctuary on hearing of the defeat at Carberry Hill. But bearing in mind Elizabeth s reluctance, not to mention England's long tradition of imprisoning Scottish Kings, the offer remained highly questionable.

Despite this, Mary overruled her advisers. She wrote to the Governor of Carlisle asking permission to enter England. Although there was plenty of time for a reply, she took a chance and on 16th May 1568, she crossed the border. As she took her first step on English soil she stumbled and almost fell.

PART III

THE COCKPIT OF EUROPE

Elizabeth had been astounded when Mary arrived in England. It not only presented problems, it boded trouble. What was to be done with her?

Initially Elizabeth considered three possibilities:

Mary could ratify her abdication and live in England. Besides laying aside her claims to the Scottish throne she would automatically be laying aside claims to the English throne and would no longer be a threat. Even so she would be a perpetual focus for unrest among the English Catholics

The second was for her to go to France. From there she would no doubt trumpet her claims and the Guise would be encouraged to invade. In fact the situation would revert to the unsatisfactory way it had been before.

The option Elizabeth really preferred was for Mary to return to Scotland but be placed under the auspices of Lord James. He would ensure she followed some guidelines, particularly over religion.

But Lord James wanted to keep all the power to himself. So he blackened his half sister's name and campaigned for her to be kept imprisoned in England. Also Elizabeth had a suspicion that a large proportion of the Scottish people would never tolerate her return while still holding sovereign power. She proved right, for a vote during a convention of Scottish nobles showed only nine in favour of her return compared to forty against.

Elizabeth's council were also against Mary being reinstated in Scotland in any form. Past experience suggested she would never abandon her overwhelming desire to oust Elizabeth.

Then Elizabeth apparently showed willing to negotiate by freeing Mary's ambassador the Bishop of Ross. She sent Sir Francis Knollys up north to Bolton, where Mary had been transferred. He was to negotiate with her personally. Mary was receptive and even talked about ratifying the Edinburgh Treaty. She hoped that her ambassador Grey would emphasise to Elizabeth that she had come seeking sanctuary. Keeping her prisoner was illegal but she was ready to stay in England and forgive all the wrongs that had been inflicted on her. Alternatively, so long as the French agreed, she was prepared to rule under the guidance of Lord James. She also agreed that her son should not marry without Elizabeth's approval. Her only complaint was that her imprisonment was unreasonably hard.

The real concern of both Elizabeth and Cecil was Catherine's reaction. They were quite prepared to wait awhile, for Catherine was dealing with a crisis arising from her refusal to let Philip's troops pass through France. When she did reply she made it clear through the Spanish ambassador that France would not interfere. Certainly she made a rather feeble official protest to the English ambassador. When she had said Mary could always come back to France, the Ambassador had asked "Will you have her head or her body?" Catherine replied "Tush, we would have her whole and alive. The Queen, my sister is so merciful and so gentle that I cannot think she will do her any harm". But when it came to the point, she showed she had no inhibitions over working with Mary's replacement – the Regent.

International opinion was much the same, that Mary had brought her woes upon herself.

Elizabeth's response to one of her complaints about her condition was to send some clothes. But they were so dilapidated it had to be pretended there had been a mistake and they were intended for her servants. Nor was Elizabeth's attitude much improved when Lord Fleming arrived with another message from Mary. She asked Elizabeth to help her get back her throne. But he then let it be known that he was bound for France and hinted that if Elizabeth did not help Mary, Catherine had promised her domicile. The veiled threat was not well received and there were unexplained delays before Lord Fleming was allowed an audience. When he did get into Elizabeth's presence she made it clear she wanted Mary to be reinstated on the Scottish throne but only when the time was right. And at that moment she did not think it was right. If meanwhile she appealed to the King of France, Elizabeth would refuse to help her in any way.

Not that Mary paid any attention. Even then she was writing to the Spanish ambassador in London declaring that if Spain would help, she was quite sure she could become Queen of England within three months. In that case, she promised, she would restore Catholicism. But Philip realised that since Elizabeth seemed to have gone as far as she dared for the moment, it would be better to let matters rest.

Mary was no less persistent in appealing to the King of France. She felt sure that with the encouragement of only a small force to free her, most of the citizens would follow their lead. But Catherine was still immersed in civil war and her feud with the Guises. She refused to take any action. Charles IX had already shown his indifference. He had thrown up his hands and made the only too real prediction: "Ah, the poor girl. She will never cease until she loses her head. I meant to help but if she will not be helped I can only see ill".

Nor did Mary despair of Elizabeth. She wrote over 20 letters pleading they should meet. She hoped to arouse pity and felt quite certain that once they were face to face she could charm Elizabeth into taking a more conciliatory attitude.

Then at last Elizabeth felt she had found the solution to the problem. She told Mary that she would graciously "protect" her but that any further action was impossible until such time as she had been cleared of the widely held suspicion that she had known in advance about the murder of her husband.

She would be put on trial.

If she was found innocent she could return to Scotland (on condition she abandoned all claim to the English throne). If found guilty, then some other action would have to be taken.

Using this adroit way of switching the reason for her detention, Elizabeth felt it wise to send an explanation to the heads of the major European countries. There was no mention of her well founded claims to the English throne. From now on she was going to be judged "by the higher law that applies just as much to princes as to commoners".

The envoy was then to go on to Lord James and tell him to stop all hostilities against Mary's followers. He must also prepare a statement of his case against her. But Cecil, probably with Elizabeth's agreement, also sent an express messenger to Lord James, making sure it would overtake the official one, warning him about the order he would shortly be receiving. It was in fact a heavy hint that whatever vengeance Lord James wished to make he had better make it quickly. He duly commandeered the absent Lord Fleming's property.

So neither Lord Fleming nor Mary's message ever reached Paris.

Mary was so sure the court would clear her that she ordered her partisans in Scotland to stop fighting. But she knew better than to trust Elizabeth. She gave her defence strict instructions that if she was not allowed to be present at the trial, they were to walk out. Mary's suspicions proved correct. Not only was she barred from the court but so were her defence team. Indeed they were not even told the exact details of the charges. Perhaps it was because they were not allowed in that they did not carry out Mary's instructions. Instead they stayed around hoping to be admitted.

Lord James, however, was not only admitted, he was allowed to give evidence.

And that was the crucial point. Early on he stunned the court by producing the first of what came to be known as the casket Letters. The papers comprised unsigned letters together with some poems, which had been found in a handsome silver gilt casket. At first Lord James produced only one letter, alleging it had been written by Mary to Bothwell and that it confirmed she had known about the murder in advance. Gradually he produced more and more. Since each new letter presented even more sensational evidence, it raised the question as to why he had not presented them all at the start. He alleged they were in Mary's handwriting, but even that was not known for sure because those submitted to the court were copies. Lord James refused to produce the originals. He wished, he said, to retain them to protect himself should the court find Mary innocent.

In several places the sense expressed in the letters was not consistent, suggesting that paragraphs had been inserted. They were written in French but included elementary mistakes in grammar and spelling such as Mary would never have made. They were supposed to have been discovered 18 months before. The fact that those who had already seen them had made no particular comment at the time suggest that the original contents were innocuous. Then when Cecil demanded that Boswell's valet, the supposed finder of the letters, should come to York to give evidence, it was found he had been one of the unfortunate minions declared responsible for Darnley's murder and had just been hanged. To cap the suspicion, once the trial was over the letters mysteriously disappeared again.

All along Mary disdained to answer the accusations in detail. Instead she made a general disclaimer.

Elizabeth decided that the introduction of the casket letters was making the trial too sensational and that it should be moved from York to the calmer environment of Westminster. It was not a very convincing reason considering this brought it in close proximity to the English parliament which was grossly prejudiced against Mary. However Mary had the wisdom to accept events she knew she could not control. She docilely wrote to Elizabeth: "Since you my good sister know our cause best we doubt not to receive presently good end thereof, where though we may be perpetually indebted to you".

Altogether the conduct of the court could hardly have been more loaded and the evidence more open to suspicion. The only real piece of evidence was a meeting Mary had held at Craigmillar with several of the leading lairds shortly before the murder. They had been discussing the problems over her husband. Mary had insisted that nothing should be done that would be against her honour but then she used the phrase "other means". It was a seriously ambiguous word.

So it was a surprise when the conference found no evidence that she was complicit in the murder of Darnley. Lord James was allowed to return to Scotland, taking with him £5,000 given by Elizabeth presumably for his "expenses".

But Scotland was still causing problems. Lord James, who was now Regent, entered into secret negotiations with Elizabeth over returning Mary regardless of what fate might await her there. "To proceed with her by justice so as neither that realm nor this should be damaged by her hereafter".

But Lord James was assassinated early the next year. In order to have a modicum of control, Elizabeth ordered The Earl of Sussex to invade Scotland and make sure the Protestant Earl of Lennox should be installed as the next Regent. The forces had instructions to hew their pathway with sufficient determination to make such supporters as Mary sill had left, reflect that perhaps they were on the wrong side. In due course the English forces reached Edinburgh and were able to ensure that Lennox was appointed Regent. But within a year he too had been assassinated.

Elizabeth decided that his obvious successor, the Catholic Earl of Mar, was preferable to some foreign Catholic. Indeed, after the discovery of the Ridolfi plot she was prepared to prop up Mar's rather precarious position with money though she was still not prepared to provide any troops. But once again she was thwarted. Mar was in turn assassinated.

No matter that Mary had been found innocent, she remained a problem. No matter whether she was returned to Scotland or France, the same objections stood. Indeed her very existence caused problems which permeated even into Elizabeth's Council. In their deliberations they had become only too well aware that at any time they might be dealing with her successor – and that would almost certainly be Mary. It was an exact replica of the situation when the Council supporting Lady Jane Grey had well in mind that Mary Tudor might come to the throne instead.

Several of the leading lords felt the ideal solution was for Mary to marry a stalwart nobleman who could be relied upon to control her. Elizabeth had already thought of this. She estimated that if such a marriage ever took place their combined powers would oust her within four months. Perhaps suspecting that just such discussions might be afoot, she made it clear that anyone marrying Mary would be committing treason.

Yet for some it remained an attractive alternative. While Norfolk had been horrified at the disclosures made in the casket letters, Maitland persuaded him that Mary was not so black as the trial had made out and that such a marriage would find favour both in France and among the English Catholics. Eventually Norfolk was persuaded to agree that the plan had much to commend it. Maitland then broke it to him that everyone thought he was the ideal person to be the groom. Eventually he was persuaded to think it a good idea – and so did Mary. They even got so far as exchanging love letters though they had never met. Norfolk was not the least dismayed over how Elizabeth might receive the plan. He felt sure that the only person prejudicing the Queen against it would be Cecil. So it seemed clear to him that he should join all the others who wished to have Cecil dismissed. Indeed he was so persuaded he was even prepared to commit treason. If Elizabeth still withheld her permission, he would have her turned off the throne and take it himself.

The errant Nobles looked to the French for support. Catherine was amenable and told her Ambassador in London to provide them with every encouragement and even give them funds. But, she instructed, if the plot failed he must be amongst the first to congratulate Elizabeth on her escape.

But now Norfolk began to have second thoughts. He was frightened the Queen might after all take offence. So he kept putting off telling her. It was being discussed and mulled over so widely and for so long that inevitably the Queen came to hear of it. She dropped some heavy hints on a number of occasions, encouraging him to come clean. Did he have any news from London? and when Norfolk said no, she persisted "You come from London and can tell me no news of a marriage?" Eventually she asked him directly if there was any truth in the rumours. Norfolk was so afraid he denied it saying, ironically as things turned out, he would rather go to the Tower than marry a woman who had set herself up as a competitor for the throne of England. In September however, Walsingham told her that the rumours were true. But still she hesitated. She was only too aware that Norfolk was a powerful man and that his supporters were powerful too. Besides she was indebted to him for having put matters right for her in Scotland

So she did no more than summon him again and make her opinion quite clear what would happen to him if the rumours did prove true "Take good heed to my pillow". And still Norfolk denied any plot.

He now feared the worst, hesitated and felt it was wise to leave court while he could. But Walsingham had been fanning the flames as he wished to have a real fire to put out. He knew how furious Elizabeth always was if any proposal of marriage were withheld from her. He told her just how far things had developed. So even before Norfolk had reached home the Queen was recalling him. He hesitated and Elizabeth had him arrested and put in the Tower along with all the others who had failed to inform her of the proposed marriage. She soon let the others go but she kept Norfolk interned for nearly a year.

Even so Elizabeth remained worried. For one thing she had noticed how the most powerful lords in the north had flocked to visit Mary on her arrival and had evidently been charmed by her charisma. Now rumours of plots to install Mary in her place were becoming increasingly frequent. Consequently she instructed the Earl of Essex to investigate. Like the others he was aware of the sticky position he would be in should Elizabeth die. He evidently did not look too closely and reported that such rumours were completely unfounded.

By November, Elizabeth was still not happy. So she sent Sir Ralph Sadler to go and size up the situation, though the official reason was to check the defences. He quickly realised that several of the Northern families, notably the Northumberlands, the Nevilles, the Cliffords and the Dacres were ineffectual in upholding the crown's authority and indeed he doubted their very loyalty. He had been given the authority to sack them from their Government posts. This was a final straw for the lords. Elizabeth had been steadily depriving them of their power. She had given the wardenship of the Northern Marches to southern lords. They were not even properly represented in the Queens Council.

Then the Marquess of Cetena arrived in London from the Netherlands. He was a senior officer in the Duke of Alma's army and had a reputation for making mischief. Elizabeth took it as the ultimate warning. She had him put under house arrest. She also removed herself to Windsor as the Castle could be more easily defended.

There, against the advice of her council, she decided to bring matters to a head. She summoned the miscreants to London. Just as her advisers had forecast, they refused. Instead they gave out a proclamation that their issue was one of faith rather than politics. They were calling for a return to the Catholic church. To make their claim seem the more genuine they dressed like the crusaders wearing white tabards with red crosses.

In December 1569 they rallied with 4,000 men and 1,000 horsemen. Considering the official muster in the north was 60,000 men it was a pretty poor effort. They advanced as far as Selby in Yorkshire. But they were surprised that none of the grumbling Catholic gentry seemed prepared to actually do anything.

In the meantime Cecil had been energetically recruiting. As everyone in Court was anxious to show their loyalty, he soon had 15,000 men under the Queen's colours. Confronted by such opposition and now lacking both finances and forces, the rebels retreated. When the Queen's men came to look for them they had melted away mostly across the Scottish border.

In this way Elizabeth brought about the end of feudalism. It was appropriately at this time that Elizabeth raised Cecil to become Lord Burghley.

After this the lords, particularly in the North, no longer held power equal to, if not more than, the Sovereign. Elizabeth refused to believe the borderers' claim that they had been motivated on religious grounds. She took uncharacteristic ruthless action. She declared them, along with their followers, to be political traitors and executed 450 of them The lords, of course, were valuable and they were lucratively stripped of their lands. With her sense of public relations, she showed the treasonable documents to the Lord Mayor telling him to relay them to the citizens of London. In particular he was to emphasise that the rebels had asked for help from Spain. Such blatant treason dissipated any question of sympathy.

It is a sad fact that while Mary's incarceration had not caused noticeable concern in the rest of Europe, the vacuum created through her absence did. Scotland was now controlled almost entirely by the Protestants. They would not tolerate invasion by French or Spanish Catholic troops. This meant, Scotland no longer held any attractions as a potential launch pad for invading England.

If England was to be invaded it would have to be direct through one of the south coast ports. To do this, a fleet would have to rally somewhere along the south coast of the channel. It must also be a deep sea port in case of high winds. The nearest was Flushing in the Netherlands. Since it had enjoyed city rights since 1315 it was virtually independent of Spanish control. So for England the region became a matter of major concern.

At the same time, Catherine lived in mounting fear that Philip might take advantage of the persistent civil wars and invade France. Her best form of protection was to divert his attention and this could be most effective by allowing the Huguenot element to become sufficiently robust to support the Dutch Protestants.

Thus, in its peculiar fashion, fate was again bringing Elizabeth and Catherine into an unholy, if not officially recognised, alliance. This time it was the realisation by both that the Netherlands was Philip's Achilles heel and that by keeping it in continuous turmoil they could keep him effectively distracted.

To this end, Elizabeth also came to the conclusion that harassing Philip's fleets was no longer sufficiently effective. So she decided to implement Cecil's policy of neighbour house burning.

Certainly the Netherlanders were in a receptive frame of mind. Their hearty dislike for the Spanish troops and the persistent pressure on freedom of conscience had turned the country into a tinder box. It had become all the more inflammable once Alva had taken over from Margaret. His reputation for ruthless suppression with bloody consequences was soon confirmed. Within a month Alva had set up the "Council of Troubles" and he imposed uniformity of the Catholic religion.

His reputation was so awesome that many of the Dutch minor nobles and gentry had not even waited for his arrival before they fled the country.

William of Orange had stayed on but had refused to take the oath of Spanish allegiance. He seriously thought of starting a resistance movement. He was already receiving considerable finance from the German princes and the Huguenots in France – not to mention Walsingham, acting as paymaster for Elizabeth. But he needed Count Egmond's support which was refused. So William fled to his estates in Germany from where he hoped to make the occasional punitive sortie into the Netherlands.

Then came an incident that brought to a head Elizabeth's determination to adopt a more blatant policy. It happened when four Spanish ships were driven by a combination of gales and Huguenot privateers into taking refuge in Plymouth. They were carrying £85,000, intended as pay for Philip's troops in the Netherlands. They sought permission to outstay both hazards. The situation could not have been more opportune. Elizabeth immediately declared that, since the money was afloat, it was at risk. This made it her duty to safeguard it properly and it must be brought on to dry land. Reluctantly, the Spanish captains agreed. Then Elizabeth declared that if such a large sum was to be absolutely safe it must be held in the Tower of London.

The Spanish ambassador immediately jumped to the obvious conclusion that Elizabeth was hijacking the money. But instead of informing Philip he got in touch direct with Alva. He told Alva to arrest all English merchant ships in the Netherlands and impound all English stock in Antwerp. Alva had only just taken over as Governor of the Netherlands from Margaret. So, even though he had grave misgivings, he complied. Elizabeth retaliated by impounding all Spanish ships in English ports and, to make a good job of it, she put the Spanish ambassador under arrest. Even better, she seized all the rest of Spanish property in England. It included a further £100,000 in bullion. Altogether she was on the way to making a tidy profit.

It turned out that the money in the ships was a loan from the Genoese bankers. As it happened, Elizabeth herself had run up a debt of £100,000 in Antwerp and no one had been interested in lending her more. So to show she was, at any rate in her own eyes, strictly honourable, she declared she would adopt it as her debt and would undertake to return the loan to the bankers in due course.

Hardly surprisingly Philip made the strongest protest. But as it happened, this was also the moment when Hawkins sailed into Plymouth after a disastrous voyage in American waters. He had failed to bring back any Spanish treasure and he had lost several of the Queen's ships. Rather than being humbled by failure he trumpeted his outrage claiming that the Spanish forces had vilely broken an agreement at Veracruz and had attacked him with an unfairly larger Spanish force. They had seized his ships and stolen all the money which, Hawkins staunchly declared, he had acquired through perfectly legal trading. It was a diversion Elizabeth could put to good use. She accepted Hawkins's claims without hesitation and whipped up popular opinion to a state whereby holding the Spanish gold in "her care" seemed nothing more than reasonable.

Elizabeth was now truly on the warpath. It also happened that 1568 was the year when the temporary arrangements over Calais, set out in the Cateau-Cambresis agreement, were due for review. Once again Elizabeth was full of hope. The situation seemed ideal. Thanks in part to Elizabeth's surreptitious supplies of money, the Huguenots had revived the civil war. Cecil had instructed Norris: "I pray you put them in comfort that if extremity should happen they may not be left.

For it is so universal a cause as none of the religions can separate themselves one from the other". In due course Catherine came to hear of this financial aid and complained bitterly. But, truth be told, over the intervening years Elizabeth's enthusiasm over Calais had cooled a bit. Also it had become clear that after 200 years the city had outlived much of its value as a base for trade and military forces. Still, Elizabeth decided, even if only as a matter of prestige, to have another try.

The treaty required that the demand should be made "on the spot". Realising the French would do all they could to prevent this, the English ambassador was smuggled in. Even from this strongpoint, initial discussion proved fruitless. Catherine simply pointed out that England had foregone her claim when, four years before, she had signed the treaty on evacuating Le Havre. Elizabeth persisted and hinted that she would settle for money. This led into a quite bizarre bargaining session. Nor were matters helped since the two men Elizabeth had delegated to conduct negotiations had quarrelled so violently they could not speak to each other. So the actual bargaining was not exactly consistent. Elizabeth had set her opening bid at 500,000 crowns. Catherine refused but offered 120,000 crowns. Elizabeth first came down to 400,000 crowns and "if the French stand on that, use all the means you can to make the said sum at least 300,000". In case of failure they were not to break off the meeting but to talk about other things. Then they were to return and offer no less than 200,000. But Catherine proved her match and in the end Elizabeth had to settle for 60,000 crowns to be paid then and a further 60,000 later.

So in the end the most important outcome of the negotiations was a treaty whereby a large number of fees and exactions that had accumulated over the years were withdrawn.

No doubt spurred by Elizabeth's high-handed behaviour over Mary, Pope Pius V decided in 1570 to complete the work of his predecessor. He had previously been the much feared inquisitor of

Milan and over the next ten years he was to show he was no less inflexible. He not only confirmed Elizabeth's excommunication but issued a bull to all Roman Catholics which declared "that they shall not once dare to obey her or any of her laws, directions or commands, binding under the same curse those who do anything to the contrary". This, he hoped, would destroy their ambiguous attitude encouraged by Elizabeth's policy of non-persecution.

Certainly it put Elizabeth into grave danger of assassination. However, he did it in such a way that he succeeded in wrong-footing himself. He so enraged the English Parliament, already highly sensitive to foreign interference, that they made it illegal to harbour or succour priests or to convert anyone to the Catholic faith. Indeed the entire country was called upon to wake up to the threat. Clergy, magistrates and squires throughout the country were instructed to keep an eye on Catholics and report any unusual behaviour. Also an old Act, making anti royalist words treasonable was reinstated.

But this turn of events also made Parliament think beyond the English boundaries. They passed yet another law whereby it was assumed that anyone who stayed abroad for more than six months had become a Catholic in exile and their lands would be confiscated.

Elizabeth next made the wise appointment of Walsingham as her Secretary of State. His brief included responsibility for the preservation of the Sovereign's person. He was eminently suitable. He combined experience in European diplomacy with a very modern concept of the spy system. He had not only built up a network of agents while he was in France but he had spread it throughout Europe. He had informants in 53 major towns spread over seven countries, including Turkey. He also proved to be most diligent. One of his most effective techniques was the agent provocateur. Using forged messages he would persuade suspected traitors to believe they had backing from a foreign country. This would sometimes encourage them to plan greater things, become rash and thereby identify themselves and provide the evidence. At home he set up a special department. It included Thomas Philips, an expert in deciphering codes and Arthur Gregory, highly skilled in breaking and replacing seals without any visible signs.

Naturally one of the first things he wanted to do was to increase the guards surrounding his Queen. She refused. Nothing, she said, should separate her from her people.

Not only this but Elizabeth had very considerable reservations over this welter of acts a frightened Parliament was introducing. She remained confident that her policy of leniency towards the Catholics would continue to maintain peace in the land. She continued to let the grammar schools teach in the spirit of the radicals Erasmus and Cole.

Indeed, most Catholics felt stronger loyalty to the Queen than to the Pope himself.

Pius, however, was not content to concentrate his wrath on Elizabeth alone. Nor was he content the quarrel should be just a matter of paperwork. He decided on a more subtle approach. He would infiltrate Jesuit priests directly into England. To this end he set up a special training seminary in Douai in Belgium. The first team were not ready until his successor, Gregory VIII was able to complete the plan and in 1574 he landed the first batch on English shore. Walsingham, much to his annoyance, could not find out exactly how many there were (in fact there were only three). But no matter how many, any one of them had intent on harming the Queen.

On landing they succeeded in becoming moles, taking refuge with the Catholic gentry who were soon equipping their large, rambling homes with priest holes. These priests became so firmly established they were soon making converts. Greatly encouraged, Gregory arranged further infiltrations and within six years their numbers had reached over 100. In Wales, however, where he tried out a parallel plan, it proved a complete fiasco. The Welsh speaking students found the

English Catholics quite incomprehensible and even during training they entirely failed to bond. On the contrary, they became suspicious of one another. So when they landed there was no mutual support and the Welsh soon found themselves stranded.

Next the Pope tried to encourage refugee leaders who had settled on the continent to plan military invasions. However the scope was necessarily limited. The French were now almost permanently involved in civil war and had no taste for interfering in foreign affairs. Worse Catherine's see-saw was, for the moment any way, favouring the Huguenots. It was clear that if those aggressive English exiles in Paris were to have any success they must undertake the task themselves. The first intimation Elizabeth had of this change of tack was in 1571 when a Scottish ship was forced to take refuge in an English harbour. On the ship was Lord Seton and among his papers were the plans for Philip to invade England. Obviously the plan would now have to be scrapped. But the danger was clear.

"Enterprise England" was the brainchild of Cardinal Allen living in exile in Paris. But having been out of England for 15 years he had lost touch with the opinion of the ordinary English Catholics. Certainly he wrote round to all those he felt might be interested but he interpreted their replies with considerable optimism. He put his plan before Philip who dismissed it immediately. "Nobody desires more than I that the matter be put in hand" he wrote to him, "but where when and how depend on the way things go in Flanders and on many other considerations". So Cardinal Allen's plan came to nothing.

Yet the Pope did find that despite all appearances the civil war in France had its advantages. It left Philip free, at least for the moment, from the threat of invasion. So he not only looked upon Philip with favour but virtually accepted him as a partner in their mutual desire to rout out heresy throughout Europe and England in particular.

Philip attached much more importance to a plan which he was hatching with his illegitimate brother Don Juan, at that time Regent of the Netherlands. Don Juan was to assassinate Elizabeth, set the imprisoned Mary free and determine the inheritance to the English throne once and for all by marrying her. However the scheme had to be set aside when Anjou, Catherine's irresponsible son threatened to lead the French Huguenots marauding the Netherlands. So instead Don Juan had to stay at home and stand by for trouble.

All these plans and plots were enmeshed with attempts to free Mary. Early on in her incarceration Mary had written "I can find no certain judgement nor know what course in the world to take in my affairs". She was only too right. Her judgement soon proved to be seriously at fault. Not only did she write all those letters making rash forecasts of her potential following but she was happy to go along with any credible plot for her release. Even more stupidly she continued irritating Elizabeth by her persistent claims for the throne. Before long even her most loyal followers were abandoning hope. Her attempts to keep contact with her son became pathetic. She sent many letters and presents but Elizabeth made sure they never reached him.

In the spring of 1569 Hawkins raised the alarm when one of his overseas contacts told him about Ridolfi, a flamboyant Florentine banker living in London who had a plan for assassinating the Queen. The banker had already received Mary's approval and she had authorised him to approach the Duke of Alva in the Netherlands who, in the plan, was to supply 10,000 men as well as guns and ammunition. They were to land at Hartlepool and free Mary. The Spanish forces would then march on London gathering disgruntled Catholics on the way. However Alva only had to look at the woeful efforts of the Northern Lords to see the prospect of gathering support on the way was not all that good. In any case, he already had too much on his plate. Under duress he eventually agreed to send in his troops but only after Mary had been released and moved to the more accessible area of Coventry.

Ridolfi then approached Philip. But Philip was not to be easily inveigled either. He no longer liked the idea of Mary regaining the throne. It would merely put back the clock resurrecting the possibility of a French, Scottish and English block to bar him from the Channel.

So he too sent a conditional reply. He stipulated that the plan must have developed much further before he would help the plotters. They must have seized Elizabeth and her Council. He reasoned this was the very earliest stage at which he could risk being seen to take an active part while, at the same time, it was the latest stage at which he could join in and afterwards still convincingly claim to have given meaningful support.

Even though he was still a prisoner in the Tower, Norfolk was also involved. One of his servants was acting as messenger to the plotters. He was intercepted carrying a lot of money which the French had intended should help Ridolfi. Under torture he revealed that a lot of incriminating documents could be found in the attic of Norfolk's house. Yes, he was telling the truth. But still Elizabeth held back. Twice she signed the death warrant and twice she rescinded it. But there was no escape, Norfolk must be executed.

But if Anglo relations with France had become comparatively friendly, those with Spain were giving considerable cause for concern. For some time Sir Christopher Hatton had been trying to persuade Elizabeth that Philip might try to conquer England by strangling the nation's trade. His solution was to encourage the seafaring escapades of Hawkins and Drake.

Cecil advocated caution. Elizabeth, though, was far from averse to the idea. She had discovered that besides bringing in lucrative profits it was also a cheap and effective way her forces could gain practical experience in combat. So she decided to invest 1,000 crowns, as well as the loan of some of the Navy's ships, in a new venture. She told Drake that not only must he, as usual, pretend she was in ignorance over his sortie but that Cecil must be genuinely kept in ignorance. She was perfectly well aware he would protest vigorously against anything contrary to the official policy of improving relations with Spain. She liked to think she could keep the two completely separate.

Drake decided the circumstances were right for raiding the Spanish treasure ports along the coast of Chile. His way took him through the formidable Straits of Magellan. This was extremely daring. But Drake made a mistake in his navigation and ended up as the first person to sail round the world. So on his return in 1780, the country acclaimed him with considerable triumph.

Better still, the expedition was a financial success. He had come back with a massive 1.5 million ducats worth of silver and bushels of jewels, all taken from the Spanish ships in the Pacific. It brought his backers a yield of 4,600 per cent. It enabled Elizabeth to pay off the national debt.

Cecil's further pleas for caution went unheeded.

Elizabeth was also considering marriage, or at least engagement. Her chequered engagement to the Arch Duke Charles had been briefly revived in 1563, on his succession to the Austro-Hungarian throne. But he was not related sufficiently close to Philip to provide a guarantee against any unwelcome attentions from France. Nor did he have sufficient forces. So this second engagement had been somewhat lacking in ardour. Any remaining hopes were finally sabotaged by Dudley. He had by this time been reinstated at Court and was still hoping to marry Elizabeth. So to further his cause he entered into an agreement with Spain. If they backed his suit against the Arch Duke and should he succeed, he would put forward the Roman Catholic cause with all the advantages of a husband's influence.

Elizabeth of course had no intentions of marrying either of them.

Once again she held all the marriage cards in her hand and it was her turn to play.

But the situation had changed. Without the Austro-Habsburg alliance, there was nothing to prevent an attack from Spain. If England was to be sure of independence, it would be necessary to counter it with an alliance with France. To Elizabeth the solution was obvious. She must marry one of Catherine's sons.

It was no revolutionary idea for when Charles was still Dauphin there had been unofficial talk of Elizabeth becoming engaged to him. Nothing had come of it and now he was married.

So by 1571 Elizabeth was dropping hints to Catherine that she might like to reconsider marrying her third son Henri. Catherine, as always, was busy with other marriage plans and was already negotiating for him to marry the still imprisoned Mary Queen of Scots But when she heard that Elizabeth was interested she was jubilant crying out "Such a kingdom for one of my children" and was quite happy for the match with Mary to be jettisoned, or at least placed on hold. But that was not all. While she was primarily thinking of the prestige, she realised it could at the same time solve another problem bothering her. For some while now she had been worried at the way Henri was being influenced by the Guise family. Only one person, in Catherine's mind, should influence her sons and that was their mother. Besides the Duke was prejudicing Henri's mind against England. That did not suit her policy. So his marriage to Elizabeth seemed the obvious solution. Elizabeth also appreciated the importance of remedying Henri's anti English sentiments. If he continued to hold them and should he succeed to the throne, as was quite possible, it would bode bad for England. At the same time Elizabeth was light of heart. She realised that, besides providing an Anglo-Franco alliance, she would be thwarting any hopes Mary might have of' regaining her liberty by marrying Henri. Conversely if she were to let the opportunity go and

Mary did marry him instead, Elizabeth would be duty bound to release her from custody with all the difficulties that entailed.

There was however one point to counter all this positive thinking. Henri made no secret of his lack of enthusiasm for the match. When first put to him he protested vociferously over "marrying an old woman with an ulcer on her leg causing her to limp" and felt he would do much better marrying Mary. The remark came to the ears of Elizabeth and it certainly did nothing to further his cause. But it had its effect in one way. After that it was noticed that whenever she danced, and the French Ambassador happened to be present, she did so with particular verve.

But Catherine was not to be easily thwarted. Henri was just as great a snob as his mother and she knew how to play upon his avarice. He had already failed for the Swedish crown and had obviously become desperate for he had gone on to try unsuccessfully for the crowns of Algiers and Cyprus. Catherine pointed out that putting up with an elderly wife, with or without an ulcer, was well worth a crown, and particularly the crown of England.

In conducting negotiations over marriage there is always the possibility the arrangements might fall through. This could make the bride appear to have been jilted. Alternatively the groom could appear to have been spurned. So, especially in such a delicate situation as this, both parties set about negotiations in the greatest secrecy. Catherine wrote all the letters personally and ensured they were sent by special messenger. When in due course the French emissary landed at Dover, he was conducted under guard to Cecil's home in London where details of the settlement were hammered out.

The French demands were high: Henri would be crowned King of England the day after the marriage and he would rule jointly with Elizabeth. He would be given an income of £60,000 a year.

Unfortunately, however, over the next few months it became clear that love was not following the proverbial smooth course. Sometimes one party would seem enthusiastic and the other cool and at other times the feelings seemed to be in reverse. But with her political intuition, Elizabeth succeeded in protracting negotiations for over a year. To further it more she started adding to her list of conditions. She must first see Henri in person. So that the rendezvous should be discreet, she would arrange to be in Kent on progress at the same time as he secretly crossed the channel.

Henri was prepared to come over for inspection but first he wanted to be sure he could hold mass there. Elizabeth refused. This threatened to be the breaking point. Catherine tried to redeem the situation by sending two portraits, one a study of his face and one full length showing his full body. However for once Elizabeth did not change her mind and the whole enterprise was called off.

But Catherine was far from letting things rest there. First she asked her ambassador in London to press Elizabeth to name her successor. She realised it might not necessarily be Mary but might well be one of the Suffolk girls. If she could be sure of this, she could have Henri marry her instead. But, of course, Elizabeth was wise to this and refused to be drawn.

Apparently completely unconcerned over the apparently embarrassing denouement Catherine quickly, almost the next day in fact, came up with the solution. Elizabeth should instead marry Henri's younger brother, Francois-Hercules, soon to become Duke Anjou. "He will not show himself" she roundly assured Elizabeth, "to be so scrupulous in the matter of religion". As a sort of sop to help things along, she invented a plot to murder Elizabeth and, in hope of thereby winning her gratitude, sent her full details. It was not necessary. Elizabeth was far too accomplished a tactician to let such trivia deflect her from her objective. Without the slightest suggestion of embarrassment, she declared she thought the revised engagement a very good idea, and switched her professional affections accordingly.

The reader may here become confused over the identity of Catherine's children. This is particularly the case as regards her third and fourth sons, younger brothers to Francis II and Charles IX. Her third son Henri was Duke of Anjou but he abandoned the title when eventually he ascended the throne as Henri III. So in this book he is referred to as Henri and, after he was crowned, as Henri III. His younger brother Francois-Hercules was first made Duke Alencon but was given the superior title Anjou together with its vast estates, soon after Henri had become King. However as references to him in this book start a mere two years before he became Anjou, he will be referred to under that title throughout.

Just to look at the 22 year age difference and the inauspicious physique of both parties it is clear the suggested union would be verging on the absurd. Added to this he was far from handsome. Walsingham, at that time Ambassador in Paris, tried to show him in the best light when he wrote "in complexion somewhat sallow, his body of very good shape, his legs long and small, but reasonably well proportioned. What helps he had to supply any defects of nature I know not." He went on: "he is void of any good favour besides the blemish of smallpox" But finally the raw truth evidently overcame him and he ended: "I hardly think there will ever grow any liking".

The French tried to reassure Elizabeth. They pointed out that, within a year or so, he would be old enough to grow a beard and this would hide his blemishes. They failed to explain, though, how this might conceal his nose which had become blue and swollen. Despite this confidence, it was thought best for a London doctor, reputed to be skilled in remedying the ravishes of smallpox, to be dispatched to attend him. But, apparently, this time his skills escaped him. Much more alarming, though, was the way the illness had warped Anjou's character. He had been a charming winning child with a sunny temperament. But the ravages of smallpox had turned him into a cunning rapacious schemer. He had become known at the French court as "The Little Rat".

To show that this time she really meant business, Elizabeth had Walsingham, who had always felt the engagement to be inadvisable, draft a new treaty which, in effect, would also constitute a marriage contract. France and England guaranteed one another against attack by a third power. While no country was specified, both sides had Spain in mind. It even defined the help to be given, notably 6,000 men at arms. Another clause specified the occasions when either country would merely agree not to assist an enemy of the other. Elizabeth wanted parenthesis to be added with the words "even if attacked on religious grounds". However Catherine felt this would cause even more unrest among the Huguenots. So a compromise was reached by having the point made in a covering letter. The treaty also included an agreement for the pacification of Scotland which meant the current situation would remain unaltered. In other words Catherine could not make any intervention on behalf of Mary. There was another useful clause allowing free trade between the two countries. After long delays and meditation, largely due to procrastination on the part of Elizabeth, the Treaty of Blois was signed in April, 1572. It was noticeable that Elizabeth had modified her views considerably over her husband being able to attend mass.

But Catherine must have become suspicious of the arrangement when she discovered that over the past few weeks Elizabeth had been in parallel trade talks with the Spanish. The discovery had caused her to feel that perhaps the Treaty of Blois lacked substance. So she asked Elizabeth if she was prepared to re-enforce the entente cordiale with a meeting. She wrote "If we had anything more precious than my son, we would offer it to you with all my heart for I have always longed to have the happiness and honour that, as I love you like a daughter, I might be able to call myself your mother". Elizabeth's reaction to this declaration can only be imagined. Catherine suggested they should meet half way at Dover.

She was right for in the Treaty of Blois, Elizabeth was acquiring all the benefits she would have obtained from the marriage without the complications of dowry and succession. Once again she had extricated herself from the bumpy road of matrimony. Now it only remained for her to extricate herself from the romantic aspect. In due course the English ambassador in Paris received two letters, classics in Elizabeth's technique. Whatever meaning could be drawn from one seemed be contradicted in the other and both were obscure and indecisive. A subsequent letter supposing to clarify the situation was much the same: "Which two declarations cannot but contain some absurdities, as we think you yourself can perceive. Therefore we have answered that either you mistook our mind or our first letters and so misreported them as we cannot think you did, or else the King mistook your words; and that where you were commanded by us to say, that the cause was very difficult (which we think you did) for so do our letters plainly direct you". The confused negotiators in Paris eventually decided that really she was declaring Anjou was too young. No one could deny that this did not make good sense.

While Catherine had more or less managed the situation, she was now beginning to find the unorthodox upbringing she had given her children was having alarming repercussions. As they started reaching the age of maturity her overwhelming insistence on their observing complete, unquestioning loyalty to her was starting to unravel. She had, apparently, completely overlooked the natural development of the teenager to wish to kick over the traces. Their complete lack of education inevitably precipitated revolt and now they were being introduced to other ideas. And just because the ideas were novel for them they found them all the more attractive.

So now not only Henri but the King were coming under the influence of other people. They included Admiral Coligny, a leading Huguenot who consequently looked leniently on the Netherlands resistance, not least because his daughter was married to William of Orange. And now this faction was persuading the King it would be a good idea to declare open war on Spain. The opinion gained further credence since the Dutch Beggars were showing considerable success in harassing Spanish shipping. It showed that as allies they could hold their own. No doubt the King was further encouraged by hints from the Dutch that in return for military help they were prepared to allocate some part of the territory to France, Germany and England. But this idea had been dashed by Elizabeth who made it clear she did not want all the long term responsibilities such an acquisition would entail. Charles, though, thought he might still be in with a chance.

He fondly imagined he was keeping these discussions secret from his mother. He should have known better. Of course Catherine got to hear about it. While the idea of irritating Philip appealed to her, the idea of a full blown war with Spain filled her with alarm. But, only too aware of her dwindling influence over her son, she did not protest too much.

In June, 1572, Charles allowed an unofficial contingent of Huguenots to cross the border. Not only were they backed with French arms but the military tactics bore strong resemblance to those classic to France.

First stop was the relief of Mons, which the Spanish now had under siege. But everything seemed to go awry. The plan depended on surprise. Somehow the Spanish got wind of it. They successfully ambushed the relieving column who were not only defeated but went pillaging all the way home. Matters were not helped when one of the besieged citizens tried to escape but was caught by the Spanish. On him was a letter from Charles. He was promising to send armies to help them. Catherine had every reason to fear that this time her son had really gone too far. Spain would now almost certainly declare war. She tried to remedy the situation by insisting the King send congratulations to Philip on his wonderful victory at Mons. She also realised this would be nowhere near enough and demanded he should also make a public declaration roundly condemning the Huguenot enterprise.

Believing the matter was settled at any rate for the moment, she set out to visit one of her daughters who had suddenly been taken ill. But she had hardly left Paris when she received a report which revealed the depth of Elizabeth's fear over French domination in the Netherlands. It indicated a growing inclination to side with Spain on the assumption that if it came to the point, France would not have the determination to carry through their undertaking. This meant Elizabeth would no longer observe the Treaty of Blois. So now if her son should take the opportunity while she was away to declare open war with Spain, France would be on her own and that would mean almost certain defeat. She dashed back to Paris to intervene. She lashed her full fury against her son for even thinking of such an idea and pointed out that the men who were now advising him to go to war had not long before had been trying to kidnap him. The King saw her point and decided to keep the peace.

Elizabeth had indeed recognised the warning. The French were becoming altogether too dominant in the Netherlands. On learning that the King was allowing unofficial Huguenot forces to cross the Netherlands border she gave the all clear for an equally unofficial force of 2,000 Flemish immigrants to join their "Beggar" brothers and hold the ports of Brielle and Flushing. She quietly reinforced this by allowing English volunteers under Sir Humphrey Gilbert to join them.

But the King and Henri were by no means Catherine's only worry. Her daughter Margot was also becoming difficult, though fortunately not on such a heroic scale. When her daughter Elizabeth had died, Catherine decided Margot must replace her sister a Philip's wife. It was the only way she could defy the Guises. No matter that Margot had previously been refused as a bride for his son. No matter his wife of whom he had been genuinely fond was only recently dead, Catherine must realise her designs quickly but without upsetting Philip. She told her ambassador in Madrid that he must not talk about Margot "unless you can do it so dextrously that he has no idea that I know anything about the proposal. Take pains also to gain for this proposal the King's confessor, pointing out to him the evil which it would be for Christendom if any disturbance of the amity between these two kingdoms should arise." Unfortunately for Catherine, the Spanish ambassador in Paris had already suspected her plans and had written to Philip about them. In any case, despite her alacrity, Catherine was too late. Philip's eye had already lighted upon Ann, daughter of the Arch Duke Charles of Austria. This union would in due course have the advantage of bringing the Habsburg family back into its former European block.

All right, then, if Margot could not marry Philip, what about her marrying the King of Portugal?

This too lay within the jurisdiction of Philip since Portugal was in effect Spain's protectorate and the two families were closely allied both politically and by royal blood.

Again there was a problem. Margot was being infuriatingly difficult. She believed she was in love with the young and handsome Duke of Guise. Her mother had told her not to be so silly, but Margot had remained obdurate. Catherine turned to the King to help bring his sister to her senses. But he had no better success. He took it so much to heart that at four o'clock one morning he got up and went to his mother's bedroom. They summoned the unfortunate girl. When she came in they put the Chamberlain on guard outside the door and submitted her to intense pressure for more than an hour. While she remained obstinate the two of them ended by roughing her up. Sensing the danger, the Guise family left court. But that did not have any effect on Margot and Catherine was irked that Philip did not seem to be doing anything to further his side of the marriage bargain. Actually he was planning for young Portugal to marry his daughter.

Then Catherine surprised everybody. She told the Pope Nuncio that she wanted Margot to marry the King of Navarre. He could hardly have been less suitable. He was not only a Huguenot but a close relation. It was generally assumed that the Pope would never agree. He didn't. And that was precisely what Catherine wanted. In her customary way she had a counter plan running in tandem. Now that the Pope was alarmed, she presented an alternative, that Margot should marry the King of Portugal. The Pope found this much more acceptable. But then Catherine told him of Philip's indifference. Thereupon the Pope brought all the pressure he could muster on to Philip. At one point it looked as though Catherine might succeed for Philip intimated that negotiations should continue. But they soon faltered and proved to be no more productive than before.

Realising this plan was not practical she returned to plan A for, in fact, she did not consider her suggestion that Margot should marry the King of Navarre was fanciful at all. She particularly favoured the idea since it would help heal the rift between Catholics and the Huguenots. So she continued preparing the groundwork and damn the Pope. She had already got so far as persuading Navarre's mother to agree to a Catholic wedding. But to her dismay she found that her first plan was being sabotaged by the second. Pope Pius V was highly orthodox and not inclined to make exceptions when asked. As anticipated, the Pope's objection to the Navarre union was strong, so strong, in fact, he utterly refused to grant dispensation under any circumstances.

As usual, Catherine was ready to do anything to have her way. She forged a letter as though it had been written by her Ambassador in Rome. It declared that Pope Pius had at last granted the dispensation and that the documents were on their way. She then told the Governor of Lyon not to let any messengers from Rome pass through the city for the next three days. This would prevent any genuine message catching up in time to stop the wedding. At last all seemed settled and with great lavishness, the marriage took place on 18th August, 1572. There had, however, been one other problem. But it had been easily overcome through quick action by the King in person. It arose during the actual service. When Margot was due to reply "I do", there was a long silence. It might have been because Margot wanted to make a dramatic pause. The King, however, feared the worst and dashing from his seat, pushed his sister's head forward so that it could be claimed that she had literally been married on the nod.

The wedding guest list had also presented some problems. One of the groom's next of kin was Coligny. He was a Huguenot of strong character, impervious to bribes and Catherine's blandishments. He had no apparent human vices or weakness which Catherine could put to use. She could tolerate that but it had become clear he had usurped her control of the King. She was so provoked she was reported to have told the Spanish ambassador she was planning to offer a free pardon and 50,000 crowns to anyone who dispatched him. He was just as unpopular among the Parisians to the extent he had for some while felt it inexpedient to visit the City at all. Instead he had wisely sought safety in La Rochelle. More alarmingly, he had assembled 30,000 Huguenots at Mons, a military manoeuvre that was ominously close to Paris.

None the less Catherine had issued the invitation and had promised him safety for the wedding. His advisers, though, warned him not to accept. But it offered him a unique opportunity to visit his forces at Mons without exciting undue comment.

While he knew only too well that she was a dangerous woman to cross, he knew, too, that most of the accusations levelled at her were part of a renewed propaganda campaign. This propaganda was, to say the least, crude. It claimed she had started committing murders as a child and, most recently, she had poisoned her brother in law so that her husband Henry could take the throne.

In more sober style it was true that recently she had developed a disturbing trait in consulting astrologers and magicians, despite the practice being forbidden by law. Then, far more serious, there had been the affair of Lingerolles. He was the chief and highly influential gentleman in waiting to Charles IX. It was he, Catherine was convinced, who had persuaded Henri against marrying Elizabeth. Earlier that year, Lingerolles had been blatantly assassinated in full daylight in a Paris street. Everyone knew who had carried out the crime but he was evidently under the protection of a very influential person. This became clear when 50 gentlemen of the court, shown by the haste of their response to be under instructions, petitioned the King for a pardon, which was also granted with remarkable speed. And everyone knew that powerful person was Catherine.

Having disposed of one adversary with such success, Catherine might well be feeling emboldened to adopt murder as a successful ploy on a regular basis. So it happened that shortly after the wedding ceremonies, Coligny was walking down a Paris street when he stopped and bent down to do up his boot lace At that moment a shot rang out from a window in a nearby house. A bullet that would otherwise have killed him merely grazed his shoulder.

Catherine heard the news of the bungled attempt just as she was starting a meal with Anjou. Her expression did not change in the slightest. She merely got up and walked to her private chambers.

But she must have immediately realised that she was now in real difficulty. The shot had been fired from a house belonging to a former tutor of the Guise. He had escaped by the back door and ridden way on a waiting horse. But he could still be caught and under torture he would almost immediately implicate the Guise family. She had no doubt that they in turn would not hesitate to implicate her.

Charles, completely innocent of the plot, was playing a game of tennis. He immediately ordered a protective cordon to be thrown round Coligny and instructed that all Catholics were to be withdrawn from the area. As soon as he could he went over to visit Coligny and promised him vengeance. He was accompanied by Catherine and Anjou who, of course, tendered their sincerest congratulations on his narrow escape and expressed their deep abhorrence of such a wicked deed.

Catherine's immediate reaction was to put all the blame on the Duke of Alba but it took only a moment or two's reflection for her to realise it would never stand up to scrutiny. She needed a foolproof way to conceal her bungled attempt. There was nothing for it. She must confess to the King. Everything depended on persuading him that all the Huguenots under Coligny were a serious danger.

All his life, the King had shown an inherent attraction for shedding blood. While still a boy he had once set his dogs onto a cow and had watched with glee as they tore the unfortunate animal to bits. In his normal and natural mood he recognised this morbid trait and would drink sweetened water instead of wine. So who better than his mother, to know how to play on this weakness. Subjected to her subtle persuasion, he eventually agreed to the murder of the few Huguenots who topped her list starting, of course, with the wounded Coligny.

It was three o'clock next morning, the dawn of St. Bartholomew's day on 24th August 1572, when unaccountably the bell of the Palais de Justice started tolling. It was the signal.

The Duke of de Guise hastened to the courtyard where Coligny was staying and personally urged his Italian and German assassins to break down the door and kill him. They threw him out of the window, but he was still alive so Guise, who was waiting in the street below, made sure by personally cutting off his head.

Despite apparent spontaneity, the massacre was well organised. The leading Huguenots were sought out first. Several were staying on the further bank of the Seine. They had been carefully listed and now were hunted down. Urged on by the blood lust of the king, even the most conservative lords were running through the streets calling the citizens to action. They joined in with much enthusiasm, murdering Huguenot women and children regardless.

Soon the massacre was spreading to other cities. The total number of victims throughout France was estimated at between 30,000 and 110,000.

Once over and Catherine had to try and justify her action with the rest of the world. So she wrote to the various heads of state setting out her version of the event. But she could not even do this in a straightforward manner. She started by writing two letters to each person. She worded the first to make it appear she had written it before the massacre. It set out the situation so that when the news actually reached the recipients they would jump to the conclusion that the Guises were to blame. In the second, dated after the massacre, she claimed the King had been horrified but unable to prevent it. The fact that the first letter had proved so timely belied any belief that it was just chance. Furthermore, on comparing the two letters they proved to be contradictory in several respects. Other points did not tie up with those facts which soon became widely known. Most telling, a body was found next day actually in the palace dungeon confirming that the King must have been well aware of his murder actually within his home. Catherine then confused the situation still further. Realising that her two previous letters had failed to do the trick she decided to send a third letter. In this she claimed that Coligny had been plotting to murder the King.

The news of the massacre was received abroad with everything from high delight to absolute horror. Throughout most of France it was received with a degree of dismay. The Catholics were revolted at the scale of the massacre. Others blamed the King for having given the Huguenots too many concessions in the first place. What is more, he had broken his word for the safe passage of the wedding guests. Certainly after the massacre he seemed noticeably more melancholy and taciturn. Others asked what else could be expected considering Catherine's Italian upbringing. Catherine herself never gave any sign or suggestion of remorse. Later still, no doubt intended for the ear of the Pope alone, she claimed the massacre had been carried out for the glory of the church. Pope Pius was happy to believe this. While he did not perhaps realise the full horror of the massacre he none the less ordered lights to be lit in the Vatican and kept burning during three days of celebration.

In Spain the ambassador was able to present his version of the incident before the official letters had arrived. It did not matter for the news was received by Philip with great glee. He was reported to have "laughed for the only time on record", happy to make the assumption that it was the result of the constant pressure he had been putting on Catherine. As an indication of his renewed confidence, especially remembering his previous experience, he had the bullion for paying his Netherlands forces sent overland through France. It also meant the army could lessen their vigilance and he could pay off his German mercenaries in Italy. He said "It is not a bad idea to set the English against the French" adding "But do not in any way try to ally me with the English" repeating yet again, "What I want is for all Christian princes to join together against England".

In England several boatloads of refugees landed before Catherine's official messenger. But Elizabeth would have already received an entirely reliable report from Walsingham. She had sent him some while before to Paris to do all he could to support the Huguenots. During the massacre his house had become a sanctuary for the English citizens and they had included Philip Sidney. So Elizabeth had no difficulty in realising Catherine's duplicity. But then Catherine asked Elizabeth to think of the executions as no more than if she had executed those who had troubled her. She was obviously hinting at Elizabeth's reaction to the rebellion of the Northern Lords. It helped Elizabeth put things into perspective for initially she had been horrified. Officially she indicated rather than expressed her displeasure by keeping the French Ambassador, who had come to tender Catherine's version of the affair, waiting for three days. She let a further two weeks pass before officially replying to Catherine. She accepted her explanations but took the opportunity to give her aspiring "mother" a homily at large. She lectured that, as a generalisation, not keeping one's word and acting against the law could be dangerous. Catherine received this with delight. It meant that at least communications between them remained open.

Among the refugees who had escaped to England was Count Montgomery. It was he who had actually driven the lance through Henri's helmet, causing his death. Though the King, on his death bed, had absolved him, the accident had none the less been held against him ever since. On the eve of St. Bartholomew's day his excellent horsemanship had enabled him to ride ahead of his would be assassins to reach the coast. Once across the Channel he found haven with his brother in law who also happened to be Vice Admiral of Devon. This connection gave him almost complete freedom of the West England ports. He had a free hand in building up a fleet to help re-enforce La Rochelle. He certainly had widespread support for, without any form of appeal, the gentry throughout England raised 20,000 foot and 2,000 horse and arms and all at their own expense. This activity was unknown to Elizabeth, or so she said. However some of the arms that formed part of the contributions could have only come from the royal arsenal.

Such sympathy was not surprising for England had been trading with the Huguenots for several years, mainly exchanging salt and wine for gunpowder.

Nor had the massacre succeeded in wiping out all the Huguenots in France. The citizens in their established strongholds were perfectly prepared to defy Catherine. La Rochelle was one of the most significant and it had locked the gates against any would be assailants. When the King sent a new Governor, they refused to let him in.

So in November Catherine put La Rochelle under siege with her two sons, Anjou and Henri taking part. They were soon making a fine mess of things by quarrelling. Not surprising really since Anjou was secretly considering going over to the enemy. He was party to a proposal that if he were to bring control of Normandy with him, Elizabeth might well think again about marrying him. Unaware of this and having appointed her children to this theatre of war, Catherine immediately went into agonies over their safety. She kept pestering the general commanding to be sure they were kept safe.

Then suddenly Catherine gave orders for the entire siege to be lifted. She offered extremely reasonable terms to the Huguenots not only in La Rochelle but in all the other cities under their control. In Catherine's mind capturing a renegade city was nothing compared to the importance of raising her son to new heights. She had just heard that she had succeeded in having Henri elected King of Poland.

In fact she had been paying an unbelievable amount in bribes and gifts to the electors. In the eventual agreement he was to bring with him all the income from his French estates, which amounted to about 400,000 florins. All of it must be spent in Poland. The French must pay the state debt and the back pay due to the army. Henri must arm a fleet in the Baltic and he must be accompanied by 4,000 troops with sufficient to pay their wages for the forthcoming year. To top it all he must refurbish the Academy at Cracow bringing the best professors from France and Italy and pay the annual expenses towards a hundred Polish students finishing their education in Paris.

For all this he did not even really get the crown, just the title. His actual administration opportunities were little more than symbolic.

Catherine had persuaded Charles to agree to this arrangement only because he had come to hate his brother with an overwhelming hate. He was jealous of the unjustified admiration Henri had won for military operations which had been planned and carried out by others. Charles had reached the stage whereby he would do anything – pay anything – just to have his brother out of the country.

Catherine's love of ostentation knew no bounds. Even after having spent all that money on winning the Crown of Poland, she now craved the title Holy Roman Emperor for the King. It too was awarded through election. Her chances were good. She could bribe three of the seven German Protestant princes and could have expected support from the moderates. Suddenly Philip threw his hat into the ring for this highly prestigious prize. He made impressive promises included affiliating the Netherlands to the more acceptable Austrian sector of the Habsburg Empire. He would reinstate the Prince of Orange and order the withdrawal of all Spanish troops. Even so, Catherine could still have won. But she was anxious not to antagonise Philip and quietly withdrew her bid.

It was six years since Elizabeth had first harboured de La Mark. For some time the Beggars had been growing increasingly unruly and recently they had overreached themselves and were attacking English shipping. So, more through irritation than any political motive, she told them to leave.

However de la Mark, now a double exile, had a stroke of luck. On leaving Dover he had sailed into a storm. In desperation he and his followers were forced to find refuge in Brielle. To their astonishment, the port offered no resistance. The Spanish forces had been called out to put down a rebellion in Utrecht. So the Beggars simply moved in and occupied the city.

They then went on to capture other "amphibious" sea wall cities such as Haarlem, Leyden and eventually the whole of Holland and Zealand. They adopted a ruthless technique. While still approaching, a town they would signal the Calvinists within, who were mostly innocuous working folk, to open the gates. Once in they would force the authorities to negotiate for a peaceful co-habitation. They then gave the magistrates the choice of either resigning or co-operating. They closed the catholic churches, took charge of the schools and preached the reformed faith, thereby removing Philip's main moral support.

For some while Elizabeth had been finding the Netherlands trade embargo Alva had reimposed on England six years before was seriously disrupting the economy. Rather than sue for peace she hopefully offered to play the honest broker. She called for a convention to resume trade negotiations between the three countries. But it did not get anywhere because the Dutch interpreted her motives as treachery and refused to co-operate.

But it did not matter. Just as Governess Margaret had experienced before him, Alva was now finding that the embargo was damaging trade as much for the Dutch as for the English. And so the negotiations, which had so worried Catherine, continued unabated. In the autumn Alba hinted it might be a good gesture if Elizabeth were to remove her troops from Flushing. She was happy to oblige.

By April 1573 both parties signed the Treaty of Bristol which returned trade virtually to the way it had been before. It so warmed up the relationship that Philip showed his appreciation by letting English traders in Spain conduct their protestant services openly.

Conversely Elizabeth's relations with the Netherlands Huguenots were rapidly deteriorating. The situation was not helped by her suspicion and dislike of the leading Dutch player William of Orange. This was made worse for Cecil, who did not share the prejudice, was seriously ill and unable to keep her on a steady path. Nor was she best pleased when William made his own agreement with the English Merchant Adventurers. Apparently unaware of her animosity, William next expected Elizabeth to help him in a cunning scheme. He was convinced that, with the help of de la Mark's outlaws and the Huguenots in the French ports, there was enough shipping to throw a ring around the Netherlands to prevent the import of salt. He calculated that after a year, the situation would become so dire Philip would at last agree to leave the Netherlands once and for all. William assumed Elizabeth would back him in this enterprise. But Elizabeth would have none of it.

Rather she suspected he was more likely to make a separate peace with France. She wrote him a strong letter. She reminded him how ruthlessly the Huguenots had been treated in France. She pointed out that if they gained power in the Netherlands, they would probably do the same there. But William paid no attention. His attention was now taken up with Catherine's wayward son.

Anjou was indeed causing not only the Prince of Orange but Catherine considerable trouble. His lack of education of just about everything except loyalty to her was revealing him to be undisciplined, inefficient, irresponsible and was soon to show he could be downright treacherous whenever the situation suited him. He had ambition together with rashness which, combined with a lack of ability, made him something of a loose cannon. Yet being the younger brother of the King of France and the possessor of extensive estates and wealth, he enjoyed almost unlimited respect and power.

By 1574 Catherine was becoming increasingly concerned over

the frequency with which he was siding with the Montmorencys as well as other enemies of the Guises. She was beginning to suspect his intentions could be bordering on treason. Indeed she was right for, though she did not know it, he had written in confidence to Elizabeth trying to disassociate himself from the St. Bartholomew massacre. He wrote that he wanted "to become leader of the Protestants of the world against all comers". Catherine's suspicions had reached the stage whereby she felt it was wise to keep a closer watch on him. She lectured him for more than six hours on his shortcomings. Of course at the time he expressed penitence but he did not really mean it. Next she caught him making plans to steal away from the court and indeed join the Huguenot forces. The King wanted to make sure of controlling him by sending him to the Bastille. But Catherine pleaded his cause and they compromised by putting him under close surveillance in the Palace.

Despite all this, Catherine dealt with him as only a besotted mother would. Against the better judgement of the King, she set out to mollify him. She made him Keeper of the Great Seal, Chief of the Royal Council and, despite behaving like a soldier of fortune, she had him made Lieut. General of the Kingdom. It was a post he had long hankered after. As an appointment, made while he was in close custody, it carried more than an element of irony. So, on reflection the King unsurprisingly rescinded the appointment and instead made him mere Commander General. It meant that Anjou's ambitions were still unfulfilled.

Then, in 1574, Charles IX quite unexpectedly died.

Henri, who had been so extravagantly set up in Poland, was now to be recalled to become King Henri III. Any worries over "cancellation of contract" fees were submerged in the humiliating manner of his escape. Far from disliking him, the Poles had rather taken to him, finding him clever and liberal minded. They had come to accept him. More particularly they accepted the money he brought with him and which he was continuing to spend as part of the agreement. As a result his departure had to be made in humiliating secrecy. He sent his jewels and clothes in advance and left stealthily in the middle of the night. Almost immediately the Poles found out and sent a troop of Tartars to fetch him back. At one point, the Tartars came so close he had to hide in a forest, whereupon he got lost. He managed to extricate himself just in time to get safely out of the country.

The Poles then began asking him when he was coming back. He stalled not daring to admit that he had no intention of returning.

However, while his exit from Poland was hasty, he was in no hurry to return to Paris and dawdled on the way.

Catherine was not slow in acquiring the power of Regent until such time as he arrived. As it happened the lawful Regent was now Montgomery. He decided this was the moment to return from his exile in Cornwall. He landed in Normandy with quite a substantial force and proceeded to advance on Paris. But he and his volunteer army were quickly defeated by the French forces. In order to diminish his perfectly legal claim, Catherine made a great show of how he had been an exile and arranged for him to be brought to Paris as a prisoner. She had him put on trial with maximum publicity. In this way she successfully covered her illegal manoeuvring to usurp his place. But she did not want to antagonise the Huguenots as a whole, especially since Henri was not yet back in the country. So despite her treatment of Montgomery, she wrote conciliatory letters to all the leading Huguenots. It was quite pointless, of course for, by this time, they did not trust her in the least.

She also found she was having to defend both herself and the King against a virulent propaganda campaign. Eventually she learnt that despite being a prisoner under close surveillance, the perpetrator was Anjou, hoping that by denigrating her, he could oust her as Regent and seize the throne while his brother was still abroad.

Despite having had to borrow heavily to carry out the siege of La Rochelle, Catherine now proceeded to pour out money on the trappings of Charles's funeral. Even the special bed for the lying in state, which went on for 40 days, cost 150,000 crowns. But by this time no bankers in Rome, Florence nor indeed anywhere else would give her credit even at 15 per cent. So she had to depend on a private loan of 5,000 francs. It paid the amount outstanding for the funeral and there was enough left over to feed her ladies in waiting. The unfortunate pages, however, had to pawn their mantles in order to buy their meals.

Henri was taking so long over his journey home Catherine could contain herself no longer. Mainly she feared that during his absence he might have shed some of his dependency on her. So she wrote urging him to take on De Retz, his late brother's Gentleman of the Bedchamber.

As the Venetian ambassador reported back: "It is the duty of the first gentleman of the chamber to stay always in the room of the King and to be always near him and so she was sure to know not only what her son did but, as it were, what her son thought. It was her custom, as I am informed, during the life of the last King, to have reported to her every morning everything the King had said and all that had been said to him, in order to take measures against anything that was being arranged against her power in the Government".

But while he might be as ignorant as his younger brother, Henri was more astute. Under increasing pressure he agreed that De Retz should keep the post but insisted that he must alternate every six months with a man of his choosing. Nor would he be expected to spend the night in the King's room. This was a slap to Catherine. She became so anxious she did not wait for him to arrive in Paris but set out in her carriage to meet him at Rouen.

After a flamboyant reunion, she insisted on holding a meeting in private. It lasted two hours and she managed to turn it into a daily event which continued even after he had arrived back in Paris. But in some ways she was too late. Despite all her efforts, he insisted that he, not she, should be the first to look at any correspondence.

As though to emphasise his independence further, on reaching Rheims and without consulting his mother, he married Louise de Vaudement. This in itself would have raised her ire. Worse, Louise was related to the Guises. However she was not only a sweet girl but her parents had been extremely strict with her. She was so timid Catherine felt sure she would prove no rival. So she had little difficulty in pretending the marriage had been made with her full approval.

Nevertheless she was heard to say in exasperation: "Sometimes the King doesn't take my word according to my intention and thinks that I am trying to palliate everything either because of love to the Guises or because he thinks I am a poor creature ruled by weakness". Although she might say this she was, in fact, still his most influential adviser and whenever a great crisis arose or there was anything of capital importance, he turned to her.

Since the negotiations over his engagement to Elizabeth had failed, Henri had, if anything, expressed increased animosity against England. Now that he had become King, Elizabeth had every reason to fear this animosity might turn into active hostility.

PART IV

1576-1587
SPANISH SILVER

Back in 1545 or thereabouts, there had been a discovery which might normally have been considered no more than a footnote to history. In fact it had a major impact on the whole of Europe. It was the patio process, whereby amalgam of mercury can be used to reduce the time necessary for refining silver. The consequent increase in the amount of bullion that could now be imported raised Philip's income. He had more within that first year than all that had been imported over the previous fifty. It meant that Philip was enjoying something around 2 million a year; this compared to Elizabeth's income of half a million.

This plethora had two dramatic effects over the entire continent. Then as now, gold was accepted as the international currency, but because the metal is useless as well as rare, the price is particularly susceptible to the law of demand and supply. So when there is too much, the value falls, leading inevitably to inflation.

However Elizabeth was able largely to counteract this through building on the trading foundations her sister Mary had almost inconsequently laid. The degree to which English trade was now flourishing had become apparent when, back in 1565, Thomas Gresham had built the London Exchange. It was intended as a more convenient place for merchants to do business instead of in the open in Lombard Street or, when it rained, in the nave of St. Paul's Cathedral. He persuaded Elizabeth to open his new building and she was much impressed though she did not grace it with the title of Royal Exchange for several to come. But it was a landmark in the sophistication of English finance, to the extent that the merchants had even come to look upon the quarrels among the countries of Europe as no more than a hindrance to their business. Traders were in fact venturing as far afield as Canada, Malay, China and Russia. They were transporting cargoes of spices, ceramics, glass, rugs, tapestries and textiles and slaves.

When in 1570 the Pope excommunicated Elizabeth, she felt she no longer owed any allegiance to the Church of Rome and this left her with a free conscience to trade with the heathen, notably the Saracens. This neatly complimented the enterprise of Drake, Hawkins and the other semi-pirates who were leading the way in exploring the globe. During his voyage round the world in 1578, Drake had made contact with the Sultan of Ternate and laid the foundations of trade with Asia. He had always traded fairly. Plunder was confined to fat Spanish galleons; indeed local traders along the western coast of South America preferred doing business with him rather than the Spanish.

Elizabeth saw clearly the way things were going. She was in frequent and friendly correspondence with Ivan the Terrible and even instructed the Earl of Essex to learn Russian. In its way, the variations in currency values brought about by Spanish inflation also brought on trading skills, to the extent that in Piacenza in 1579 there was the first ever international fair for clearing credit notes. The traders were dealing in nearly 400 different coins and they were now helped by the introduction of conversion tables.

In England the Levant company was formed in 1578 and in 1581 Elizabeth gave Edward Osborne and Richard Staper incorporation as a company of Merchants and she backed it by appointing an ambassador for the Levant. Two years later the trading area was extended to include Aleppo, the Persian Gulf and India. Elizabeth later helped to consolidate this by providing naval backing for the East India Company.

In 1583 Elizabeth appointed the first English ambassador to the Ottoman Empire. This however also revealed how trading, regardless of the Pope, could still bring its embarrassing moments. It was not so many years since both Charles V and Philip had been fighting the infidel. Elizabeth was now trading with them, not just in luxury goods but in tin and lead, which could only be used for armaments, notably for casting cannons.

She now found herself not just in papal disgrace but in danger of being ostracised internationally. She had to send Christopher Rarkins to convince Rudolf II, who was now Archduke of Austria as well as the Holy Roman Emperor, giving her usual excuse that the merchants were acting independently and, of course, that she had had no knowledge of the matter.

In 1587 new ground in international finance was broken when Banco della Piazza Rialto was founded in Venice. It was the first such major institution to be backed by the state. This not only ensured security, often lacking among the normal moneylenders, but it broadened finance on a European scale. Instead of complicated bills of exchange and the physical transportation of coin, transactions could be completed simply by cheque.

Philip too had awakened to the potential for income other than importing silver. He declared himself to be King of Ceylon and Goa. He did this without even bothering to refer to the papal authority, which had originally so cavalierly divided all the lands beyond Europe between Spain and Portugal. He went on to form a company specifically for importing pepper from Asia.

It had for some time been apparent that Anjou's relations with his brother, the newly crowned Henri III, were just as strained as they had been with the former King and there was no let up over the strictness with which he was still confined within the Louvre Palace.

Here Elizabeth sensed an interesting opportunity, so she told her ambassador in Paris to report on the situation.

Catherine, of course, guessed the real intention for his visit and gave the ambassador a hard time. On one occasion she deliberately insulted Elizabeth by dressing one of her dwarfs to look like her and make objectionable remarks about her relations with her "riding instructor" (Leicester being Elizabeth's Master of the Horse).

Another time she naively tried to impress His Excellency with a blatantly staged "chance" meeting. He was in her rooms when Anjou apparently happened to come in and, as though quite spontaneously but completely out of context, declared his loyalty to the his brother the King. Then Navarre came in and said the same. Even if the Ambassador had not drawn his own conclusions, some Huguenot court officials beside him nudged his elbow to make it clear how fictitious it all was.

However the Ambassador did manage to meet Anjou on his own who told him his life was in danger and his only hope was to bribe the guards and escape. This was sufficient for Elizabeth, and she started sending Anjou money. She was careful to send it in small amounts so that if any single contribution was intercepted it would be considered more as "pocket money" than the means of financing anything so expensive as bribing his way to escape. For the same reason, such a small sum was unlikely to be associated with someone with her considerable financial resources.

Catherine had only been able to persuade Henri to allow Anjou to remain in the palace rather than the Bastille after he had promised he would keep his word and not abscond.

He didn't and he did.

As soon as Elizabeth's money reached £20,000, he bribed the guards. Then one evening, muffled in a large cloak, he walked past them to where a coach was waiting and sped off into the night.

Catherine's first thought was to accuse him of treason and arrange his kidnap, but he forestalled her by writing to the King assuring him of his loyalty. He then made a direct appeal to the public by declaring he had risen in defence of the ancient laws which had been violated by foreigners, a snide remark against the nouveau Guise family. Such a wide and popular appeal ruled out any attempt at kidnap.

The Huguenot forces had already been planning to make him their commander-in-chief and Elizabeth assisted matters by sending more money for them to recruit mercenaries from Germany

So almost before he knew what was happening, Anjou found himself in the incongruous position of being Lieutenant General of France and at the same time head of a dissident army of 30,000 men who were prepared to fight whomever they were told, including the French. Navarre and Conde joined him and with such able commanders it was easy to manoeuvre the troops until he had Paris encircled and it was clear he could easily starve the city of supplies. The king had to capitulate, and in May 1576 the brothers signed The Peace of Beaulieu. It soon came to be known as "The Peace of Monsieur" after Anjou, because he was so palpably the greatest beneficiary. It transferred even more estates to him, bringing in an amazing annual income of 300,000 livres. Navarre also did nicely under the treaty, for he got back his wife's pocket kingdom and was allowed to manage it without interference. But the most far reaching clause pardoned the Huguenots and gave them back freedom of worship.

For the moment, Catherine hoped to disguise the humiliating situation and told the King to make a pretence at reconciliation and express undying love for his prodigal brother. So to the world, all was apparently in sweet harmony. Only Elizabeth was not well pleased. All her money had been spent by the Huguenots with surprising speed, yet had added little to the discomfort she had intended for the King.

Catherine soon came to learn that Elizabeth had largely financed the enterprise. She wrote that she had heard that her son had been offered large sums of money to pay for troops. Of course she realised the offer must have been made by some of the Queen's more reckless subordinates and without her knowledge. She also tried to calm the English Ambassador, assuring him that France was no more in a position to declare war on England than England was on France.

For Anjou, in his new-found freedom, the prospect looked bright. Philip's ill-paid troops had sacked and pillaged Antwerp and several other towns. As a result all the Dutch had come together under the leadership of William of Orange.

William had been impressed by Anjou or, more particularly, the large army he had at his command. At the same time, Anjou had made no secret of his ambition to join the Netherlanders and help them gain freedom from Philip. Regardless of his deplorable reputation, William offered to make him "Defender of the Faith and Count of Holland and Zealand", a title which was as empty as it was long. But Anjou's prime motive remained to own a more substantial piece of real estate which he could call his own realm, so he surprised everyone by turning down an offer which normally he would have found irresistible. Actually he had no regrets, for he felt sure that sooner or later he would only have to drop a hint for the offer to be renewed.

More importantly, he had conceived himself a far better plan. He would marry one of the King of Spain's daughters. He hoped that in temporarily rejecting the honour he would gain Philip's approval. As a start he wrote to the Pope offering to use his forces to repress the Huguenots in the Netherlands - no matter that they were still his allies.

But it was no use. When his proposition was placed before Philip it was received with marked indifference.

This, however, was the marriage Catherine had been trying to arrange for so long. With her facility for turning any opportunity to her advantage, she wrote to Philip commending Anjou's idea. She backed her suggestion by pointing out that under the present situation, there was Anjou in charge of an army on his eastern state while on his western border there was the formidable French force in the Azores. She left it up to him to see he was in an uncomfortable pincer situation.

Philip countered her barely-veiled hint at a stroke when he had granted the Dutch almost all the demands they had put forward in the Pacification of Ghent and had agreed to take out the Spanish troops within 20 days and all the foreign mercenaries as soon as he had been paid them. This left the Dutch as a fairly content coalition of faiths, so that they were for the moment indifferent to Anjou's blandishments.

The Guises had been furious at all the concessions the Huguenots had wrung from the King in the Beaulieu treaty. The Montmorencys were furious too, not so much over the leniency but because they felt belittled, since Catherine had forgotten to consult them during her negotiations. It was an unusual and formidable alliance.

So with Philip's encouragement, the Guises announced the formation of the League of the Holy Trinity. It was, in fact, the Catholic League under a new name. Their declared intent was to protect the King from the heretics. Their real intent, however, was to force the King to go back on the treaty of Beaulieu. Everyone realised that this new League was being formed primarily for the benefit of the Guises. Yet despite their unpopularity, many people felt they had to join, even if they did so with considerable reluctance.

The League thrived prodigiously and soon had branches throughout the country. Indeed it became a potential threat to the King, so Catherine advised him to join it. This way he automatically became the senior member and was able to claim a right to the leadership. It caused another lurch in Catherine's see-saw policy.

At the same time the Catholic cartel within the court came to the conclusion that the real strength of the Huguenot cadre lay in the close friendship between Margot, her brother Anjou and her husband Navarre. One way to nullify their potency would be to break up this trio. On assessing their characters, the Guises decided this could best be done by casting aspersions on Margot's morality. Her brother would almost certainly side with her, while Navarre would believe the worst and, as her husband, would feel affronted. It would all lead to a furious quarrel. The plot seemed all the more promising because the King already had a low opinion of his sister's morals, while Catherine was furious with her because she thought she was wielding more influence over the King than she was.

The ideal moment came when the King was out walking. One of the Guise minions in his party spotted Margot's carriage. Indeed it could hardly be missed, for it was heavily gilded and upholstered in yellow velvet. It was outside the house of a courtier. The Guises had little difficulty in persuading the King that they had caught her virtually "en flagrant". She was, in fact, merely attending a service at a nearby abbey. On her return to the palace, the King immediately ordered her to come to him and, without further inquiry, nor giving her a chance to speak, ordered her to leave the court. Next morning, anxious to justify his hasty action and prove her adultery, he dispatched 60 of his guard to follow her. They were to inspect the bed in which she had just been sleeping for any suspicious signs of adultery, but nothing incriminating was found. Some of her party were brought back for further questioning, but they too said nothing to incriminate her.

Still the Catholic faction were not satisfied with their success. Anjou must also be incriminated. One day they convinced the King that proof of Anjou's treason could be found that very moment in his apartment. The King immediately went down and personally started searching the room. He thought he saw Anjou concealing a piece of paper up his sleeve and angrily demanded that he should see it. Anjou refused and, against all etiquette, the King snatched it from him. To his mortification he found it was in fact a *billet doux* Anjou had received from Madame de Sauve. It was only the honour of a lady that had compelled him to defy the King's command.

This made the King look ever more foolish. Partly to try and justify himself and partly as a way of curbing Anjou's confounded tricks, he determined that this time Anjou must be sent to the Bastille. But while Catherine might well be having no truck with Margot, Anjou was still her dear boy, so she exercised her art of persuasion and the King yet again ended up just re-imposing Anjou's close confinement within the place.

All this while Philip's problems with the Netherlands had been continuing unabated. Then he had what he thought was a bright idea. He decided to ask Margaret to come out of retirement and become Governess of the Netherlands again. This time she would be working in conjunction with her son Alexander whom he had already appointed General in charge of the Spanish forces. Margaret must have been aware that over the 18 years since she had last occupied the post Europe had undergone a seismic change. During her first term the leading European powers had in effect been using the Netherlands as a way of tweaking the tail of the King of Spain to keep him out of mischief. Since then there had occurred the enforced departure of Mary from Scotland, transferring its strategic value to the deep water port of Flushing capable of servicing an invasion fleet and situated in an independent area of the Netherlands. Margaret now found that far from having charge of Europe's Tom Tiddler's Ground she was now in Europe's cockpit for war.

This shift of emphasis was well illustrated by the growing contempt in which Elizabeth was holding Spain. At one point she had not even bothered to replace her ambassador in Madrid, though this may in part have been in protest. Her ambassador had been told that his servant could not attend a Protestant service. He had lost his temper and expressed his opinion of Spain, Catholicism and the Pope in no uncertain terms. Philip had expelled him.

By the time Margaret arrived in 1578, her son Alexander had already taken on the leading Calvinist Dutch Prince William of Orange and with considerable success. In the Treaty of Arras Alexander had persuaded the southern provinces of the Netherlands to support Philip and Catholicism and in return he had agreed to withdraw the hated Spanish troops.

Margaret arrived just in time to be hit by the Calvinist reaction to Arras, particularly by the Dutch Holland, Zeeland and Utrecht. They signed an agreement of Utrecht which set out their determination to retain the freedom in religious belief as had been decided barely two years before in the Pacification of Ghent.

Philip felt sure that mother and son were just the team to put a final end to this perennial problem. He specified her job as bringing the bickering provinces to accept allegiance to Spain.

The Dutch, however, resented it as they thought Margaret had been appointed to stop them making an alliance with Anjou.

And now, here on her doorstep, Anjou was just about to appear in person.

His escape three years earlier had convinced Elizabeth of his potential value when at liberty. The Philip/Don Juan scheme had impressed upon her that the full power of Spain was now bent upon her assassination. Only Anjou's escape from the Louvre and his threat to create havoc in the Netherlands had prevented Don Juan from leading the invasion which would have cost her life.

So once again Elizabeth was only too happy to start sending him money. By the summer he had accumulated sufficient funds, and one night Margot had a lute case brought into her apartment, where he was waiting. The case contained a rope, and so he was able to lower himself down the palace walls. Margot was so anxious to remove all clues of her collusion that she almost wrecked the whole plot. She decided it would be good to burn the rope, but it set the chimney on fire and the next thing she knew palace staff were hammering on the door anxious to put it out. She managed to convince them that she could see to it herself and the danger was averted.

So Anjou had time to make sure of his escape, which was not discovered till the morning. This time he took refuge in the Huguenot stronghold of Dreux. Catherine had little trouble in tracking him down and once again tried to make him see reason and persuade him to return to Paris. Anjou realised that if he did so, he would be playing right into the hands of the King, who this time would almost certainly put him in the Bastille. If, on the other hand, he stayed where he was, the Huguenot forces at his disposal ensured they would not dare capture him.

Catherine was really frightened, for Philip had already made it clear that he held Henri responsible for the actions of his wilful younger brother. She pleaded with Anjou that if he crossed the border into the Netherlands Philip would declare war on France. She also pointed out that Elizabeth had gone into alliance with the Protestant princes of Germany, so that now they would almost certainly refuse to finance any invasion. Catherine also pointed out that it was wrong to raise forces without the King's consent. The fact that she made this point, and presumably believed it would have some effect, shows just how much the mother was besotted with her son.

Having failed in persuasion, she next tried bribery. The last time Anjou had escaped she had tried to win him back by heaping honours upon him, culminating with his appointment as Lieutenant General, so there was nothing more she could add in that line. Remembering his failure to marry Philip's daughter, she next decided to lay before him a list of nubile princesses, hoping that marriage might induce him to settle down. In her list she bypassed the Princess of Saxony and the Princess of Cleaves as not being of political value. Much more to the point, there was the daughter of the Duke of Florence or, better still, there was the lovely daughter of the Duke of Mantua, who would bring as part of her dowry a nice piece of land south of the Alps. Best of all there was the Princess of Navarre, who would bring with her the province of Franche Comte.

But Anjou would have none of it. Instead he declared his intention of liberating Artois and Hainault from the thralls of Philip. Ignoring all his mother's pleadings, in July 1578 he led his hastily-gathered troops, who were now in fact little more than a rabble, across the border into the Netherlands. He was enthusiastically backed by the French nobility, who saw an excellent opportunity for plunder. Unfortunately they were so enthusiastic that they were unable to resist these activities while still within the French frontier. No matter; the Dutch were happy to overlook the past so long as Anjou was able to bring his forces onto their side. In accepting the title of Hereditary Sovereign to the United Provinces, he promised to supply 12,000 men at his own expense for three months and if after that time the war had not ended, he would increase the total to 35,000 and finance them for as long as the war might last.

In 1580 Philip made a dramatic move. He invaded Portugal. He had long held considerable influence in his neighbouring country and it had not been difficult for him to forsee an opportunity.

A year or two before, King Sebastian, along with a large number of Portugal's male aristocracy, had been killed fighting the Moors at the Battle of Jarnac. He was succeeded by his great uncle Cardinal Henry, who was certainly not eligible for fighting. He was aged 67, deaf, toothless, half blind and racked by tuberculosis. In fact he was virtually senile. In this state of health he was horrified at the prospect of succeeding to the throne. However, nobody paid any attention to his protests and no one was surprised when after barely two years he had died.

The Portuguese had named his successor as Don Antonio de Cato. But Philip declared a claim of sorts as he was Sebastian's nephew. Even more to the point, Philip was half Portuguese. No sooner had the old man died than Philip invaded. While the Portuguese populace did not approve, the aristocracy was not totally averse to Philip and he received positive support from the business and mercantile sectors and also from the Jesuits. Don Antonio did not stand a chance. He fled to the north coast, where he was taken aboard an English ship and deposited on the Portuguese outpost islands of the Azores. Although outside the mass of Europe, the Azores were of value, being the first outpost for ships returning from the Americas. These islands provided the key for all Spanish navigation in the Atlantic, eliminating the need to go to the Indies or pass into the South Seas. Don Antonio declared: "If this summer we had only four English galleys here we could have collected more than ten millions of gold".

Catherine sent French ships to warn off any attempts Philip might make to capture him, or rather the Azores. She justified her interest with a tenuous claim for the Portuguese throne for herself. She said she was descended from a mid-thirteenth century king. The Spanish contemptuously dismissed this as just another example of the merchant's daughter's burning desire to have herself associated with royalty.

Elizabeth had more practical grounds for objection. Along with the occupation, the Spanish had taken possession of the Portuguese Navy. While the English fleet did not amount to much more than

40,000 tons, the Portuguese had a significant fleet of between 200,000 and 300,000 tons. Moreover it came to Philip along with possession of Portugal's long seaboard. It presented a formidable combination, especially since this was the era when the centre of European sea power was shifting from the Mediterranean to the Atlantic.

Obviously the development had not been lost upon Catherine and it further increased her fears over France being invaded by Philip.

They were fears multiplied because she felt she was losing control over her family and that meant France was becoming dangerously vulnerable. The King had deliberately set about diluting the power not only of his mother but of the old families, many of whom were loyal to Catherine. They already disliked Henri because of his strong distaste for war and his effeminacy. He indeed seems to have been sexually deviant. While a teenager he had been very much a ladies' man and had had a serious romance with the Duchess of Cleaves. Now he was alienating the old families again by surrounding himself with a number of effete *nouveau riches*. Their pursuit of extreme fashion, with their long crimped hair tucked up beneath their little bonnets of velvet, was in itself offensive. They wore them with six-inch starched ruffles so that they "looked like the head of John the Baptist on a platter". They quickly became known as the Darlings, though a more appropriate translation would be "the Dainty Ones". To underwrite the permanency of their status, the King gave them large amounts of land.

What particularly annoyed the old families was that these upstarts had not had time to prove themselves. They were all as young as the king. Anne d'Arques was made Duke of Joyeuse at the age of 20. Even more influential was the son of a major army official who was given 10 important offices of state and created Duke of Epernon and Admiral of France all before he was 27. Inevitably, because they owed their status and estates entirely to His Majesty, these favourites became sycophants. They praised him outrageously and agreed with whatever he said. Now he had no one with real political expertise to give him genuine practical advice.

Seeing the danger, Catherine tried to make friends with the Darlings. They simply ignored her – and so did the King. While he gave banquets and balls, she never even received an invitation. Sometimes there were weeks, even months, between their meetings.

But what made Catherine even more alarmed was the outward change in the King's character. He had always been subject to difficult moods and the Darlings soon learnt how to play upon them. They played upon his religious scruples and encouraged him in fasting and even in self-flagellation, an unfortunate practice he had picked up in Poland. The next moment all would be given over to pleasure.

Unfortunately these extremes were there for all to see. One day he would be in the street playing cup and ball and the next making his way to church in a hair-shirt and with a great ebony yolk around his neck. He built a hermitage at Vincennes and spent more time playing the hermit there than ever he did in the palace carrying out duties as King.

Not only was it the king causing Catherine concern. Her daughter Margot was also being difficult.

Her marriage had been in trouble for some time. Navarre had just disposed of his third mistress in as many years and was now establishing his fourth. This did not particularly worry Margot, until she learnt that he was trying to get rid of her and install this latest mistress in her place. This was too much. She tried to poison him, but bungled it, and then she literally had a shot at him – but missed. Next she sold her jewels and everything else she had in order to raise two companies of soldiers and fortify a citadel of defence – or more realistically of defiance – within Navarre's mini-kingdom. But it was a feeble effort and within six months she had gone broke and was thrown out by the citizens, who were fed up with all the pillaging by her troops.

Once again Catherine thought she could mend the family rift through marriage. Margot should divorce Navarre and marry the Duke of Lorraine, one of the Guise brothers. This would provide a strong link between Catholics and Huguenots. But why just one link? Upon this Catherine's imagination ran riot, with a veritable carnival of marriages. Conde, who was a Huguenot, could marry the daughter of the Duc de Guise; and, come to that, Conde's sister could marry the Duke of Neves, a Catholic who was tending to ally himself primarily with the King. The only difficulty was that none of the parties concerned took her idea seriously. The Duke of Guise told Philip "I would sooner see anyone dear to me dead than consent to such a plan and I am certain that the Duke of Loraine and the Duke of Nevers will feel the same way.

Anjou was also running into difficulties. He was beginning to rue the day when he had so rashly committed himself to liberating the Netherlands. Indeed, the terms he had accepted for the honour of being a "Defender" were not those that any level-headed person would have agreed to. The situation was aggravated by inefficiency and extravagance. His loose control and lack of leadership enabled the military staff he had gathered around him to steal and pillage. The campaign reached the second stage of his agreement without any suggestion that the end was in sight. Before long he was running out of money for the troops' wages, so it was hardly surprising they started drifting off in droves. And all this time, Alexander of Parma was outwitting him at every turn. By January 1579 Anjou realised that all was lost. He was writing home to Mummy begging that he might be allowed to return to Paris.

Some time before this, Elizabeth had come to the conclusion that matters were becoming critical. Catherine, under pressure, had recently signed the Treaty of Nerac. Once again she was pacifying the Huguenots. But more to the point, Elizabeth realised that hitherto the

Huguenots had been largely exercising Catherine's attention. With the treaty in place Catherine now had time to think of relations with England in more robust terms. Indeed Elizabeth was beginning to regret having let the genie out of the bottle. Anjou, too, was becoming surprisingly successful. There was always the possibility that, together with his mother, he might squeeze the Spanish out of the Netherlands altogether. This would mean the vital port of Flushing would fall into French hands, something Elizabeth feared as much as she feared it being occupied by the Spanish.

She pondered the situation and decided the best way she could bring him under her control would be to fall back on her ever effective ploy and become engaged. This would have the additional advantage of weakening France, since it would feed the jealousy already existing between the King and his brother. Finally such a move would scotch the still-existing prospect of Anjou marrying Philip's daughter.

When Elizabeth broached the subject, Anjou was more than delighted at even the smallest prospect of becoming King of England and fell in with her plans immediately. Now, with the dangers facing him when he returned to Paris, he felt he could ensure his safety by taking up Elizabeth's invitation.

As Anjou had anticipated, the King's first reaction had been to put him under lock and key. No wonder Elizabeth sarcastically remarked that she hedged her invitation with the remark she was not prepared to take a husband with irons on his feet. Catherine was, of course, delighted to have her darling back and in penitent mood and was at her most persuasive.

In the end and largely because of Elizabeth's remark, Henri agreed to stage a welcome, hailing Anjou as the provident brother. But Catherine was not fooled by Elizabeth's plans and told the Venetian ambassador: "I will tell you confidentially what I wouldn't say to anyone else. The Queen of England is a very astute person and always manages to look after her own interest. She got hold of my son, who is young and won't listen to my advice".

Despite severe doubts, she considered such a prospect was worth encouragement no matter how remote it might seem, but she also adopted her customary policy of pursuing an opposite plan along parallel lines. So while again professing great joy at the prospect of Elizabeth becoming her "daughter", she pointed out to Philip that since he might find such an engagement unacceptable, he might like to think again about agreeing to his daughter marrying Anjou.

When Elizabeth broke the news of her intention to her council, they were aghast. Hatton burst into tears and the people made it clear they did not like the prospect of returning to the time when they had a foreign King. But Elizabeth was apparently determined to go ahead. She was further encouraged when Anjou confirmed his intent by sending his best clothes in advance. Better still, he said he would be sending Jean de Simier as his wooer in proxy to warm his place. de Simier proved to be an enormous success, "a most choice courtier, exquisitely skilled in love toys, pleasant conceits and court-dalliance". He entranced Elizabeth, who would not allow a word to be said against him. He completely captured her heart when he raided her bedroom and took away her nightcap, which he sent to his master as a token of love.

Leicester, who had for some time renewed his dalliance with the Queen in the hope of eventually marrying her, considered all this to be a disaster. He tried to prevent Henri from giving Anjou a passport. When de Simier learnt this, he let drop to Elizabeth that Leicester had secretly married one of her ladies-in-waiting. If there was one thing that could be counted upon to arouse Elizabeth's wrath it was anyone who married one of her maids in waiting without her knowledge. The move certainly had the desired effect. She had Leicester put in the Tower. To show her sincerity, she had de Simier sign the terms of marriage, but astutely she also insisted that he should sign a paper allowing proceedings to be postponed for two months, time necessary, she assured him, for her subjects to become amenable to the idea. Indeed Elizabeth was so convincing over her sincerity that de Simier wrote to Anjou urging him to come over as soon as he could.

Catherine, however, retained her initial suspicions and asked Elizabeth to make a definite statement. Elizabeth replied that she could not do so until she had seen her prospective husband in the flesh. So when in August 1579 Anjou duly arrived, he was received most warmly and given five days of feasting. The flesh, however, left much to be desired.

On the face of it, of course, the whole project was absurd. Elizabeth was now well over forty and, in those days, that meant an old woman. But with marriage more a political ploy than a love match, the idea made sense and child bearing, though important, was not essential. But Elizabeth had two good reasons for carrying out the charade Physically Anjou remained just as repulsive, but maturity had given him a degree of style. He had a very smooth way with the ladies: "He takes the hand of one and pulls the ear of another and in that way passes a good part of his time". He could also write very good love letters. Elizabeth did not seem to be at all put off by his unfortunate appearance and revelled in his gallantry. She called him her 'Little Frog' after the pearl ear rings he gave her. But a more practical reason was that the longer she played the game, the more she was fanning the intense jealousy between the brothers. She also knew she could count on the English Parliament to provide a reason for breaking off the engagement whenever she felt it necessary. The people had no wish for a return to those dreaded times under Mary Tudor when the country had been in thrall to a foreign power. So plans for any immediate marriage were by mutual consent, left in the air.

Largely due to the Duke of Parma's increasing success, William of

Orange had come to realise that he could no longer continue his resistance without help. So he approached Henri, offering him an honour with the usual snappy title: "Defender of Liberty of the Belgians and Liberator of the Netherlands against the tyranny of the Spanish". Henri declined and as second choice and, despite his despicable record and the poor quality of his men, the title was offered to Anjou, on the one condition that he had the support of Henri in writing.

Anjou had no doubts on that score. He was only too well aware how much his mother and brother feared he might return to France and raise havoc, as when he had threatened Paris. He proceeded to blackmail them into supporting his enterprise. In a moment of confidence, Catherine told the Venetian ambassador that even though Anjou had been granted lands with an income far larger than legal limits allowed, "He is not content either with the King or with me because in truth he has too ambitious a mind".

And so in 1580 Anjou arrived triumphant in Antwerp with the requisite letter in which his brother promised he would "aid him with all his power and league himself with the Netherlands as soon as they shall have effectively received you as their Prince and Lord". Buoyed up with his new-found importance, Anjou, in a moment of bravura, proclaimed he would march and relieve Chambray, which was under siege by the Spanish. It was a typically wild boast, bringing with it the immediate fear that Philip would carry out his threat that should France become involved in the Netherlands he would declare war. So Catherine had no difficulty in persuading the King to pretend he was doing his best to restrain his wayward brother.

Officially Henri forbade Anjou to proceed. He instructed French authorities everywhere that if they found any soldiers acting without his warrant, "They should be cut into pieces". Not that anyone acted on these drastic instructions. Indeed Catherine was sending him money and the King sent Marshal Artus de Cosse to advise him. Thanks to de Cosse,

Anjou was able at last to execute his promise. But soon Anjou, had typically become over-confident and had started ignoring de Cosse.

Then things began to go badly wrong, so in October, in the hope of winkling more money out of Elizabeth, he raised the subject of marriage again. To make sure he was not rebuffed, he openly invited himself to London. Elizabeth was certainly no lovesick maid. In later years she confided in the Spanish ambassador: "An old woman like me has something else to think about besides marrying. The hopes that I gave I would marry Anjou were given for the purpose of getting him out of the Netherlands States. I never wished to see them in the hands of the French".

Elizabeth thought she was fully aware of what he was up to and determined that she would not make him another loan. She also realised she was challenging the danger that should their apparent amours go awry, it could at this late stage provoke a Franco-Spanish alliance. Elizabeth's agreement to take the risk on renewing their acquaintance may well have been tinged with the realisation that at forty-eight, this must almost certainly be her last opportunity to indulge in her favourite pastime of flirting. His love letters were sufficiently florid to encourage her: "on the brink of this troublesome sea I kiss your feet"

The Venetian Ambassador was shocked at Elizabeth's behaviour after his arrival. He reported that she had been seen early in the morning, taking cups of broth to him while he was still in his bed. Even more blatantly and in front of the whole court, she kissed Anjou full on the mouth and told the Ambassador he could tell his master that they were engaged. *As these new* negotiations became extended and Anjou stayed longer and longer, she began to find him tiresome. She hoped to get out of the situation with dignity. Far from it, she soon found herself conducting a sort of unedifying auction as she kept introducing more and more demanding conditions so as to remove all reasons why he should continue to stay, while he made more and more conciliations so that he could.

First she made it clear that she was not prepared to finance Anjou's sorties in the Netherlands. Then she said that France must guarantee to come to her aid if England was attacked by Spain. But Henri was so anxious to be rid of his brother once and for all that he kept accepting her new demands. In short, Elizabeth found herself entrapped by her own caprices. Finally she declared that she wanted Calais back. Even then she was afraid Henri might agree, but this proved too much and negotiations were broken off. Yet Anjou stayed on and of course, his brother was in no mood to order him home.

At last Elizabeth broke it to him that he ought to forget her in exchange for her money and hopefully offered him 60,000. He accepted and, according to her ladies in waiting, she skipped with delight at the prospect of finally being rid of him. But though Anjou was weak, he was no fool. He decided that Elizabeth would pay more, and to her horror, he declared that he loved her so much that after all he could not possibly leave her and all her marriage terms would be accepted. "This stopped the skip in Elizabeth's step". However she knew that his love, though unbounded, still had its limitations. First she tried appealing to him. Did he really mean to "threaten a poor old woman in her own country?" For a moment it looked as though she might have won. Anjou broke down in tears at the very thought, and Elizabeth had to lend him her handkerchief. But he still refused to leave.

Elizabeth, who had been so determined that she would not lend him anything, now had to raise the stakes. Then she had a stroke of good fortune. A message came from William of Orange offering Anjou the title of Duke of Brabant. It was even grander than all the other Dutch distinctions, and better still it entailed estates. So Elizabeth accompanied him to Canterbury and bade him a heart-rending farewell. She declared she was utterly distraught with grief and swore she would never be happy till he returned. Then, to make quite sure this would never happen, she followed it up with a letter in which she declared that while she loved him dearly, on reflection her greatest desire was to keep England at peace and their marriage would tie her to fighting on behalf of another country. It was something her people would not stand for, so she could not for the moment see her way to marrying him.

He duly arrived in the Netherlands for the third time and went right away to Antwerp, where he was installed with all pomp as the Duke of Brabant with William of Orange himself placing the ducal mantle over his shoulders, solemnly declaring "I must secure this robe so firmly, my Lord, that no man may ever tear it from your shoulders".

By this time it had become clear that Philip's idea for a great team was not working. Partly it was because when Margaret arrived, Alexander had already cooked up an intricate mixture of military and the political and the consequent success made him resentful of intrusion by a second person, even if it was only the political side. Also Philip had failed to appreciate the psychology of mother and son working together under pressure. The natural inclination of an adult son is to consider his judgement superior to that of his mother. Additionally Philip had failed to understand that two strong personalities rarely form a happy partnership.

Alexander had already asked Philip to recall his mother and Philip had refused. Now, after two years, Margaret herself had had enough and in 1582 she too asked Philip to relieve her of her post. This time Philip felt he had to accept.

As regards Anjou and his latest Dutch honour, Catherine and the King were delighted that her son had found Brabant a replacement interest and one which still kept him outside France. Catherine's greatest fear now was that he might make a mess of it and lose Brabant or, perhaps he might become bored. In either case he might return to Paris with his army and cause more mayhem.

The only way she could think of making sure he stayed in the Netherlands was for France to declare war on Spain. Her old fear that Spain might win was as nothing compared to the relief she felt through removing the threat of her son returning to Paris and endangering the King.

As it happened, her idea found widespread support in court circles. Many of the nobles were still mortified over the humiliation of the atrocities the Spanish had inflicted on them in the Azores. Against this, the Pope was expressing dismay at the idea of two Catholic countries at war.

Consequently the King did not take his mother's advice.

Before long, Anjou found he was running out of money again. The King had had enough and refused to help, but Catherine's heart was melted and she began to send him some of her own. That, of course, was not nearly enough. He wrote to Elizabeth with the piteous story of how his brother would no longer send him money and he would have to abandon his Netherlands exercise unless she sent him 30,000. As he had hoped, Elizabeth was glad to have some control over him and obliged. Shortly after, he pleaded for another 20,000, which Elizabeth also duly provided.

Then this incorrigible man disgraced himself beyond all civilised protocol. He changed sides, blatantly betraying his allies. In a despicable plot, he tried to seize control of all the principal cities on behalf of the Spanish. As a sort of prototype, he marched his French troops into Bruges. On reaching the city centre, they suddenly called out "Let all Catholics take arms and help us against the Protestants!" In his plan, the officers were then to seize the city for the Spanish. However both Catholic and Protestant citizens banded together again and with considerable determination prevented the soldiers from returning to barracks.

His intention had been to replicate the "coup" in several other major cities but they met with similar opposition. In Antwerp, a Frenchman had already warned the citizens. They slammed the City gates on the 1,500 soldiers and threw stones at them from the roof tops, then took up arms until the Spaniards had all been killed. Anjou's treachery had backfired and Alexander was able to take control of Zutphen, all of Waes and finally Bruges and Ypres.

For the moment Catherine, desperate for the good name of her son, tried to place all the blame upon the ingratitude of William of Orange, but then it emerged that Anjou had also been in negotiations with Alexander, offering to surrender the crucial points in the military defence plans in exchange for the control of Brussels. In an even more dastardly move, he wanted to surrender Cambrai for a handsome sum of money. Even Catherine was reduced to utter shame over such blatant treachery: "The mere rumour of it brings to me and all France so much shame and infamy that I almost die of displeasure and dislike even to think of it".

Never abashed, Anjou tried to redeem his situation by offering his troops to fortify the Netherlanders, but they had had more than enough and told him to go home.

And this he did. His ever-indulgent mother forgave him and persuaded the King to do the same, but it was not many months before consumption overtook him and in 1584 he died.

Naturally Catherine was struck with grief. The King was not. Surprisingly, Elizabeth also mourned Anjou and she was reported as having cried for three weeks.

Within the year, William of Orange was also dead, assassinated at the behest of Philip, who had put a price of 25,000 crowns upon his head.

The death of Anjou brought the House of Valois ever nearer to its end. It also brought Henri Navarre in direct line to the throne. As he was a Protestant, this was something all the Catholics in France, not to mention Philip in Spain, were desperate to prevent. The very day Anjou had died the King had told Navarre he could assure himself of the throne and bring peace to the nation, if only he would declare himself a Catholic. A grim indication of what would happen were he not to do this had been shown through the Catholic reaction on the signing of the Treaty of Monsieur.

But Navarre refused.

So in December 1584 and in the greatest secrecy, the Guises met representatives of the King of Spain at Joinville at the heart of the Guise estates and where they were unlikely to be discovered. There they signed the Treaty of Joinville. In effect, it amounted to treason. Initially they avoided this by saying the charges were against the King's ministers, not the King personally. They were careful, too, to incorporate a eulogy to Catherine. The real gist was that within a month of the death of Henri III, the League of the Holy Trinity would issue a manifesto. The Cardinal of Bourbon, who was one of the Guise family, would become King. The superiority of his claim lay in that he combined being a Cardinal of the Roman Church with being First Prince of the Blood. Once this was announced, the Guises would conduct an offensive until both France and the Netherlands were rid of the Huguenots once and for all.

The entire concept was to be financed by Philip, flush with all his silver. He agreed to provide the Guise with sufficient arms for 17,000 men. He would also pay the Guises 50,000 ecus a month, starting immediately civil war broke out. He would, of course, give full recognition to the League. In return for his support Philip would have the City of Cambrai returned to him. In practice, it meant the control of France would be held by Philip, with the Guises as his puppets.

The conspirators immediately started preparing the ground by issuing pamphlets and sermons vilifying Catherine. But her intelligence network had already detected the increased activity. She immediately realised it would completely undermine anything Henri could do to prevent Philip from having complete control of the Netherlands.

Once again she summoned her energy and put her faith in her powers of persuasion. She decided to tackle the Guises first and negotiate with them in their Nancy stronghold. They kept her waiting more than four weeks. Admittedly this delay was in part due to her ill health. Physically, life was very painful for her. Gout was causing her acute pain in her side. She had a bad cough, earache, toothache, pain in the arm and frequent headaches. She was so ill she often had to conduct negotiations from her bed. But her determination remained intact. When the Cardinal Bourbon tried to play her game and made out he was too ill to go to her, she threatened to take a litter and come and see him.

The Guises knew that while they wanted to keep Catherine engaged, they must not seem too close to her or they would raise the King's suspicions. In the words of the Cardinal: "Little by little without anyone finding it out you will gradually take to yourself the power and authority of both". However after a further two months Catherine realised they were just playing for time so that they could strengthen their arms, so she temporally fobbed Philip off with an agreement virtually banning the Huguenots from France, not that she had the least intention of implementing it. Next she turned her attention to the Huguenots. Pope Gregory had taken it upon himself to excommunicate Navarre. The move aroused widespread indignation at such blatant interference in what was essentially an internal affair.

Navarre gained a further advantage through his retaliation. With considerable cheek, he put up a poster on the Pasquino statue in Rome defying the Pope. Catherine still believed her best hope lay in trying to persuade him to convert to Catholicism. Even after all these years, she still could not understand that honour and conscience govern a person's faith rather than negotiation and manoeuvring. When she turned up on his doorstep, Navarre also kept finding excuses to postpone a meeting. After three months she realised that he, too, was playing the waiting game; he was seeking more time in which to build up arms.

It now became clear that both sides had used her to their own advantage. It was a situation she would never have tolerated in her youth. It was yet another sign that, with the frailty of old age, her negotiating powers were failing. And now it was the turn of the King to lose power. The Nuncio succinctly summed up the atmosphere at court: "Here there is war within and without - religious factions - political factions - Catholics and Protestants - Politiques and Leaguers... The hate of the people for the government is great and the King, in spite of his power, is poor and his prodigality makes him poorer. He shows remarkable piety and at the same time detests the Holy League. He is about to make war on the heretics and is jealous of the success of the Catholics. He wants the defeat of the heretics and is also afraid to have them defeated. He fears the defeat of the Catholics and desires it. These conflicting feelings make him distrust his own thoughts".

Under intense pressure from the Catholic League, Henri was forced to remove all the privileges he had extended to the Huguenots even going so far as to have Navarre excluded from the throne and declare that the aged Cardinal de Bourbon was his true heir.

The outlook in the Netherlands also looked bleak. Now that William of Orange and Anjou were both dead, the Duke of Parma's armies were encountering little opposition and the Dutch rebels were becoming really hard pressed. But on the other hand, the Dutch were at the same time showing willing when they offered Elizabeth sovereignty. If she had been a man, she might well have accepted it. But while Elizabeth was greedy for flattery, it did not extend to a greed for honours. She realised that if she accepted, it would be without any practical advantage. It would merely raise Philip's ire still more. Instead she secretly sent her secretary, William Davidson, to the Netherlands to negotiate the Treaty of Nonesuch. In this she actually committed herself to providing 4,000 troops to relieve Antwerp and agreed to keep them at her expense for a further three months. She also agreed to loan the Dutch 126,000 until the end of the war. But, as usual, although Dutch success was vitally important to her, she still required her reward. When peace returned, the Dutch would give her Flushing. This time she was as good as her word and in December 1585 Leicester landed in Holland leading a considerable force of volunteers.

She still did not want to increase Philip's animosity any more than necessary, so she gave Leicester what must be one of the most extraordinary orders for any commander going to war. He must "avoid at all costs any decisive action with the enemy".

In their ignorance the Dutch hailed him as their saviour and accorded him a great welcome. Elizabeth had foreseen this too and warned him, as her emissary, not to accept any honour the Dutch might offer. On landing Leicester found the situation dire. He arrived too late to save Antwerp and now Alexander was advancing on Holland and Zealand in the south. In the north east, though, the Huguenots were still holding on to Groningen. Initially Leicester succeeded in repelling Alexander at Grave. However his forces were severely undermanned. Added to which, while he himself was merely extravagant, his officers were embezzling on a colossal scale. Elizabeth had fixed a cap for the total cost of the war at £126,000 (£126,180.10s, to be precise). It proved a fictitious amount and soon she was wondering how it could be that though she poured in £24,000, then £52,000, leading to a final total of £160,000. Even so the men on the ground were not being properly paid; they were even starving.

Then Leicester did a foolish thing. The Dutch invited him to become their Governor General and in direct contradiction to orders, he accepted. Elizabeth, still anxious not to be too closely associated with Protestantism in Europe, was furious. "We could never have imagined" she wrote, "had we not seen it fall out in experience, that a man raised up by ourselves would have in so contemptible a sort broken our commandment". But she did not want to offend the Dutch, so a compromise was reached to the utter humiliation of Leicester. She instructed that the post was to be officially redefined by placing the Governor General under the direction of the Estates General. This way she could not be associated in a direct chain of command.

To make her disapproval completely clear, she ordered Leicester's humiliation. She instructed an emissary to read out her letter of disapproval before a full session of the Dutch Council of State, so that all would know about it. She also instructed that Leicester must stand close by throughout the proceedings. Not even this retribution meant that Elizabeth had forgiven him, and she took the earliest opportunity to recall him. But once back at court his charm and magnetism persuaded Elizabeth to forgive him. He was lucky too, for the full harvest of his incompetence only became clear after he had left. He was able to – and did – put all the blame on those of his deputies still in the Netherlands. Part of the problem was the plague. Before long it had reduced the English troops by half, too few, in fact, to maintain all the garrisons. Deventer had to be surrendered.

At the same time Alexander was gaining advantages politically; he was subtly playing on the fragile alliance between the Huguenots and the Catholics. Soon he had them at loggerheads again. Then he laid Sluys under siege. Flushing would be next. Desperate not to let the deep sea port fall into Spanish hands, Elizabeth accepted all Leicester's excuses and in 1587 she sent him out again with reinforcements of

5,000 men and a further £30,000 in cash. Sluys fell almost as soon as Leicester had landed, so he could hardly be blamed for that. Part of his job now was to counter Alexander's policy and try and reconcile the various Dutch groups and renew the alliance. But he was ham fisted. He unwittingly allied himself to one of the political parties and thereby offended all the others. He offended the people of Holland and Zealand by trying to prohibit their trade with Japan. All in all, from a practical point of view, he was less Alexander's hindrance than his aid. To cap matters, it was not long before he was quarrelling with his subordinates.

After he had been out six months, Elizabeth refused to send any more help and instead recalled him for the second time. Now she had to look for another way of keeping the Netherlands pot of trouble bubbling. Here again she could no longer look to France for help. By now William of Orange's brother Maurice of Nassau had got the Dutch in hand and once again Alexander was at bay.

Eventually Philip was to overreach himself. First of all he weakened his Netherlands presence by ordering his troops to start preparing for an invasion of England. At the same time he ordered part of his army to invade France. It was altogether too ambitious, and Maurice was able to cut off Philip's fortresses on the Maas. Even so it was another ten years before the Dutch could at last claim that the United Provinces of the Netherlands were genuinely free from all Spanish control.

Compared to the Netherlands, Scotland had become of little relevance to England. In 1582 the young King was kidnapped by the Ruthven family and held prisoner for a year. Elizabeth's council urged her to take advantage of the situation and invade, but she merely promised to use her influence and did nothing more. Instead she waited till his release before signing a treaty with him allying Scotland with England rather than any other country. In the unlikely event of an invasion, he was to provide forces – for all that was worth. But with it he sold his soul. For these small tokens he was to receive a pension of £4,000 a year. There were to be pensions, too, for several of his advisers. As things turned out, it was a move well timed by Elizabeth. It would not be long before she would be glad of his indulgence over his mother.

Over so many years of incarceration, Mary's attitude had inevitably changed. Used to the strong family links that surrounded her during her upbringing in France, she failed to realise that her son had forsaken her. In fact his tutor, George Buchanan, had brought him to hate her as a harlot who had helped murder his father and then married the murderer. She was not to know Elizabeth had her letters, and even the presents she had sent him, censored or confiscated. So when the Regent Morton had been assassinated, Mary had rejoiced, believing that her son was at last abandoning the heretics who had brought him up and that he was planning to declare war on England so as to release her. All that was necessary, she believed, was the support of Spain. She had grown less concerned over Scottish affairs and had no idea how hopeless her cause had become.

Due to the machinations of Walsingham, her French contacts were now largely illusory. He had infiltrated her Council in Paris. Maddison Gray, her ambassador to London, had come to the conclusion that his interests were better placed with Elizabeth than with his incarcerated mistress. Walsingham was continuously uncovering plots to put her on the throne of England. None of them were very serious, but they were becoming so numerous that he, and indeed Parliament, felt there was always the danger that one of them might succeed. So Walsingham lay in wait for a plot which he felt sure he could nurture until it incriminated Mary convincingly. He had Mary removed to Chartley, where she was in effect held incommunicado and where Walsingham could exercise better control.

In 1586 he felt he had at last found the right plot. It was being hatched by a young Catholic called Anthony Babington. It was uncomfortably close to Elizabeth's person, for six of the fellow conspirators were Catholics actually at court. They were all from the younger generation who had not experienced the ruthless days under Edward VI and did not appreciate the Queen's latitude. They were sending messages hidden in the bungs of beer barrels. The brewer was in the pay of Philip, but he was also in the pay of Walsingham – and Walsingham was paying more.

At last came the moment to pounce. One of Babington's notes had just the incriminating phrase he needed: "the usurping competitor (meaning Elizabeth) must be dispatched". All he needed now was for Mary's corroboration. She fell into the trap when she replied: "When all is ready, the six gentlemen (those at court) must be set to work and you will provide that on their design being accomplished, I may be myself rescued from this place". It not only involved Mary in the plot to escape and take the throne but it showed she was conniving at Elizabeth's murder.

Even with this evidence, Walsingham wanted to make doubly sure. He forged a postscript in which Mary was supposed to be asking for the names of the six conspirators in Court. The French ambassador was also suspected of being in the plot and Walsingham had him confined to his house. A commission of 40, including the full Council, went to Fotheringhay, where Mary had been moved, and there they duly found her guilty.

The execution was postponed until Parliament had been consulted. Elizabeth did her best to influence them against calling for the death sentence "and now though my life hath been dangerously shot at, yet I protest there is nothing hath more grieved me than that one not differing from me in sex, of like rank and degree, of the same stock, and most nearly allied unto me in blood, hath fallen into so great a crime... and even yet, though the matter become thus far, if she would truly repent, and no man would undertake her cause against me, and if my life all depended thereupon, I would unfeigned, most willingly pardon her".

She even wrote to Mary herself: "You have in various ways and manners attempted to take my life and to bring my kingdom to destruction by bloodshed. I have never proceeded as harshly against you but have on the contrary protected and maintained you like myself. The treasons will be proved to you and all made manifest. Yet it is my will that you answer the nobles and peers of the Kingdom as if I were myself present. I therefore require, charge and command that you make answer for I have been well informed of your arrogance. Act plainly and without reserve and you will sooner be able to obtain favour from me".

Parliament hesitated, particularly because they were unsure what would be the reaction of James VI. After all, it was quite likely that he would become King of England within their lifetime and it was his mother they were about to condemn to death. But James showed little inclination to help save his mother. For instance, he could have threatened to break off the Anglo Scottish alliance. But he had merely said: "It was meet for her to meddle with nothing but prayer and serving God". However, for appearance he wrote a strong letter to Elizabeth. It did infuriate her, but in the wrong way, because he included some crude remarks about her mother's execution. Elizabeth always held her mother's memory in great respect. However James's complete indifference to his mother's fate became clear when he sent a message expressing pleasure that Elizabeth had survived the plot.

As for Catherine, she also showed complete indifference, so it was evident that France would not take any action. Only Henri acted, but that was merely to write asking for his sister-in-law to be spared. Unfortunately Elizabeth so disliked him that it had the reverse effect and merely hardened her heart. So only Elizabeth's signature now lay between Mary and her execution. While Mary's plotting against Elizabeth's life may have formed part of the problem, the other part lay in Elizabeth's scruples. Execution would be an act contrary to her fundamental principle: the sanctity of an anointed sovereign. It is the heart of the coronation ceremony and confirms the approval of God. It was interpreted as giving the sovereign the absolute right to rule. So naturally it was a belief considered sacrosanct among all monarchs. If it were to be broken, kings and queens everywhere would become vulnerable.

However, over the years Elizabeth had modified her views. When the Pope had condoned attempts to assassinate her he was breaking the mysticism. He had, in effect, put all crowned heads into "open season". There was another point that caused Elizabeth to hesitate. She felt sure that Mary's existence was the only thing preventing Philip from launching an invasion. She also realised that Mary would probably try and do everything possible to have herself acclaimed a martyr to the Catholic faith. Consequently Mary's one great fear was that she should die in obscurity. This, of course, is exactly what Elizabeth would have preferred, and she started testing the possibilities.

First she told her ministers that she would be glad of any means to be rid of this turbulent woman and hinted it would be well if her life was ended in some nefarious way. She had in fact, tried to enter such a conspiracy with the Earl Morton four years before. He had a reputation for villainy which made him the obvious choice to do the deed. It was well known that he had played a major part in the murder of Bothwell.

He did agree in principle. However he suspected that if it was done in secret and later uncovered, Elizabeth would place all the blame upon him. So he insisted that she should be clearly associated with the deed by supplying 2,000 English soldiers to be on guard at the execution. Then, before any agreement could be reached, Moreton was dead.

The reaction by Elizabeth's council to this current proposition was quite different. They still held to the principle that an anointed sovereign was sacrosanct. They were horrified. They would have nothing to do with it.

She then tried her gaoler, Sir Amyas Paulet, suggesting he might in some way shorten the life of that Queen who was threatening the life of his sovereign. Paulet had told Walsingham that he would kill Mary rather than hand her over to any rescue attempt. He considered that to be no more than his duty as gaoler. He was even prepared to follow Elizabeth's earlier instructions, and when Mary had been taken ill, he had stolen into her apartment and confiscated her money. But when it came to cold-blooded murder, no. That was completely against his Christian principles. He wrote to the Queen: "I am so unhappy to have lived to see this unhappy day in which I am required by direction from my most gracious Sovereign to do an act which God and the law forbidith."

There is no doubt that the problem was taking its toll on Elizabeth. She was having to fight against her fundamental principles for her own safety. Her handwriting over this period became ragged. And still she dithered over making the final decision. She had the death warrant drawn up, but refrained from actually signing it. Finally, stooping to dishonour yet again, she chose a day when Cecil was ill and his assistant Davidson was in attendance on her. That day she finally signed the deed, telling Davidson to set the great seal upon it and take it to Walsingham with the ironic remark "I fear the grief thereof will go near to killing him outright".

Still afraid of the possible accusation of having butchered a martyr, Elizabeth gave orders that all the attendants except those closest to her should be dismissed. Nearer the execution date, her private chaplain was banished. In a cold, calculating move, which Mary might well have been interpreted as an insult, Elizabeth chose to replace him with the Bishop of Peterborough. He was a particularly stalwart Protestant.

So it was on 7th February 1587, the eve of the execution, that Mary was told she would not be allowed to have any of her attendants present. It was feared that they might demonstrate or, even worse, they might rush forward and dip their kerchiefs in her blood, thus providing the church with relics. However for once Paulet relented, and in the end he agreed to allow them to be present, but only after Mary had strictly instructed them not to cause any trouble.

But Mary still had her triumph. When, she took off her seemly black gown, preparatory to kneeling before the block, she revealed a scarlet petticoat. Her attendants then stepped forward and gave her sleeves, so that she was prepared to die entirely dressed in the colour of blood; the liturgical colour of martyrdom. When the Bishop started praying for her soul, she began out-praying him in Latin. After he stopped, she switched to English, praying for all Catholics in England and for Elizabeth herself.

Once the execution had been carried out, still afraid of being accused of having caused the death of a Catholic martyr, Elizabeth made strenuous efforts to disclaim all responsibility. She had only signed the warrant "for safety's sake"; She never meant it to be sent; she placed the blame on Davidson and had him impeached by the star chamber and committed to the Tower. At first she blamed Cecil as well. Fortunately, knowing his mistress well, Cecil had taken the precaution of putting the signed warrant before the council, and at his request they had endorse it.

It was several months before she felt sure there was not going to be any immediate violent reaction among the English Catholics. Only then did she re-instate Cecil at court. Fortunately it still left time for him to point out that Davidson's execution would cause widespread reaction against her.

James described the act as a "preposterous and strange procedure", hardly a damning condemnation. He also cut off communication with

England. That was the least he could be expected to do. There were rumours that he was plotting with the French.

Cecil wrote to his secretary pointing out that past experience showed the French would be unlikely to support him if it came to the crunch. He suggested James would do much better working in collaboration with England. Elizabeth also wrote explaining her version of the circumstances behind the "unintended" execution. How much James believed her, and presumably it was not much, is not known. But no doubt remembering his pension, he confined his protests to saying he felt he must draw attention to how aware he was of the anger among the Scottish people that their Queen should have been executed by a foreign power.

Catherine was still pursuing her matrimonial dreams, though circumstances now demanded that they should be on a more modest scale. Indeed this time, after some false moves, she succeeded in marrying off her favourite granddaughter. Her first choice for husband had been the Duke of Nemours. Catherine started negotiating with his mother, and the dowager Duchess agreed to the match and even to a Catholic service. But then Catherine had what she thought was an even better idea; her granddaughter should marry the Grand Duke of Florence. Admittedly arrangements for the earlier wedding had already reached an advanced stage, but money was of no importance to Catherine when it came to seeing family advancement.

She pacified the outraged Duchess with a gift of 100,000 scudi, which was comfortably more than the costs the Duchess had already spent. Next she persuaded the Grand Duke of Florence to accept her granddaughter on payment of 600,000 crowns and her property in Tuscany. The wedding took place and there was dancing in her apartments. It was about the last moment of joy in her life.

The growing power of the Guises, now that they were backed by

Philip, stirred Elizabeth into action. She sent Navarre £15,000 and dispatched Sir Horatio Palavicino to Germany to raise £23,000 mercenaries to help Henri of Navarre defend himself. Cecil and Walsingham together had to persuade Elizabeth that this was a ridiculously low budget. In any case it was too late for that year's campaigning season, so Elizabeth agreed to loan Navarre double the amount which he felt sufficient to prove his salvation.

With both the Guises and the Huguenots now well financed, Henri felt he could let them fight one another until both parties were completely exhausted. Then he could mobilise his own forces, considerably enlarged with mercenaries, and step in to dictate his terms to both parties. Full of confidence, he set out to raise his own troops and left Catherine as Regent of his Kingdom. While she may have lost much of her political power, Catherine now showed that at 68 her dynamism in organisation remained as strong as ever. "I would never have believed the trouble she takes, even beyond the natural limits of the strength of her age, unless I had seen it and the great zeal she shows and her hopes that the outcome of it all will be good".

She arranged supplies and conducted defensive tactics to prevent the Huguenots from attacking in the rear. She took precautions against any hostile fleet that might be hovering off the coast of Brittany. She instructed a company of gendarmes to stay in Normandy in case of revolt there. She organised a scorched-earth policy against the German mercenaries. Grain was brought into strongly-fortified cities. As for the rest, mill wheels were thrown into the rivers and all blacksmith forges and equipment were destroyed.

But the King's hopes were dashed. The Huguenots' hired mercenaries merely marched around France living off the peasants and failing to fight anyone before they went off home. So instead of the Guises being seriously weakened in battle, they remained as strong as ever.

Now fearing for his life, the King forbade the Duke de Guise to enter Paris, but in complete disregard he arrived. He lulled the King into a false sense of security by having only seven people in his retinue, but it quickly transpired that over the past few weeks he had been dribbling supporters into the city. They now emerged, so when the Duke set out for the Louvre to present his compliments or, nearer to the point, his demands, he had around him 30,000 supporters. Under such circumstances, the King did not dare arrest him. To his credit, he limited his precautions against the threatening crisis. He could have called on the Swiss mercenaries, whom he still had to hand, and conducted a violent defence. Instead he insisted that the safety of the Parisians must take priority and appealed to Guise not to massacre his passive troops. His advisers did not know what more could be done. He lost his temper and, gathering about him such regality as he still had, left and was about to try and humiliate Guise when Catherine took him aside. She pointed out that all Paris was behind the Duke. So when Guise eventually left the Palace it was with all the swagger of having the King surrender to his demands. Thereupon the Guise followers put up barricades and took control of the city, causing Catherine an indignity that would have been unthinkable in earlier times. On her way to negotiate with the Duke, his supporters refused to let her carriage forced to take a litter. The King had to negotiate. Wisely, he handed the discussions over to his mother. Then, while she was still negotiating, he slipped out of Paris to take refuge in Chartres. This left Guise free to take command of the château of Vincennes, the arsenal and the Bastille. Henri's flight merely postponed the day of reckoning.

Now Catherine embarked on the very last of her missions of conciliation. Normally she held the opinion that "Time brings often more things than one would think and those are praised who know how to yield to save themselves", but now she was forced to admit "I have never been in such trouble before nor with less light to see my way out of it. Unless God puts his hand to it I do not know what will happen".

She had never before shrunk from meeting a serious situation head on. Rather, she would extemporise. But now the best she could do was to persuade Guise to meet the King at Chartres. The resulting agreement gave Guise all the power he craved, short of the crown itself. The King agreed to return to Paris and to acknowledge Cardinal Bourbon as his heir presumptive. He also agreed to field two armies to fight Navarre and the Huguenots.

Henri then broke his word. Instead of going to Paris, he went to Blois. There he called a meeting of the Estates. Next, without warning or consultation with anyone, he dismissed his eight closest advisers, most of whom had been appointed by Catherine. He dismissed them overnight, telling them to go immediately to their homes and stay there until he told them they could come out. To show his independence, he replaced them with men who were virtually unknown but whose loyalty he felt he could rely upon. None of them was a Guise or a Montmorency. He told them not to appoint any subordinates who had served in the previous council and that they were not to go near Catherine.

Catherine was furious, but recognised that the final vestige of her authority had been stripped from her. In fact it made no real difference, and during the weeks leading up to Christmas, the King continued to dance to the Guise tune.

Everyone realised that the struggle was now for the crown itself. It called for drastic action, and Henri took it. The Duke was well aware of the danger surrounding him. By December 1588 he was receiving numerous warnings against attending the next Council meeting. Some were direct; some were mysterious, as when he found a note in his napkin. The night before the crucial meeting, he received nine separate warnings not to attend it. His response in each case was "the King won't dare". None the less, Guise kept a large bodyguard around him, so he had no fears when he attended the council.

During the meeting he received a summons to attend the King in his bedroom. As he entered an ante room, eight of the Kings' men raised their hands in salute. He was not to know that in their loose sleeves they concealed unsheathed knives. When he opened the door to the King's room, he saw eight assassins facing him. Realising the situation, he turned, but his escape was blocked by the men he had just passed.

The King's caution in having so many assassins proved fully justified. In the subsequent fight, Guise punched two of them in the face and knocked four more to the ground. When at last the King had Guise lying dead at the foot of his bed, he crowed like the coward he was, "Look at him, the King of Paris. Not so great now." He had the Cardinal of Guise murdered next day.

For once Catherine had no foreknowledge of the murder. In fact she was resting in the room below, and made enquires as to what all the noise was about. Her daily routine over the last five months of her life was almost a return to the years she had spent as the docile wife of Henri II. She wrote numerous letters trying to arrange considerations for her friends. It was left to Henry of Navarre to put her life into true perspective when he said "What could a woman do, left by her husband with five little children in her arms and two families of France who were thinking of grasping the crown, our own Bourbons and the Guises? Was she not compelled to play strange parts to deceive first one and then the other in order to guard, as she did, two sons who successfully reigned though the wise conduct of that shrewd woman. I am surprised that she never did worse."

The Pope did not look so kindly upon the murder of Guise and excommunicated the King. The Sorbonne declared him to be a murderer, and the League became openly revolutionary. Since he could hardly expect the Guise family to remain his ally, the King had to join forces with his heir, Henry of Navarre. But even before the year was out, he was himself assassinated by a crazed monk. Navarre claimed the throne as Henri IV and the new Duke of Guise revived the civil war.

PART V

ELIZABETH HOLDS THE FORT 1588-1603

All this while Elizabeth happily continued to harass Philip by raiding his ships. Drake was encouraged to emerge from retirement and was soon ready with another major flotilla. The destination was the West Indies; the intention, to capture Spanish silver. It obviously had the Queen's backing, for 20 large ships would have been beyond the scope of any private enterprise.

Through clever deception, Drake led Philip to believe he was coming to raid a Spanish port. Finding he did not have sufficient ships to provide adequate protection, Philip panicked and commandeered all ships at that moment anchored in his ports, regardless of nationality. They included some English. Elizabeth was furious and demanded – and got – financial compensation. Meanwhile Drake sailed smoothly past the Spanish coast to reach a totally unprepared West Indies.

But Philip had had enough.

Elizabeth's suspicion that once Mary was dead Philip would go ahead with his ambition to invade England proved correct. He now had the money to carry it out. But there was added fervour in his mission. Since there was no Mary to put upon the throne, he felt that as husband of the former Queen of England he had strong claims himself, and duly made it known that he should become King.

One of the first incidents that made Elizabeth realise how serious matters were becoming happened while she was in Greenwich Palace. Her attention was drawn to a ship passing up the Thames and routinely firing a salute. On a whim she sent for the Captain, who was returning from Spain. He told her how he had seen 27 galleons in Lisbon which were "not ships but floating fortresses". So the messages Walsingham's agents had been sending back, messages warning that the Spanish fleet was far larger than anything needed to defend the Netherlands, looked as though they might be true.

Some of Elizabeth's Councillors were not so sure. They, like Catherine, thought the fleet was destined for Rochelle, others for Flanders, but still most agreed that it was destined for England. Elizabeth started to prepare. She had already shown again her aptitude in choosing the right person. Some years before Hawkins had become "respectable", in that he held a commercial licence and was in semi-retirement. But she had appointed him to be treasurer of the Navy. At last there was a realist in the post, and he ensured the arm was brought up to strength. Soon he had built a number of medium and small boats. Altogether the English were now able to muster 44 ships. Nineteen of them were major fighting ships and they were to be supplemented by armed merchantmen and privateers, 40 of them over 100 tons.

The London city merchants showed a gratifying degree of patriotism. They asked what help they were expected to provide. When they were told it was to finance 5,000 men and 15 ships, they responded by providing funds for 10,000 men and 30 ships. But then, of course, they were the main beneficiaries of the raids on Spanish shipping, and were anxious the trade should not be disrupted.

Most of the other English townships complained bitterly over their share of the burden. In contrast Philip was advised that he would need all of 500 ships. The figure brought him up to reality. He had let his navy deteriorate to the extent that there was now no cannon shot to be found in his entire arsenal. When he placed an order for major ship construction, he learned that 90 per cent of the materials required had to be imported. There had to be copper from Hungary and gunpowder, only available from Germany or Italy. Even such major accessories as the sails and oars could only be made in Italy. And, most demeaning of all, he had to go to England for tin.

These widespread components well illustrated the fundamental differences that had developed within the European navies. Up to this time, both Spanish and French naval power had been centred in the Mediterranean. The warships depended on slave oar power, which was only practical in comparatively calm waters. Those Spanish ships which did incorporate sail were designed essentially for cargo. In a sea surrounded by land, most sailors still had no need to calculate longitude. Navigation did not amount to much more than hugging the land and guesswork. In contrast the English ships were built from experience, through having a long seaboard facing the Atlantic.

With his part-time interest in boatbuilding, Hawkins introduced designs which revolutionised warfare tactics. The customary battle manoeuvre had been to fire just the one broadside, for the guns were placed so close together that it took too long to reload them. The troops would then jump into the rigging ready for when they became locked together with the opposing ship. Then they would board and fight on the combined deck area as though on a battlefield. To make things easier, the ships were designed with a high fo'c'sle, or tower, so that snipers could shoot down upon the decks.

The drawback was that should these ships venture into the heavy swells normal in the Atlantic they were in imminent danger of turning turtle, so Hawkins designed the low "race build" ship. This was about three lengths longer than their breadth and the fo'c'sle was much lower. He also brought the masts further forward and made the sails flatter, which made the ships not only faster but much more manoeuvrable.

All this was additional to the major revolutionary ideas Henry VIII had previously introduced for his warships. One was to mount the ship's cannon along the length of the ship so that their number could be considerably increased. As a result they could fire broadsides, keeping the enemy at a distance with quite devastating results. This was despite the fact that gunnery was still a highly inaccurate procedure. It was a shortcoming soon to be proved in the battle of Gravelines, when the English fired 100,000 rounds of grape shot but only 20 Spaniards were killed. The main damage was through reducing the sails and rigging to tatters, thus rendering the ship a floating hulk.

The wealth of knowledge held by individual English seafarers was tapped, largely because they held a social advantage. The Spanish aristocracy at this time held their sailors to be socially inferior and little more than slave drivers. They were given orders without being properly consulted. In contrast, sailors from Devon and Cornwall such as Drake and Hawkins had made fortunes, were accepted in court circles and, indeed, duly knighted. So although the English combined fleet facing the Armada was under the command of Lord Howard, a man of high rank, Drake was also consulted, and indeed his opinions were frequently the ones acted upon.

Elizabeth at last realised that it was advisable that the raids should concentrate less on booty and more on hampering Philip's preparations with the Armada. So the next sortie comprised 17 vessels with instructions to raid the shipping in Lisbon and the Azores. It had the backing of the City of London, which meant that despite the spoiling intent, the primary purpose still remained the capture of Spanish treasure.

Drake started off by crashing into Cadiz harbour, for the first time using fireships. But it turned out there were only a few supply vessels in the harbour, so their destruction made little difference to Philip's war preparations. Worse, they did not offer up much in prize money.

Drake then sailed to St. Vincent and set up a base at Sagres. From there he went on to the Azores, where he captured a major prize ship worth £140,000, a healthy profit. This rather overshadowed the political value, for he had also drawn the Spanish admiral Santa Cruz temporarily away from command of the now almost complete Armada. Even so, it meant the date on which the Spanish fleet was scheduled to put to sea had to be postponed.

All this time, Elizabeth had been making unofficial contacts outside conventional diplomacy. She was hoping to carry out her own personal coup to pacify Philip. She had opened up several avenues of secret negotiations, and was placing particular hope in a Flemish merchant living in London who was in direct contact with Parma. Her negotiations had been dragging on for some time without any notable progress, yet still she thought she could make a personal triumph. Fatefully, she ordered Drake to reduce the pressure and indeed forbade him to carry out any more raids on the Spanish.

It was also in hope of keeping her secret negotiations going, that she recalled Leicester after only six months of his far from successful Netherlands campaign.

Lord Howard, as Admiral of the Fleet, was the only person with the nerve and social position sufficient to upbraid her openly: "For the love of Jesus, Madam, awake thoroughly and see the villainous treasons round about you against your Majesty and your realm and draw your forces round you".

Elizabeth's astonishing naivety was, of course, a godsend to Philip. He gave instructions that all the strands of negotiations then being conducted should be protracted for as long as possible. The ploy proved successful beyond his greatest expectations. Despite Howard and her Council's warnings, Elizabeth remained stubbornly assured, right up till the end of June. When it eventually became clear, even to her, that she had been hoodwinked, she excused herself by insisting that it was Parma who had first extended peace feelers. She herself had, of course, been highly suspicious, but, appreciating that peace was "the Gift of God", she had feared that her suspicions might spoil a chance for peace. She had, so she said, sent commissioners but found that they were being trifled with. This version of events caused Cecil, Howard, Walsingham, Drake and everyone else in the know to smile behind their fingers.

Philip's plan for the Armada was exactly as had been widely expected. The fleet was to sail from Cadiz up the channel to Calais, where they would collect additional forces to be landed in England. But the Marquess of Santa Cruz warned Philip that a large proportion of the ships assembled in the Netherlands, ready to join the Armada, were not seaworthy. Then Santa Cruz suddenly died, and there was further delay while the Duke Medina Sidonia was appointed as his successor.

In July 1588, Philip again ordered the fleet to sail, but the weather was quite unsuitable. The ships had barely reached Corunna before they had to take refuge in harbour. With few experienced men surviving his earlier decommissioning, the Spanish fleet was now manned largely with novices. Their morale was at a low ebb and a formidable proportion took this opportunity to desert. Medina Sidonia urged Philip to postpone the operation yet again.

Philip's retort was typically curt: "I have dedicated this enterprise to God. Get on then and do your duty". He was further encouraged by news of the night of the Paris barricades. It reassured him that there was no need to fear the French might take advantage of his vulnerability while all his ships were at sea.

Although only too well aware of the need for guarding the nation,

Elizabeth and her Council were, unbelievably, still holding potential booty to the fore in their calculations over the coming invasion. Drake's original instructions, authorised by the Queen, were to split the English fleet in three and attack the Armada even before it had left Spanish waters. They could then go on to capture any cargo vessels within the area. But then, with thoughts of plunder still uppermost, the orders were changed. The fleet was to be divided into four parts. One was to be stationed between Dover and Calais. The second was to be stationed off the Cornwall and Irish coasts to cut off the Armada's escape route once it had entered the straights. The third part was to remain hidden and then, taking advantage of the Armada's absence, attack the coastal shipping off Portugal. The fourth was to go to the Azores and intercept cargo ships returning from the Indies.

When Drake received these instructions, he immediately realised how absurd they were. For a start, Philip's fleet was so large that it would have no trouble in knocking off the two English sections supposed to attack it. Drake sent back an alternative plan in which the entire English fleet was to be concentrated on the Armada itself. Elizabeth received the details and was, of course, indecisive. Although she could have reasonably assumed that the Armada was on its way, she none the less ordered him back to London to discuss the plans further.

At last Drake won her over and she agreed. Then, after he had left London, she, true to form, sent him counter orders; he must not attack the Armada but should concern himself solely with protecting the English coast. Nor was Drake helped when he found that, presumably due to the Queen's niggardliness, the supplies still were not assembled and stowed. Fortunately the prolonged Spanish delay provided another desperately-needed respite, providing sufficient time for the fleet to be fully prepared to sail.

In true Mediterranean fashion, on 28th July 1588 the dense mass of Spanish ships could be seen from the coast of Cornwall as they hugged the English shore on the way to pick up additional forces at Calais. Fortunately, however, they failed to appreciate the double tide in Southampton Water and in the turmoil Howard managed to chivvy them from anchoring in the Solent. Instead they had to go on to the Calais Roads on the south of the Isle of Wight. There they learned there would be further delays before the 17,000 troops, supposed to be waiting for them, would be ready to embark.

As Drake had forecast, the Spanish ships were too many for the English to attack straight on. That night Howard sent in six small fireships. To make them even more fearsome, he had their guns primed so that they went off haphazardly as the flames engulfed them. Though none of them made contact, their fearful appearance against the night sky caused panic. The huge unwieldy Spanish galleons cut their cables and chaos followed. They looked for an opportunity to reassemble in the shoals of Flanders, but the Dutch had removed all the sea marks.

Come the dawn, they could see the English fleet bearing down upon them. Not only were they still in complete disarray but Drake had got onto their windward side. The gales exposed a part of their heeling hulls which would normally have been under the waterline. Well practised in firing from a distance, the English were able to hold them. Altogether, due to the genius of Drake and with not a little help from the weather, Gravelines proved an out-and-out victory.

On land, the Lord Lieutenants had been alerted of their responsibilities for mustering a total of 26,000 foot soldiers to be assembled at Tilbury under the command of Leicester. They were to be supplemented as soon as possible by a further 20,000 men. Elizabeth proved her courage and just how magnificently she could rise to an occasion.

As she rode down to review the troops dressed in white with her orange wig uncovered she looked right royal, carrying a small silver truncheon. She ran a real risk of assassination, but this did not deter her from mingling with the men, rallying their spirits and making her famous speech. In truth, the words so often quoted are more likely to have been written for some later melodrama. But whatever she actually did say she most certainly hit the right note and showed she had lost none of her talent for playing on popular sentiment.

She also showed brazen impudence. The men were not to know that, purely for the sake of economy, she was already exposing them to unnecessary risk. Only three days before she had specified that those men living in the area, and they amounted to about a third of the force, should be stood down. Yet she had no idea how many Spanish troops would be landing, nor whether Parma was sending a large second force from Flushing. As it was unlikely the reserves could be reassembled in time, she was exposing her army to potential massacre.

This time Elizabeth got away with it, but her niggardly attitude proved really disastrous for her unfortunate sailors. Weeks after the battle, Howard was urgently pleading for money to pay the men off and to land the battle casualties, whose numbers were soon being increased by the plague. But Elizabeth's purse strings remained drawn tight. Certainly the navy was still needed to patrol. But she also appreciated that the longer the men were kept at sea the more would die and the fewer she would eventually have to pay.

Meanwhile the scattered Spanish fleet could only escape by sailing into the treacherous North Sea and round the coast of Scotland. Again a lack of knowledge of the area took its toll. They did not understand the Gulf Stream and it was carrying them north and east, so that they turned south too soon. Added to this, blind adherence to Mediterranean habits proved too strong. Despite warnings, the Spanish captains persisted in hugging the land, so many ships were dashed on the rocks along the Irish coast. It brought the grim total of Spanish losses to about 100 ships at a cost of 5,000 lives and £400,000.

Following the defeat of the Armada, Elizabeth's first idea had been to capture the Spanish treasure fleet, but then she learned how many ships had survived and were now safely back in port. She changed her policy, placing less emphasis on prize money and accepting the need to prevent as many as possible of the remaining Spanish ships from sailing again. Consequently Drake was able to polish his routine, entering the Spanish ports and destroying ship replacements, sometimes while they were still under construction.

However, this was not in itself very remunerative. Since Elizabeth still preferred to put up only part of the cost of any treasure expedition, she had to share the venture with sponsors from the City. The prize money also determined the crew's bonus. It was therefore not surprising that the expeditions tended to favour the plunder aspect of their work, and she found that the sailors were not always carrying out their instructions with all the diligence she could have wished. She tried having one of her clerks of the council sail with the fleet to make sure her orders were carried out, but Drake disregarded the clerk and paid no attention to his protests.

Drake's first major sortie, to completely dismantle the remnants of the Armada, was to Santander and San Sebastian, where it was thought that the Spanish ships had taken refuge. Only after wreaking havoc there did his orders allow him to proceed to the more profitable target of Lisbon. It was also suggested that he might re-establish Don Antonio, but Elizabeth had learned to be rather sceptical over the prince's claim that under his leadership the populace would immediately rise up and join the English in freeing Portugal from Span, so she insisted that before landing they must establish that there was adequate support within the country. Only if it really seemed sufficient could they go ahead, throw out the Spanish and install the Prince.

Inevitably, Elizabeth changed her mind and sent a message telling Drake not to enter the harbours. Once again she was too late, for he had already set sail. Not that it mattered, for Drake chose to ignore the plan he already had. Instead he sailed to Corunna, where, indeed, he found five ships and duly dispatched them. He then bypassed Santander and San Sebastian, since they were rather out of his way. Instead he went straight on to take the fat prize of Lisbon.

The plan was to launch a combined land and sea attack. The troops would be landed 45 miles north of Lisbon and would then advance on the city. It would form half of a pincer movement, which would be completed when the Navy entered Lisbon from the sea. Things did not start well, as the land siege train did not materialise. It was Elizabeth's responsibility; either she was carrying out one of her economy drives or she simply forgot about it.

The next setback occurred when the leaders in Don Antonio's party betrayed him and the locals refused to rise up in support. Instead of Philip feeling the pincers, Drake found he had lost 11,000 men, so he called off the whole campaign.

After a week of deliberation, Drake and his men fell to temptation and sailed on regardless to the Azores. But they were out of luck. A southerly wind blew the fleet ignominiously back to England. On his return Drake had to explain why his troops had been decimated, none of the objectives had been achieved and, most damaging of all, there were very small returns for the £100,000 that had been invested with him.

Elizabeth decided against any more naval-assisted operations.

But it only needed a year to pass before her desire for booty was rekindled. She became interested in a private enterprise organised by Raleigh and Howard. This proved far more successful and captured a carrack stuffed with spices, silks and jewels from the East with an estimated value of £250,000. Of this Elizabeth took £80,000, which just about doubled her income for that year. It left £60,000 for distribution among the investors. The remaining £110,000 was absorbed by "slippage", which showed that it was just as difficult to impose financial control in the Navy as in the Army.

Throughout the last ten years of her reign, Elizabeth concentrated on thwarting Philip and his crusades by supporting Henri IV on land rather than on sea. Since the murder of the Duke of Guise and his powerful brother the Cardinal of Lorraine in 1588, Philip had decided he should be ruling France. His first idea was for his daughter Isabella Clara to be made Queen, on the strength of her being Catherine's granddaughter. Then he had a better idea. Instead of influencing France indirectly, he would actually invade the country. So in July he ordered Alexander to cross the border into France and stop Henri, who was threatening to take Paris from the Guise Catholic faction. Alexander did this successfully before returning to the Netherlands, but the precedent of invading another country, even for such a short period, had been set.

In October 1590, Philip had a stroke of luck. Hawkins, who had been posted along the coast of Brittany to prevent Philip from landing at Brest, was once again tempted by the glister of gold. Chasing what seemed to be easy booty, he left Brest unguarded and Philip sailed in and took Crozon on the western side of the Bay of Biscay, right opposite the Cornish coast.

Admittedly Henry IV had proved himself extremely competent at improving conditions in France. This had extended to the Army, which had become much more professional. However Elizabeth had never been particularly impressed by Henri IV, so it went much against the grain to realise she must help him if the Channel ports were not to fall into the hands of the Spanish.

Early in 1591 she landed 3,000 troops in Brittany, intending to supplement them with an equal number from the Netherlands. Together, so went the plan, they would be able to impart a short sharp surprise which would knock Philip's forces out of France. But the

Dutch strongly objected to the withdrawal of troops from their area. The consequent delay meant that the short sharp shock was neither sharp nor short. The attack staggered on for two more years which can only be described as chaotic.

The prime reason was a diversity of interests. Essex was in charge of the English forces and was bent on besieging Rouen, while Henri was concentrating on besieging Chartres, and neither paid particular attention to the other. Matters were made worse through a series of misunderstandings and changes of mind.

Soon the inevitable outbreak of disease was drastically reducing the already inadequate number of English until Essex had only 1,000 men left fit to fight. So Elizabeth tried juggling the troops stationed in Normandy, Brittany and the Netherlands. In addition to the forces commanded by Essex she had 3,000 troops under the command of John Norreys wandering around Brittany, and another force under Lord Willoughby also in Northern France.

After a year she realised that if they were to be of any use at all, she would have to make up the numbers considerably. No wonder she expressed her frustration over Essex's behaviour: "Where he is or, what he doth or, or what he is to do, we are ignorant", she wrote. At the same time Henri sought to galvanise his forces and asked Elizabeth for 7,000 troops....... even 5,000 would do. But by this time even this was way beyond her resources.

Despite such confusion, English troops did save Dieppe and Brittany from occupation by Philip. Once Henri had said, "Religion is not changed as easily a shirt". But by the middle of 1593 he had become so desperate he took the step he had for so long eschewed. He announced his conversion and was received into the Catholic church. In a moment of indiscretion he explained that "Paris was worth a mass". He was genuine, though the Pope evidently thought he was not for he refused to absolve him from his excommunication for heresy.

This was the moment for which the whole of France had been waiting.

The Parliament of Paris passed a law ruling out all thoughts that the crown should go to Philip's daughter. More importantly, the large number of Catholics who heartily disliked the ambitious family of Guise quickly transferred their allegiance. At the same time, Henri successfully retained the loyalty of his Huguenot allies by allowing them freedom of expression and the right to hold public office. He also paid for the troops that had been defending the 150 cities which had Huguenot governors. With enormously enhanced prestige, he won a series of victories and in March 1594 he was at last able to enter Paris in triumph.

But while Henri was celebrating his triumph, the English had every reason for extreme concern. When the Spanish had retreated, they had still managed to retain Crozon. Almost immediately Philip was seen to be converting the port into a fort. If he was allowed to complete it, he would dominate the considerably more significant port of Brest, directly opposite the English coast.

Elizabeth realised the emergency and said she would send a force of 3,000. No she did not. She changed her mind and reduced it to 2,000, but with some help from the French, the English successfully ousted Philip and the danger was averted.

Another matter that still prevented Henri's triumphs from being complete was Philip's continued occupation of Cambrai. Henri knew he could not take it alone, so he approached Elizabeth for help. She refused, so he hinted he might be driven to making peace with Spain. This certainly had the desired effect, and Elizabeth sent over Sir Henry Upton to try to persuade him against doing any such thing. She could have hardly guessed the result, for it entailed an astonishing conspiracy. Sir Henry had for long been the protégé of the Earl of Essex, who did not feel Elizabeth attached sufficient importance to his hawkish policy towards Europe. So before Sir Henry set sail, the Earl persuaded him not to let the French know of the Queen's offer of help. On the contrary, he must encourage Henri to keep up his threat. This, Essex felt, would help the Queen become more sympathetic to his point of view.

Then matters took a bizarre turn. While still in Paris, Sir Henry became seriously ill. Realising he was dying, he confessed to Henri that Elizabeth would indeed send help. Henri sent the Duke of Bouillon to ratify the alliance, but he need not have bothered, for the Spanish army then set siege to Calais.

Once again it proved an explosive spur to action. Elizabeth immediately sent Henri 2,000 troops, but as was only to be expected, she demanded that once freed, her beloved Calais should be returned to her. This and her other offers and counter-offers dragged on until, yet again, her procrastination caused her to miss the opportunity, and Philip used the delay to capture Calais from the French.

No doubt taking advantage of Elizabeth's humiliation, Henri persuaded her in April 1596 to sign the Treaty of Greenwich. This bound her to supply him with 4,000 troops for six months. She even agreed to pay for them. In return France would give support if England was invaded by Spain. As though Elizabeth could be so easily tied down. She then made it clear that it was only a loan which Henri must repay when the troops left. Henri then persuaded the Dutch to sign as well, thereby making the Treaty of Greenwich a three-nation agreement. But the incorrigible Elizabeth insisted further on a secret clause. The 4,000 troops were really to be only 2,000.

As it happened, Elizabeth actually did have good reason to withhold the 2,000 troops. They were needed when that autumn Philip turned his attention back to Ireland and launched a flotilla of 98 ships. Then one of those storms that seemed to dog Philip's every move sank a third of the fleet off Finisterre. The residue returned to Spain after a loss of a further 2,000 lives.

While Elizabeth was forever changing her mind, it would seem that once Philip had made up his, he was incapable of altering it, regardless of logic. No matter that the first Armada had been a disaster, his supply of silver was still providing him with immense riches, and he remained convinced that he was carrying out God's will. And so he set about building a new Armada. Within two or three years Sir Walter Raleigh was warning the English Parliament that whereas previously one ship in the English fleet could beat ten in the Spanish, now they were just about evenly matched.

This second Armada set sail for England in 1596. Unfortunately God still did not seem to be in support, and the fleet met another disastrous storm. Even a third Armada, launched thirteen years later, met the same fate. Indeed it made Philip bankrupt for the third time, so that even he must have begun to doubt he was on the right evangelical course.

Philip's attempt at the invasion of Ireland had, however, had the advantage of drawing Elizabeth's attention there. Over recent years she had not given it much thought. Indeed she had never given it much thought, and frankly it would have been better if she had left it that way.

But now she was an old woman. Despite all the flummery and artistry to make her look less than her 63 years, she was beginning to feel them. Her health was bad and she had outstayed her time. Of all the young men who had surrounded her during those early days, so full of promise and gaiety, Robert Dudley had died in 1588 and Sir Philip Sidney had died as nobly as he had lived on the battlefield of Zutphen in 1585. Robert Earl of Essex had died on service in Ireland in 1558. Thomas Teenage, who at one time she had favoured almost as much as Leicester, Sir Francis Knollys – they were all were dead now. The man upon whom she had most depended, William Cecil was also dead. While he lay dying she had visited his bedside and with her own hands fed him soup, a gesture she could only have made to an old friend; a far more meaningful acknowledgement of her indebtedness to him than the highest official decoration.

Even her lifelong protagonists were gone. Catherine de Medici had died in 1589 and Philip in 1598. The younger generation surrounding her were every bit as handsome, courtly and talented as their parents had been. Their veneration was if anything even more marked and she just had to look around for all within her view to fall on one knee. But she could not share memories of past experiences with them, nor reminisce with them. It was a recipe for loneliness.

And then from out of all this there emerged a ghost to mock her. When the first Earl of Essex had died in Ireland, his son had been brought up by his stepfather, the Earl of Leicester, who introduced him to Elizabeth as a highly presentable young man of 21. There was so much about the lad – a small gesture, a fleeting expression – which brought the memories flooding back. What had started as indulgence towards him soon changed into something more. Before long he had become her close companion. He was her dancing partner in the evenings, and would play cards with her late into the night. Perhaps because the romance with young Anjou had set a precedent in overlooking extremes of age, the close friendship seemed acceptable without scandal. But while young Essex had the looks, the spirit and the energy of his father, his ambitions far outdistanced his ability. He was dashing beyond rationality, all the time winning wide admiration, but his brave conduct was more often plain foolhardy.

Soon the relationship took on a set pattern. He would wheedle and cajole some concession from the Queen or gain permission to go off on some adventure. In his absence she would feel responsible for him and agonise over his safety. Then he would exasperate Elizabeth by failing to carry through her wishes, sometimes even ignoring them entirely, and he would be recalled under a cloud. But once back at court with his charm and boyish swashbuckling, he would win his way back into her favour.

The first expedition of this ilk had been little more than a schoolboy prank, when he had tried to persuade her to let him join Drake's ambitious raid on Lisbon. She had refused, so in direct contradiction to her wishes, he had escaped from Court and managed to persuade Drake to take him on board the Swiftsure. By the time Elizabeth's messengers had reached the port to bring him back, Drake had set sail. Essex distinguished himself by leading his men on a protracted and difficult march to back up the naval attack on Lisbon, but it all came to nothing.

Soon after this he joined his stepfather in the Netherlands. He so distinguished himself at the battle of Zutphen that he was knighted on the field, before Leicester was recalled in disgrace. In 1591 he badgered Elizabeth into giving him command of 4,000 men to set siege to Rouen. There he was so rash he both infuriated and alarmed her and he returned to England having failed to raise the siege. By 1596 he was back storming Spanish ports, this time Cadiz, but again the objective was not achieved.

Now, in 1599 and against her better judgement, Elizabeth once more succumbed to Essex's persistent requests and appointed him Lord Lieutenant of Ireland. It was a tough assignment and she had originally intended to send the far more experienced Sir Francis Knollys. The English had been virtually ousted from Ireland. Only Leinster remained in English hands. Under the circumstances even the 16,000 troops Essex raised were none too many. In contrast, the staff he assembled for himself was far too large. He made matters worse by spending enormous sums of the Queen's money, yet after three months there was still nothing to show for it. Far from engaging with the enemy he realised Tyrone had a vastly superior army.

Although it was against Elizabeth's express wishes, Essex opened negotiations. Worse, just after receiving instructions not to, he agreed a truce, occasioning a virtual status quo. The next lot of instructions were appropriate for a naughty boy; he was not on any account to return to England until he had completed his task. Yet a few days later he was brushing the ladies in waiting aside as he burst into the Queen's room even while she was still at her toilet. She had not had her hair dressed, so that her baldness was ruthlessly exposed to his gaze.

This time Elizabeth's patience snapped. She paused for reflection, for he was very popular among the people of London, but almost inevitably she decided he must be brought to trial for "great and high contempts and points of misgovernance" in Ireland. Essex was found guilty and stripped of some of his titles. But most damaging of all, Elizabeth refused to renew his sinecure of tax on the import of sweet wines. This made him virtually bankrupt.

His hot-headedness now took a turn bordering on madness. An unsuccessful appeal to King James in Scotland for support in removing his enemies at court indicated the dangerous way his mind was working. The tendency he had always had towards disobedience now teetered into treason. With the encouragement of his more hot-headed companions, he drew up a drastic plan; to seize the court, the Tower of London and the City. Then he would confront the Queen and force her to banish his enemies at court.

For several years Cecil had been schooling his son Robert to take over from him, and in 1596 he had been officially appointed Secretary of State. Robert had got wind of the plan and the Queen sent for Essex to come and explain himself. Instead, Essex held the messenger captive and realising he could no longer take the court by surprise, marched with his supporters to the city. While he was there, trying to obtain the help of the Lord Mayor, Robert barred the streets, making any further advance or retreat impossible. The only way home was along the Thames. This left him devoid of most of his supporters.

Once he had reached home Robert put his house under siege, and there was nothing he could do but surrender. While Elizabeth showed surprising lenience towards his followers, she had no option but to order his execution.

With these ghosts haunting her and the inevitable feeling that she was alone on the wrong side of the divide, she virtually became a recluse. A courtier reported, "she sits in the dark and sometimes with tears to bewail Essex". One day in March 1603 she simply had cushions laid upon the floor. She lay down upon them and virtually willed herself to die.

Considering the way she delayed decisions until the last minute and even then changed her mind, and considering how, apparently on a whim, she would reject the considered opinions of her advisers, it seems strange that her contemporaries – and even her enemies – held her in such esteem. Towards the end of her reign, Cecil, the father, summed up his feeling for her by saying "She was so expert in the knowledge of her realm and estate as no counsellors she had could tell her what she knew not before" and "When her counsellors had said all they could say she would then frame out a wise counsel beyond them".

On her death, the Pope declared "She is certainly a great queen, and were she only a Catholic would be most dear to us. Just look how well she governs. She is only a woman, a mistress of half an island, yet she makes herself feared by all". A courtier in the court of Philip declared "Everyone is amazed to see how cleverly that woman manages in everything. They say that the King thinks and plans while the Queen of England acts. Only England preserves its spirit and increases its reputation. I think that other princes should exchange advisers with the Queen because she alone assaults with impunity the most powerful crown in the world".

Certainly Elizabeth left Europe, and particularly England, in a far safer situation than when she had inherited the throne. Philip had been caged, though it had been largely due to nature. Due to Elizabeth's erratic support, the Netherlands had gained strength to embrace genuine freedom. Death had cleared France of that 'something of the night' that had shrouded Catherine and her sons for so long. And now it had emerged tolerant of both England and the Huguenots.

Whenever Elizabeth had been pressed to name her successor, she had given some very practical reasons against it: "I know the inconstancy of the people of England, how they either mislike the present government and have their eyes fixed upon that person that is next to succeed". Sometimes she would say: "They are more prone to worship the rising than the setting sun". In more sombre mood she said that to name her successor was "to require one in mine own life to set my winding sheet before my eyes. Think you that I could love my own winding sheet?"

She was well aware that to name her successor could easily lead to serious conflict, so Robert, using the utmost discretion, with all his communications in code, coached James in the way to win Elizabeth's approval. He did so with considerable skill. When James was congratulating her after the Armada, he signed his letter "Your natural son and compatriot of your country". It had its effect, and in replying to another of his letters Elizabeth wrote "So trust I that you will not doubt but that your last letters are so acceptably taken as my thanks cannot be lacking for the same but yield them to you in grateful sort".

She almost certainly had a shrewd idea that Robert had arranged things in much greater detail, as indeed he had. There had been an awkward moment when the Queen happened to spot the newly-delivered diplomatic bags from Scotland, and demanded that they should be opened so that she could see the correspondence immediately. With great presence of mind, Robert opened the bag and seemed to recoil from the contents. He explained that they smelt nauseating and must be dried and aired before anyone could handle them. So fortune ruled the day. Without fuss or controversy, the Crowns of England and Scotland were united and Europe, too, was united in peace and for many years to come.

INDEX